Noted, but no
ap

JR Spe.

·H A R T·
PUBLISHING

OXFORD AND PORTLAND, OREGON
2014

Published in the United Kingdom by Hart Publishing Ltd
16C Worcester Place, Oxford, OX1 2JW
Telephone: +44 (0)1865 517530
Fax: +44 (0)1865 510710
E-mail: mail@hartpub.co.uk
Website: http://www.hartpub.co.uk

Published in North America (US and Canada) by
Hart Publishing
c/o International Specialized Book Services
920 NE 58th Avenue, Suite 300
Portland, OR 97213-3786
USA
Tel: +1 503 287 3093 or toll-free: (1) 800 944 6190
Fax: +1 503 280 8832
E-mail: orders@isbs.com
Website: http://www.isbs.com

© John R Spencer 2014

John R Spencer has asserted his right under the Copyright, Designs and Patents
Act 1988, to be identified as the author of this work.

Hart Publishing is an imprint of Bloomsbury Publishing plc.

British Library Cataloguing in Publication Data
Data Available

ISBN: 978-1-84946-671-4

Typeset by Criterion International, Quito, Ecuador
Printed and bound in Great Britain by
Page Bros, Norwich

Table of Contents

Table of Contents

Table of Contents

Table of Contents

Preface

John Spencer worked at Cambridge for over forty years. He lectured, supervised – and entertained – students in tort, contract, crime, medical law, and criminal procedure and evidence. The case notes reproduced in this volume – and selected by John himself – were all written for the *Cambridge Law Journal*. With the exception of the last note, which is somewhat longer, the articles are taken from the case note section of the CLJ. Regular readers will be aware of the constraints imposed by the CLJ editors on authors: 1000 words and no more, although the complexity of the cases and the prolixity of the judges have meant that the CLJ recently relaxed this rule to 1500 words. The case notes reproduced here provide a master-class in the incisive, engaging note. Written with students in mind but also intended for the consumption and edification of a wider audience, John has cajoled, lambasted and encouraged the judiciary to see things his way.

In a questionnaire return, one student crossed out John's name and replaced it with Victor Meldrew, the curmudgeonly star of BBC sitcom, *One Foot in the Grave*. As these case notes show, John certainly sees the absurdities of life – the reliance by a jury on a Ouija board to find out who done it, being one – but, unlike Victor Meldrew, John has a wicked sense of humour, and a capacity to reduce a rapt audience to fits of laughter as he tells one of his (risqué) jokes. He even made the Queen smile when she opened the new Law Faculty Building, with his suggestion that the SAS kindly cleaned the windows. Perhaps less known is John's skill as a puppeteer. He does a mean Punch and Judy show. The picture on the front cover shows one of his own, hand-made puppets of Mr Punch.

John is also a pugilist. He is not afraid to take on the anti-EU brigade,[1] and most recently Nigel Farage,[2] and any others who cross him. The picture on p 7 shows John's correspondence with his

---

[1] JR Spencer, 'Who's afraid of the Big Bad European Public Prosecutor' (2011–12) 14 *Cambridge Yearbook of European Legal Studies* 363, 374 ff.

[2] http://www.cambridge-news.co.uk/Education/Universities/Cambridge-Universitys-Prof-John-Spencer-denounces-comments-by-UKIP-leader-Nigel-Farage-on-EU-justice-as-muddled-and-confused-20131210060004.htm

insurance company over its refusal to reimburse his travel expenses following a cancelled trip to Paris.

John's voice rings out clearly in these notes. There are some wonderful turns of phrase, including my favourite 'the common law should move by little steps, like centipedes and corgis, not leaps and bounds, like kangaroos'. But more importantly the case notes demonstrate John's commitment to the underdog, and his strong sense of justice. They also reveal his breadth of knowledge – children's evidence, comparative law, crime, tort, contract, medical law, even some legal history – catholic tastes as befitting a traditional Oxbridge don. This volume is not intended as a critical appraisal of his work. That is a matter for others. However, it is meant to provide a showcase for some of his finest short writings over the years. For those wishing to know more, a full list of John's publications is attached as an Annex.

Catherine Barnard
Trinity College, Cambridge
1 January 2014

Tribute

"I am honoured to have joined the scores of Cambridge law students taught by this amazing teacher before he retired. Professor Spencer's commitment to our learning was perhaps best epitomised when the law faculty plunged into darkness from a blackout in Michaelmas term, and Professor Spencer, without missing a beat, continued on lecturing under the subtle glow of laptop screens. We will miss you!"

Anonymous, Law Tripos Questionnaire 2011–12, Part IA Paper 4, Law of Tort

Generations of Cambridge students from 1970 onwards, myself included, will endorse this opinion wholeheartedly. The Cambridge Law Faculty is lucky to have many fine teachers among its members but John Spencer has been one of the very best. John's fluent, and often highly entertaining, articulation of the most complicated scenarios and his ability to convey them in terms instantly intelligible to all make him a great teacher. But John is no empty showman: when he speaks, people listen with great attention and pleasure because the quality of his incisive analysis shines through.

Cambridge law students often have only the haziest sense of the eminence of their lecturers and even Faculty members do not always appreciate the full extent of their colleagues' achievements. One of the privileges of being Chair of the Faculty is having the opportunity to learn more and then to blow the trumpet for colleagues who are too modest to do so for themselves. In John's case, the full blast would be long and loud and only an edited version can be given here. The high notes include: a distinguished academic career in Cambridge (Fellow of Selwyn College (1970), University Assistant Lecturer then University Lecturer (1973–91); University Reader (1991–1995); University Professor (1995–2013)); a long list of important publications in English and in French (including 11 books and over 200 articles, chapters, notes and other publications) that have shaped the scholarly debate in a number of fields and had an impact on judicial decision-making and on public policy; academic and professional honours (such as the Chevalier de l'Ordre des palmes académiques, honorary Queen's Counsel, and honorary President of the European Criminal Law Association (UK)); visiting professorships in France and Italy;

11

regular invitations to train the senior judiciary of England, France and Italy; holder of major academic leadership positions within the Faculty (including being Faculty Chairman between 1995 and 1997 when the Faculty was settling into its new building); and responsibility for major Faculty strategic innovations (such as student exchange programmes under Erasmus/ Socrates scheme with Poitiers, Utrecht and Regensburg; and from 1999, the Joint Degree (*Double Maîtrise*) with the University of Paris II).

Throughout the course of his academic career John has been extensively involved with a number of projects for law reform, ranging from campaigning with the NSPCC and other bodies for changes in the law relating to children's evidence through to recent heavy involvement in public discussions about the UK's stance with respect to opting out of EU police and criminal justice measures. John's EU work has made him a regular visitor to the Committee corridor of the Palace of Westminster, as an invited expert witness.

A list of impressive achievements says something important but does not tell the whole story. I got to know John well in the period when he was Chairman of the Faculty and I was the Secretary of the Faculty Board (now Academic Secretary). There was a lot to do, but it was also great fun. The inevitable petty bureaucracies that come with administrative responsibilities had their own quite special silver lining because no-one does exasperation quite like John.

I am personally delighted that John's retirement is being marked by the publication of a collection of his Cambridge Law Journal casenotes. These notes are models of lucid and succinct legal analysis and I know from personal experience that editors of the Cambridge Law Journal have often pointed new note writers to them as outstanding examples of how to say something that matters within a tight word limit. We are immensely grateful to Catherine Barnard, Lesley Dingle, and Felicity Eves-Rey for their work in putting this collection together, and to Richard Hart for overseeing its publication.

Eilís Ferran
Chair of the Law Faculty
University of Cambridge

Foreword

This is a collection of comments on decided cases that I have written for the Cambridge Law Journal over the last 43 years. The last is a lengthy criticism of *L'Estrange v Graucob*, a well-known case on the law of contract. This was my first published article and, despite its age, I believe it is still sometimes quoted. The rest are short notes, which appeared in the "Cases and Comments" section of the journal between 1970 and 2013. Of those that I wrote, most are reproduced in the pages below, but not all of them. There were some, which on re-reading, struck me as not very good, and others which now seemed to be of little interest because they were about battles fought long ago, and long ago forgotten – and for these reasons I have left them out.

When he was an old man, Somerset Maugham wrote a preface for a new edition of an early novel that he had written half a century before. With tongue in cheek, he told his readers how the author, who "had been dead for many years", was "not only a foolish young man", but "supercilious, cock-sure and often wrong" – concluding "If I met him now I should take an instant dislike to him." I confess to having some of the same feelings on re-reading some of the earlier things I wrote. But as this book is published on my retirement, and to commemorate the course of my career, it would be dishonest for that reason only to delete them.

This collection was the brain-child of my old friend and colleague Catherine Barnard, who has faithfully supported me in a range of academic projects over many years. I am most grateful to her for thinking of it, for persuading Hart Publishing to produce it, and then for undertaking the work of putting the collection together. As Cambridge colleagues will recognise, the collection is modelled on the similar collection that Catherine and others put together to mark the passing of our much-loved and much-respected colleague, Tony Weir; but this time, she had to face the added complication of my continued existence. I am also deeply grateful to Richard Hart for allowing Catherine to persuade him to publish the book. And I would also like to record my gratitude to the staff at Hart Publishing for producing it with the skill and speed which has made it a pleasure to publish a number of other books with them in the past. A final word of thanks is due to Cherry Hopkins for her professional proof reading, to Leslie Dingle in the Squire Law Library for helping to locate the earlier material electronically, and Felicity Eves-Rey, in the Law Faculty office, who provided a large amount of practical help in putting the typescript together with her usual calm, cheerful manner.

John Spencer
Selwyn College
19 December 2013

The Rescuer as Defendant – Reversal of Roles
Matthews v Maclaren
CLJ 1970, 28(1) 30–33

The good ship "Ogopogo", navigated by a drunk, is not as it sounds, either something out of a Tripos paper or else the start of a dubious after-dinner anecdote, but the setting for *Matthews v MacLaren* [1969] 4 D.L.R. (3d) 557, which came before Lacourciere J. in the Ontario High Court.

MacLaren and his friends had what is politely called a drinking-bout at a yacht-club before he invited them to join him as his gratuitous passengers on his pleasure-boat, the "Ogopogo." The party, including Matthews and one Horsley, sailed merrily across Lake Ontario, until Matthews accidentally fell in. Immediately MacLaren manoeuvered the boat in order to rescue him, but because he was drunk he did it clumsily and Matthews drifted out of reach. The delay was desperate because the water was icy cold, so Horsley bravely jumped in to save him. Unhappily both he and Matthews died, and their widows sued MacLaren under the Ontario Fatal Accidents Act.

Everything which the judge said about Mrs. Matthew's claim is *obiter* because he found as a fact that Matthews had died of shock and cold before anyone could have rescued him. Whether or not the other elements of the tort of negligence were present, MacLaren's acts had not caused his death, which was entirely due to his falling overboard. In this respect the case is like *Barnett v Chelsea and Kensington Hospital Management Committee* [1969] 1 Q.B. 428, which was not cited to the court. Nevertheless Lacourciere J. discussed at length what his decision would have been had Matthews lived long enough to be rescued, and here is the chief interest of the case, because he would have held MacLaren liable.

There was no doubt that MacLaren had handled the boat very carelessly, so the judge held, nor that the death of Matthews would have been a foreseeable result. The doubtful question was whether this was a situation where the tort of negligence could ever arise at all. Was MacLaren, a potential rescuer, in a duty of care situation, owing a "notional duty" to rescue the drowning man? Lacourciere

J. began by stating the general rule that the law imposes no duty to rescue, and he cited *Vanvalkenburg v Northern Navigation Co.* [1913] 19 D.L.R. 649, where in an identical case the master of a ship was held to owe no such duty. Nowadays it is a crime for the master of a ship not to help those in distress at sea, both in Canada and in England (Canada Shipping Act, s. 526; Maritime Convention Act 1911, s. 6 (1)), but the judge said this gave no civil remedy here. So he went on to cite several American cases, including *Harris v Pennsylvania Railroad Co.* (1931) 50 F. 2d 866, where, contrary to *Vanvalkenburg's* case, a duty to rescue had been held to exist at common law. He referred to Prosser, Fleming and Salmond to show that there is such a duty where there is a "special relationship" between the parties. The existence of such a relationship was a question of law, and he accordingly held that there was such a relationship between the master of a ship and the crew and passengers. So MacLaren was bound to make a reasonable effort to rescue Matthews.

If this is the law, how do you tell if there is such a "special relationship"? Lacourciere J. spoke loosely about a "quasi-contractual duty" and an "implied contract". This gets us nowhere. Perhaps the answer is that someone owes a duty to rescue a person, wherever failure to do so can be fairly described as a bad method of doing some larger transaction involving that person. For example, in the present case failure to try to rescue his passenger could fairly be described as a bad way of conducting a boating party. This is admittedly a bit vague, but it is supported in *Winfield*, 8th ed., p. 47, and is also how a similar problem was approached in Roman law (D.9.2.27.9).

Mrs. Horsley's claim succeeded. After citing the usual passage from *Donoghue v Stevenson* [1932] A.C. 562, Lacourciere J. relied on the usual authorities to show that the "neighbour principle" now applies to make those who create a danger liable to those who are hurt rescuing people from it. He seemed to have no trouble in deciding that MacLaren had created the danger, although he was really trying to rescue Matthews from a danger Matthews had accidentally created for himself. So, disposing of defences of *volenti* and contributory negligence, and finding Horsley's action reasonably foreseeable, he held MacLaren liable.

16

If this part of the decision is meant for volunteer rescuers as well as for those who owe a duty to rescue, it is unfortunate. Common sense dictates that rescuers ought to be encouraged by law, but according to this case they get kicks as well as ha'pence. The first kick is that although someone who callously refuses help is not liable, he becomes liable if he charitably tries to help, but fails to use reasonable care. This is Prosser's view, and Lacourciere J. adopted it as a second ground for finding that MacLaren would have been liable to Matthews had Matthews lived longer. By doing so Lacourciere J. extended the rule, too, because it originally only meant that the rescuer was liable if he made the victim's plight worse, while Lacourciere J. took it to mean that he was liable if he failed to make his position better. The second kick is that he said the rescuer is also liable to anyone else who, like Horsley, gets hurt in the rescue. Not only does he owe such a person a notional duty of care, but it seems that he must behave extremely carefully to discharge it. The policeman who tries to stop a runaway horse but fails, and then is sued by the man the horse trampled and the man the policeman bumped into as he ran out to stop it, is unlikely to bother next time. Perhaps this is unfair criticism since MacLaren was bound to attempt a rescue, and so was not the usual good-hearted volunteer rescuer, while the plaintiff Horsley was. But this should have been pointed out.

Could Mrs. Horsley have sued if MacLaren had not been bound to try to rescue Matthews? In *Videan v B.T.C.* [1963] 2 Q.B. 650, a rescuer recovered damages where the person he rescued was unable to sue. But a rescuer can only sue where the defendant created the danger. Even if we accept that MacLaren created the danger to Matthews when he failed in his bounden duty to rescue, it is surely going too far to say that he created the danger to him by failing to rescue him when he was not bound to do so.

Noted, but not invariably approved

Rescuer as Defendant – Reversal of Roles Reversed
Matthews v Maclaren
CLJ 1971, 29(2) 193–195

The unfortunate Ogopogo, the subject of an earlier case note ([1970] C.L.J. 30), has been reversed – or is the word "capsized"? – by the Ontario Court of Appeal. The decision is reported as *Horsley v MacLaren* (1970) 11 D.L.R. 277, and as *The Ogopogo* [1970] 1 Lloyd's Rep. 257.

The case, which concerns both the duty to rescue and liability towards rescuers, arose out of a boating accident on Lake Ontario. MacLaren, the defendant, took Matthews and Horsley for a trip in his cabin-cruiser, and Matthews accidentally fell in. MacLaren manoeuvered the boat to try to rescue him, but the trial judge, Lacourciere J., was satisfied that he did so in a clumsy manner because he was drunk at the time, and that he wasted precious minutes in pulling Matthews out of the water. Since the water was extremely cold, the delay looked desperate. Fearing for his friend, Horsley tore off his trousers and jumped into the lake to save him; but his efforts were in vain, as both he and Matthews were killed. Mrs. Matthews and Mrs. Horsley sued MacLaren under the Ontario Fatal Accidents Act.

At first instance, it was held that MacLaren owed a duty to do all that a reasonable master of a vessel would do to try to rescue Matthews, and that he had negligently failed in this duty; nevertheless Mrs. Matthews' action failed, because it was found as a fact that Matthews had died of shock and cold as soon as he fell into the water and before he could possibly have been saved, whatever MacLaren had done. However, the action by Mrs. Horsley succeeded. The judge held that it was a reasonably foreseeable consequence of the delay caused by MacLaren's negligent navigation that someone else would be driven to risk his life in an independent rescue attempt, and that there was no reason in law why the widow of that someone should not be able to sue.

Now the defendant has successfully appealed against the decision in favour of Mrs. Horsley, the judgment of the Ontario Court of

Appeal being delivered by Schroeder and Jessup JJ.A., McGillivray J.A. concurring.

The court began by saying that Horsley was a "rescuer," and that "rescuers" who get hurt can only sue those who have caused the danger from which they are trying to save the victim. Was MacLaren the author of Matthews' danger? The court was certain that MacLaren could not possibly be so called unless he owed Matthews a duty to help which he failed to perform, so the first thing that Mrs. Horsley had to show was that the defendant owed a duty to help Matthews.

The court stressed that the common law recognises no general duty to help those in trouble, but said that a duty may arise if the parties stand in a special relationship to one another. Both Jessup J.A. and Schroeder J.A. agreed with Lacourciere J. in holding, despite earlier cases to the contrary, that such a relationship now exists between the master of a vessel and his crew and passengers. However, the court did not entirely agree with Lacourciere J. about the meaning of the loose term "a duty to rescue". Jessup J.A. thought that it meant a duty to do all that a reasonable man would do to help the person in danger, and he said that Matthews had clearly failed to carry out this duty. Schroeder J.A. also spoke about a duty to make a "reasonable effort". However, he also said that people in MacLaren's position must not be judged by a harsh standard, and unlike Lacourciere J. and Jessup J.A., he said that here MacLaren had not failed in his duty. So whereas Jessup J.A. would judge a rescuer by an objective standard of behaviour, apparently Schroeder J.A. would judge him by the subjective standard of what was reasonable for this man in this situation.

Here the court digressed to give its opinion on the liability of a volunteer rescuer – someone who, unlike MacLaren, owes no duty to help, but who voluntarily does what he can. Lacourciere J. had quoted with approval some American authority which he took to mean that although no one owes any duty to help another in distress, once he makes the effort, he owes a duty of care, and if the attempt miscarries, he may be liable for failing to rescue the victim. This idea was strongly criticised. According to the court, a volunteer rescuer is only liable if he is careless and so makes the plight of the victim *worse*; he is not liable if through his carelessness he merely fails to make his position *better*. Thus if X sees Y drowning and tries to rescue him by harpooning him, he will be liable; but if he merely throws the life-ring in a careless way and misses the drowning man he is not liable.

At this point, however, the academic interest of the case almost evaporates, since the appeal succeeded not on a point of law, but because the trial judge was reversed on his findings of secondary fact. As has already been said, Schroeder J.A. decided that MacLaren had not navigated the *Ogopogo* carelessly at all. In addition to this, both he and Jessup J.A. said that it was not reasonably foreseeable that Horsley would jump into the lake to save his friend, since he had been expressly warned to stay inside the cabin before the trip started. This seems a little odd. It would have been unforeseeable that Horsley would bravely jump into the lake if he had been renowned as a mean coward who regularly watched with passive equanimity whilst little children drowned in lily-ponds and blind old ladies walked into open manholes – but would this have prevented him from suing if he had risen to the occasion just this once? The question, surely, was whether *someone*, not this precise man, was foreseeably likely to attempt a rescue in this way. However, for better or for worse, these findings of fact disposed of Mrs. Horsley's case completely.

But for these new findings of fact, it is impossible to say what the answer would have been. Jessup J.A. would have found for Mrs. Horsley, since he accepted Lacourciere J.'s theory that if X owes a duty to help Y in trouble and fails to do so, X is considered the author of Y's danger, and may be liable to the volunteer who is injured when he comes to the rescue. Schroeder J.A.'s remarks, on the other hand, suggest that he would have found against Mrs. Horsley in law as well as on the facts. McGillivray J.A., who held the casting vote, said no more than "I concur", so the talking-point remains open.

Widening Scope of Defence of Contributory Negligence
O'Connell v Jackson
CLJ 1972, 30(1) 27–31

The Law Reform (Contributory Negligence) Act 1945 has consistently received a broad interpretation from the courts. Two recent decisions follow this trend.

In *O'Connell v Jackson* [1972] 1 Q.B. 270 the defendant drove his car from a side-street without looking, and knocked the plaintiff off his moped, causing him severe injuries. At first instance, Payne J. found the defendant wholly to blame and gave the plaintiff full damages. The defendant appealed, arguing that the damages should be reduced by reason of the plaintiff's contributory negligence in failing to wear a crash-helmet. Counsel for the plaintiff countered this by trying to prove that it was not careless to fail to wear a crash-helmet. She cited *Hilder v Associated Portland Cement Manufacturers* [1961] 1 W.L.R. 1434 and *MacDonnell v Kaiser* (1968) 68 D.L.R. (2d) 104, where the court refused to reduce the plaintiff's damages for contributory negligence because of his failure to wear, in one case a crash helmet, and in the other, a seat-belt. The Court of Appeal easily distinguished them, however, because in neither case was it proved that the failure to take precautions increased the injuries sustained. Having no doubt that it was careless of this plaintiff not to wear a crash-helmet, and being satisfied that he increased his injuries by not doing so, the Court of Appeal reduced his damages by fifteen per cent.

The judgment of the Court of Appeal is short, and Edmund Davies L.J. seems to have thought the matter was rather obvious. However, the facts raise a fundamental point about the nature of contributory negligence. The plaintiff's failure to wear a crash-helmet in no way contributed to the occurrence of the accident; it merely increased the damage he suffered. Could this amount to contributory negligence? A strong case could have been made to the contrary, and it is surprising that counsel for the plaintiff conceded that such conduct could be contributory negligence, and argued the case solely on the issue of carelessness. *Winfield and*

Jolowicz on Tort, 9th ed., p. 110, say categorically that to amount to
contributory negligence, "It is essential... that the plaintiff's lack of
care for his own safety should be a contributory factor *to the accident
which caused his damage*", and dicta in various cases support this, for
example, those of du Parcq L.J. in *Lewis v Denye* [1939] 1 K.B. 549.

On the other hand, a stronger case can be made for the opposite
view, which was taken for granted by all concerned. There are
at least two English cases where something has been held to be
contributory negligence which augmented the damage but did not
cause the accident. In *The Scotia* (1890) 6 Asp.M.L.C. 541 there
was a collision between the ships of P and D, in which P's ship was
damaged. His ship might have been saved had P left someone on
board, but because of his negligent failure to do so, it sank and was
a total loss. Although the collision seems to have been entirely due
to D's negligence, P's damages were reduced on the grounds of his
contributory negligence. The same principle underlies *R. A. Brand
& Co. v Barrow (Samuel) & Co.* (1965) 109 S.J. 834. Directly in point
is a Canadian case, *Yuan v Farstad* (1966) 66 D.L.R. (2d) 295, where
upon proof that P's injuries in a motor-accident would have been
less severe had he worn the seat-belt provided, the Supreme Court
of British Columbia reduced his damages because of contributory
negligence. Furthermore, Professor Glanville Williams argues in
Joint Torts and Contributory Negligence (p. 292) that the Law Reform
(Contributory Negligence) Act ought to apply to negligence
which contributes to the damage but not to the accident, and the
conclusions of Prosser (*Torts*, 3rd ed., p. 434) point the same way.

The case will not thrill the motor-cycling public, but it will be
welcomed by practitioners because it gives a clear answer to a
question which often arises from motor accidents. It is submitted
that the answer is welcome not only because it is clear, but also
because it is right in principle. Now that contributory negligence
no longer forms a complete bar to action, it would be pointless
to complicate the matter by dividing it further than necessary
into potentially difficult categories of operative and inoperative
contributory negligence.

Lumsden & Co. v London Trustee Savings Bank [1971] 1 Lloyd's Rep.
114 concerns an innocent stockbroker plaintiff, P, and an innocent

banker defendant, D. The apex of the eternal triangle was a rogue, X, who came to England on a visit from Australia, took temporary employment as an accountant with P, and who, *per* Donaldson J., "is now, I understand, engaged in a much longer and involuntary stay here". X opened a bank account with D under an assumed name similar to that of one of P's customers. Then he stole cheques which P had made out in favour of this customer, forged them to make them appear payable to himself under the false name, and paid them into his account with D.

D handled P's cheques in good faith, but he certainly committed the tort of conversion by doing so; thus he was liable to P unless he could establish the defence given to the collecting banker by the Cheques Act 1957, s.4, which exonerates him if he acted "in good faith and without negligence". Donaldson J. held that this defence failed, because D had been careless in allowing X to open the account without proper references and identification. Therefore D was liable to P for the value of the cheques. What is really interesting, however, is that Donaldson J. went on to hold that the Law Reform (Contributory Negligence) Act 1945 applies to the tort of conversion, and accordingly he reduced P's damages by ten per cent., because the careless manner in which he wrote his cheques facilitated their forgery by X. This is the first case in England where contributory negligence has been allowed as a defence to conversion, and it comes as a surprise to everyone. What is even more surprising is that counsel for the plaintiff, like counsel in *O'Connell v Jackson, supra*, was prepared to concede the point!

It is generally agreed that the Law Reform (Contributory Negligence) Act does not enable a defendant to set up contributory negligence as a partial defence to any torts except those where it might have been a total defence before 1945. (See Professor Glanville Williams, *op. cit.*, Chap. 13.) Donaldson J. accepted this. Therefore it is remarkable to find that he went on to hold that contributory negligence is a possible defence to conversion. If one rule of law seemed certain, it was that the plaintiff's conduct, however negligent, provides no defence to an action in conversion unless it estops him from asserting his title to the property in question. Estoppel may be either by direct representations made by P to D, as in *Henderson v Williams* [1895] 1 Q.B. 521, or by negligence. It is only estoppel by negligence which concerns us here. To amount to estoppel by negligence, the cases show that two things have to be proved: (a) that the negligence was the direct cause of the particular transaction in which D converted the property, and (b) that D was someone whose interests P was bound to protect. Furthermore, if D can prove estoppel, this is a complete defence, and if he cannot, then it is no defence at all; there is no room for partial estoppel and apportionment of damages.

A line of strong cases to this effect stretches from *Bank of Ireland v Evans' Trustees* (1855) 5 H.L.C. 389; 10 E.R. 958, where the Lord Chancellor said: "there must be something that amounts to an estoppel, or something that amounts to a ratification, to make the negligence a good answer", through *Farquharson v King* [1902] A.C. 325 to the present day. In the more recent cases contributory negligence was not even raised, presumably because counsel in cases like *Central Newbury Motor Auctions v Unity Finance* [1957] 1 Q.B. 371 rightly thought the defence to be closed by the half-dozen or so House of Lords cases which preclude it. In view of these, the solitary New Zealand case relied on by Donaldson J., *Helson v McKenzies* [1950] N.Z.L.R. 878, where the court reduced a lady's damages for the conversion of her handbag by reason of her contributory negligence in leaving it around where the defendant could convert it, seems a little unconvincing.

Despite this unpromising background, however, Professor Glanville Williams suggested in *Joint Torts and Contributory Negligence*, p. 210, that contributory negligence should be a defence to certain cases of conversion. His idea was expanded by H. W. Burnett in (1960) 76 L.Q.R. 364. The idea now seems to have found its way into Holden, *Law and Practice of Banking*, cited with approval by Donaldson J. Professor Williams suggests drawing a distinction between those cases of conversion in which the defendant withholds property or the proceeds of property belonging to the plaintiff, and those cases where all he has done is to handle the plaintiff's property, innocently and without profit. In the first class of case, it is admitted that the authorities preclude any defence of contributory negligence falling short of estoppel, whereas in the second class of case, of which the *Lumsden* affair is an example, it is argued that there is nothing to preclude a defence of ordinary contributory negligence.

Can this distinction be supported? With due respect to all concerned, it cannot. In the first place, the cases do not permit it. If we divide the decided cases on conversion into the two classes suggested, we find that those involving conversion by mere handling are nearly as uncompromising in refusing to allow a defence of contributory negligence as the cases which we are thereby distinguishing. To start with, *Bank of Ireland v Evans' Trustees*, which Professor Williams admits to be a "stumbling-block", seems to be a case of handling rather than withholding. The same is true of *Staple of England v Bank of England* (1887) 21 Q.B.D. 160, where again general contributory negligence was rejected as a defence. Even more in point is *Arnold v Cheque Bank* (1876) 1 C.P.D. 568, because the facts are much the same as those of the present case. The plaintiff's servant stole a bank-draft which the plaintiff was sending to someone else, and paid it into an account with the defendant bank. The court would not allow the defendant to set up the plaintiff's negligent treatment of the cheque as a defence, and was quite scathing about the suggestion. In fact, the only case that bears the distinction out is *Helson v McKenzies, supra*, where the conversion consisted of the defendant's handing the handbag over to the wrong person, and this case is not strong authority. It is a majority decision on contributory negligence, the dissenting judge alone considering whether the defence was properly available. The majority were not alive to any distinction such as Professor Williams suggests, and seemed to think that contributory negligence was a defence to *all* cases of conversion – which is obviously wrong.

Secondly, Professor Williams' distinction is not supportable on the ground that it distinguishes the cases on their merits. Is it any more equitable in practice to give the plaintiff full damages when his negligence has led to the defendant innocently withholding his chattel, than to give him full damages when the same negligence has led him to handle his cheque? Certainly not. In practice, the cases where the defendant merely handles the property usually involve banks, which can afford to pay damages in full and allow or insure for the risk, whilst the withholding cases usually involve private individuals who have innocently bought stolen motor-cars, and who are probably unable to pay damages at all. If contributory negligence ought to be a defence to conversion – which it probably ought – then it should be a defence to *all* cases of innocent conversion. Such a change would have to be introduced by statute. The fate of Devlin L.J.'s similar proposal in *Ingram v Little* [1961] 1 Q.B. 31 suggests that this is unlikely to happen.

Trespassers will be Prosecuted – Wooden Lie Comes True
Brittain
CLJ 1973, 32(1) 10–14[3]

The Court of Appeal has brought criminal trespass to life. The new monster, like Frankenstein's, has been made from an assortment of unsavoury remains which should have been decently buried long ago. These are the crimes of forcible entry, and conspiracy to do an unlawful (but non-criminal) act.

The first step in the gruesome story is *Brittain* [1972] 1 Q.B. 357. Brittain and his friends, equipped with a pint mug, tried to gate-crash a bottle-party to which they had not been invited. Annoyed at the host's refusal to let them in, they flung their pint mug through the window and forced themselves through the door. Petty sessions stuff, one might have thought, and likely to lead to fines for criminal damage and common assault, and a judicial "raspberry" from the Bench. For some reason, however, the defendants were indicted with forcible entry contrary to the Forcible Entry Act 1381, which provides (in Norman French) as follows:

---

[3] Since this and the next note were written the legal world has greatly changed. The ancient offences the contours of which were discussed in them were abolished by statute long ago, and various new statutory offences have been enacted to replace them; and the higher courts no longer think it proper to resurrect and stretch ancient criminal offences to meet modern problems. But they are still interesting as a reminder of how the legal world was 40 years ago.

> The King defendeth that none from henceforth make any entry into any lands and tenements, but in case where entry is given by the law; and in such case not with strong hand, nor with multitude of people, but only in a peaceable and easy manner...

They were tried at Assizes, convicted, and sentenced to nine months' imprisonment. The defendants appealed against conviction, arguing that a crime under the Forcible Entry Act requires not only an incursion made with force, but also an intention to take possession of the premises invaded – an element of course absent from this case. Cairns L.J., delivering the judgment of the Court of Appeal, rejected this contention, holding that the word "entry" in the Act must be given its "ordinary meaning". Accordingly the convictions were upheld.

There are three reasons why the interpretation which the Court of Appeal gave to this ancient statute is dubious. In the first place, "entry" is not a term with an "ordinary meaning" when it appears in a statute, but a legal term of art. Jowett's *Law Dictionary* defines "entry" as "the act of going in land, or doing something equivalent, *with the intention of asserting a right in the land*", and adds a secondary and equally technical meaning for the word as used in the crime of burglary. Secondly, the works of most legal writers who bother to deal with forcible entry suggest that in this context, the word "entry" bears the first of Jowett's meanings. Dalton's *Countrey Justice* (5th ed., 1635, p. 196) appears to suggest the contrary, but Wood's *Institutes* (1722), p. 426, Blackstone's *Commentaries* (iv), ch. XI, 8, Stephen's *Digest of Criminal Law* (1877), Article 79, and *Russell on Crime*, 12th ed., p. 279, all define the offence in terms that make it clear that the defendant must assert some kind of right against the land. Hawkins says:

> It seems certain, that if one who pretends to a title to lands, barely go over them, either with or without a great number of attendants, armed or unarmed, in his way to the church, or market,... without doing any act, which either expressly or impliedly amounts to a claim of such lands, he cannot be said to make an entry thereinto within the meaning of these statutes. (Pleas of the Crown (1716), Book I, ch. 64, s. 20.)

27

Thirdly, the historical context of the Forcible Entry Act 1381 suggests that Hawkins is right. In the middle ages it was all too common for men to assert title to land by force. The various Forcible Entry Acts were passed to restrain this social evil, and to persuade the King's subjects to settle their disputes in his courts instead of resorting to mayhem in furtherance of their claims, valid and invalid. This is clear from the works of ancient writers such as Lambard (*Eirenarcha* (1581), p. 145) and Pulton (*De Pace Regis* (1609), p. 34), and is the view of legal historians today (e.g., Milsom, *Historical Foundations of the Common Law*, p. 135; Simpson, *An Introduction to the History of Land Law*, p. 39).

In view of this, surely the Court of Appeal was wrong to treat the absence of a single reported case of forcible entry where the defendant did not assert some right against the land as mere historical accident. The reason is the same as the reason why there is no reported case of arson by flooding – because the crime is about something different. By turning forcible entry into forcible trespass the Court of Appeal has widened the offence enormously.

The second step in the creation of a crime of trespass is *Kamara* [1973] Q.B. 660. As a political protest, Kamara and his friends invaded the Sierra Leone High Commission. This led to their prosecution on two counts, one of unlawful assembly, and the other of *conspiracy to trespass*. They were convicted on both counts, and like Brittain, appealed to the Court of Appeal. They strongly argued that there is no such offence as conspiracy to trespass, but the Court of Appeal, in a judgment delivered by Lawton L.J., held that there was, and upheld their conviction both for this offence and for unlawful assembly.

It was a surprising result to reach, because there is a clear and well known case, *Turner* (1811) 13 East 228, which holds that conspiracy to trespass does not exist. The decision was said to be wrong in *Rowlands* (1851) 17 Q.B. 671, but since *Rowlands* has nothing to do with conspiracy to trespass, it can hardly have overruled the earlier case. Anyway, the court in *Rowlands* did not criticise the rule of law the case laid down, but said that Turner was wrongly acquitted on the facts, since he had conspired not merely to trespass, but to commit the crime of unlawful assembly as well. Furthermore,

Turner was approved by Lord Coleridge C.J. in *Mogul S.S. v McGregor Gow & Co.* (1888) 21 Q.B.D. 544.

Nevertheless, Lawton L.J. treated *Turner* as no longer authority, and thus was able to agree with counsel for the Crown that conspiracy to trespass does exist. Indeed, Lawton L.J. gave counsel for the Crown even more than he had asked for, since he rejected his submission that the offence was limited to cases involving deliberate annoyance, or injury to the public interest, or riot and disorder. The only limitation he appeared to accept was a requirement that the trespass be intentional or reckless. He even held that an agreement between two ramblers to cross a farmer's field without permission was a criminal conspiracy. This thought did not worry him, he said, because "the common sense of those who are concerned with the administration of criminal justice" would make a prosecution unlikely.

Lawton L.J. reached this remarkable result by adopting the well worn definition of conspiracy as "the agreement of two or more to do an unlawful act, or to do a lawful act by unlawful means". A tort, he continued, is an unlawful act. Therefore an agreement to commit trespass to land, which is a tort, is a criminal conspiracy. This must be so, he said, because to hold the contrary would "be to flout the commonly held opinion of many generations of our ancestors".

There is a fallacy in this. It is true that a conspiracy is an agreement to perform an unlawful act, but, with due respect to Lawton L.J., it is *not* true that *every* agreement to perform an unlawful act is therefore a conspiracy; a duck is a creature with two legs, but that does not make every creature with two legs a duck. Every writer seems to agree that, in this context, "unlawful act" has to be defined restrictively with reference to decided cases (e.g. Kenny, *Outlines of Criminal Law* (2nd ed., 1904), p. 288, R. S. Wright, *The Law of Criminal Conspiracies & Agreements* (1873), p. 64, Glanville Williams, *The Criminal Law—The General Part*, § 221). If this were not so, conspiracy would include "any form of immoral, unpatriotic, disloyal, or otherwise objectionable conduct which involves a plan concerted by two or more persons". (Stephen, *General View of the Criminal Law*, 1863, p. 149.) Adultery, for example, is an "unlawful" act which is usually preceded by agreement between two persons, and would appear to involve the crime of conspiracy! With due respect to Lawton L.J., it is *his* view, and not the contrary, which flouts "the commonly held opinion of our ancestors". They thought a notice saying "Trespassers Will Be Prosecuted" was a wooden lie, and they said so – see, e.g., Maitland, *Justice and Police* (1885), p. 13.

There can be no doubt that the combined effect of *Brittain* and *Kamara* is to widen the criminal law in an important respect. Before they were decided, trespassers could not be prosecuted. Now they can – where they force their way in, like *Brittain* – or where they trespass in pairs, like *Kamara*. In neither case is there a statutory maximum punishment. Furthermore, because of the fiction, piously restated by Lawton L.J. in *Kamara*, that the law has not really been changed but merely declared, the change in the law has retrospective effect. There can hardly be a single "squat" or "sit-in" since these disorders began which has not become an indictable offence *ex post facto* – to the joy of those who have been sat in on, and the shock of the sitters-in.

Behind these two cases lies an important constitutional issue. Whether or not trespass to land should be a crime is a controversial matter of penal policy, involving questions of civil liberty. Issues of this kind are for Parliament, not the courts, to decide. There was talk of introducing a crime of trespass during the last General Election, but this has not been followed by action in Parliament. Had the matter been raised in Parliament, it would have been decided after those opposed to the change had been able to air their views and influence the outcome – as in the Republic of Ireland, where a Forcible Entry and Occupation Bill was introduced in the Dail in 1970. Instead, the Court of Appeal has quietly done on the side what the Government either dared not or chose not to do.

Leave to appeal to the House of Lords was granted in *Kamara's* case, but refused in *Brittain*. It is much to be hoped that both decisions will eventually come before the House of Lords, because if two decisions deserve to be reversed, these are they. If this does not happen, it will finally prove that England needs a comprehensive criminal code before the principle *nulla poena sine lege* is part of the common law.

Criminal Trespass – Wooden Lies Reach the House of Lords
R. *v Kamara*
CLJ 1973, 32(2) 187–190

In an earlier note ([1973] C.L.J. 10), we saw how the Court of Appeal had created a new offence of criminal trespass. The first stage was *Brittain* [1972] 1 Q.B. 357, where the court held that any violent trespass to land amounted to the crime of forcible entry, and that intention to take possession of the land was not an ingredient of the offence; thus they upheld a prison sentence on a lout who gate-crashed a bottle-party in a disorderly manner. And the second stage was *Kamara* [1973] 1 Q.B. 660, where the court held that any trespass *by two or more in pursuit of an agreement* involved a criminal conspiracy; thus they upheld a suspended sentence on a group of men who, as a political protest, invaded the Sierra Leone High Commission. Both decisions were criticised in the earlier note, and fervent prayers were uttered that the House of Lords would reverse the pair of them. Both cases have now received some attention from the House. Predictably, perhaps, neither has been reversed.

The contribution of the House of Lords to the *Brittain* saga was the purely negative one of refusing leave to appeal. (Information kindly provided by the solicitors.) This is a pity, because the Court of Appeal reached its decision in almost total disregard of the authorities (see earlier note). Not only has further discussion been stifled; *Brittain* received honourable mention obiter when *Kamara* reached the House of Lords. So this undoubted extension of the criminal law looks as if it is here to stay. In *Kamara*, on the other hand, the House of Lords produced a judgment (*Kamara v D.P.P.* [1973] 3 W.L.R. 198) which considerably cuts down the scope of the Court of Appeal decision – although it upheld the convictions nevertheless.

The Court of Appeal, adopting the words let drop by Denman C.J. in a misguided moment in *Jones* (1832) 4 B. & Ad. 345, defined conspiracy as an agreement "to do an unlawful act, or a lawful act by unlawful means". From here, it reasoned that since a tort is an "unlawful act", any agreement to commit an intentional tort must

31

be a criminal conspiracy – a horrifying thought. Fortunately the House of Lords disagreed with this. Lord Hailsham said:

> ... the Denman antithesis does not mean that all acts which can be described as unlawful are indictable if done in combination. If it did, all illegal contracts, all acts which are in fact tortious however innocent or trivial, and all agreements in the execution of which contracts are broken, might be indictable at the prosecution of any individual, and not merely of the police. The authorities simply do not bear out that view.

Thus at last the point has been made that Denman C.J.'s statement, while a valid *description* of conspiracy, is not – and was never meant to be – a *definition* of the offence. Nothing is a conspiracy unless it is an agreement to do an unlawful act, but something is not a conspiracy merely because it is an agreement to do an unlawful act. This part of the decision is most welcome.

The rest of the decision is more controversial, however. The House of Lords refused to take the fundamentalist line it earlier took with affray in *Button* [1966] A.C. 591, and would not prune conspiracy back to agreements to commit crimes rather than torts. Lord Hailsham went on to say:

> Trespass or any other form of tort can, if intended, form the element of illegality necessary in conspiracy. But in my view, more is needed. Either (1) execution of the combination must invade the domain of the public, as, for instance, when the trespass involves the invasion of a building such as the embassy of a friendly country or a publicly owned building... Alternatively (2) a combination to trespass becomes indictable if the executive of the combination necessarily involves and is known and intended to involve the infliction on its victim of something more than purely nominal damage.

When does a tort "invade the domain of the public"? This looks very vague, and the examples given to explain it hardly help. The invasion of an embassy is both specific and serious, but what .about a "publicly owned building"? Presumably Lord Hailsham had something like the Houses of Parliament in mind, but the phrase is equally apt to cover a "squat" in a council house – or even the invasion of a telephone box or municipal urinal, if such places can really be "invaded"! However, the matter becomes clear if we read the rest of the judgment. Lord Hailsham appears to be saying that an agreement to commit a tort is a criminal conspiracy when, quite apart from its tortious aspect, it amounts to a conspiracy to effect a public mischief. And vague though "public mischief" is, it is a piece of vagueness already present in the law of conspiracy. So limiting conspiracy to commit a tort to cases where the tort is also a public mischief at least avoids extending conspiracy any further. Thus this part of the decision is not so alarming as at first appears.

If we also read the second limb of Lord Hailsham's test with the rest of his judgment, this too is fairly clear. He says it is also a criminal conspiracy to agree to commit a tort which is intentional in three distinct senses. First, it must be intentional in the sense that the defendant is aware that he is infringing the rights of others; thus if he believes he has the right to do what he plans to do, this "claim of right" is a good defence. Secondly, the intention must extend to every element of the tort; thus where damage must be shown, as in nuisance for example, there is no criminal conspiracy unless damage is intended. And thirdly, whether or not damage is an essential element of the tort in question, the tort must be intended to inflict "something more than purely nominal damage" on its victim.

What are we to make of *Kamara* in the House of Lords? It is certainly a great improvement on *Kamara* in the Court of Appeal, compared with which the House of Lords decision reads like something published by the N.C.C.L. Furthermore, Lord Hailsham's exceptionally lucid judgment takes a line on conspiracy which, if controversial, is a supportable interpretation of a highly obscure bunch of authorities. (See Davies, Dashwood and Trice in [1971] Crim.L.R. 342.) On the other hand, the decision that, despite *Turner* (1811) 13 East 228, an agreement to trespass can be an indictable conspiracy still smacks of criminal trespass by judicial legislation – especially if we examine what Lord Hailsham means by a trespass inflicting "more than nominal damage". The land itself need not be damaged, apparently; it would seem to be enough if the owner is to be deprived of the enjoyment of his property, either indefinitely – "squats" – or temporarily – "sit-ins". (See [1973] 3 W.L.R. at p. 208.)

Conspiracy remains a most unsatisfactory offence. The Law Commission, in its recent Working Paper No. 50, says "The extended form of conspiracies to do acts other than crimes ... is one which we feel has no place in a modern system of criminal law." And the same goes for the Statutes of Forcible Entry, and for all the other antique aces which the judges pull from their sleeves to play in games which they are really keen for the defendant to lose.

Belt up! – The Widening Scope of Contributory Negligence
Froom v Butcher
CLJ 1976, 35(1) 44–47

Failure to use an available seat-belt is contributory negligence for which a plaintiff's damages may be reduced, even if the collision in which he was injured was entirely the defendant's fault. This is the ruling of the Court of Appeal in *Froom v Butcher* [1975] 3 W.L.R. 379, a decision which thus settles the seat-belt controversy unless and until the matter comes before the House of Lords.

Lord Denning M.R., in whose judgment his brethren concurred, began with a brief review of the dozen or so conflicting decisions at first instance. Then he squarely faced the main legal issue – the point conceded by the plaintiff and thus largely going by default when in *O'Connell v Jackson* [1972] 1 Q.B. 270 the Court of Appeal held it to be contributory negligence in a motor-cyclist not to wear a helmet (see [1972A] C.L.J. 27). *Can* conduct amount to contributory negligence if it does not help to cause the accident, but merely augments the damage that results? Lord Denning said that it can. So it was relevant to go on to consider (a) whether or not the plaintiff was negligent not to have worn his seat-belt, and (b) how far, if at all, this should reduce the damages recoverable. After examining a mass of technical evidence, Lord Denning had no doubt that wearing a seat-belt, although it might increase the risk of injury in some rare cases, on balance greatly decreased the risk of injury. This fact was widely known and should have been appreciated by the plaintiff. Overruling the trial judge, Lord Denning said that it was no answer to the allegation of contributory negligence for the plaintiff to say that, contrary to the evidence, he believed that seat-belts were useless. His failure to wear his seat-belt was therefore negligent. Then by how much should the damages be reduced? Lord Denning answered this as follows. "Sometimes the evidence will show that the failure made no difference.... In such cases the damages should not be reduced at all. At other times the evidence will show that the failure made all the difference. The damage would have been prevented altogether if a seat belt had been worn. In such cases I would suggest that the damages should be reduced by 25 per cent. But often enough the evidence will only show that the failure made a considerable difference... In such cases I would suggest that the damages attributable to the failure to wear a seat-belt should be reduced by 15 per cent."

Lord Denning's judgment is so clear and so comprehensive that it leaves little for a commentator to add. However, there are three unconnected points which deserve to be discussed.

The first of these is the way in which the Court of Appeal tried to prescribe in advance the percentage by which a plaintiff's damages should be reduced in this sort of case. As the apportionment of damages for contributory negligence is usually treated as a matter for the discretion of the court in question, it is possible to raise academic objections to this. Nevertheless, in practice this piece of clear guidance is surely very welcome. The courts have decided that the apportionment of damages where there is contributory negligence depends on two main factors: comparative blameworthiness, and comparative causal contribution to the damage. Because these factors often pull in opposite directions, and no one knows which of them is then supposed to trump the other, in such a case as this virtually any apportionment can, in abstract terms, be logically supported. In a situation which is likely to recur frequently, therefore, a clear rule seems highly desirable. Practitioners will thank the Court of Appeal, and heave hefty sighs of relief that the greyest of all grey areas has resolved itself into black and white.

The second point for discussion is the practical effect of the decision. No doubt the consequence will be that many persons injured in road accidents will receive less compensation than would otherwise be payable. On this account the decision is likely to be criticised, especially as the hardship to the victim will not in practice be balanced by any greater fairness to the defendant. Although in theory reducing the victim's damages for his contributory negligence relieves the defendant of the unjust burden of having to pay for injuries for which the plaintiff is himself to blame, in practice the defendant could not care less, since it is not the defendant but his employer or insurer who really foots the bill. As Professor Atiyah points out, contributory negligence falls much more heavily on the plaintiff than negligence falls on the defendant, and for this reason a decision which extends the scope of contributory negligence will be said to be unwelcome. As a comment on compensation for road accidents, this criticism is entirely just. However, critics should remember what the function of the tort of negligence is meant to be. Compensation alone may be the object of some torts, but torts of fault liability are surely designed to serve a double function. Thus the tort of negligence is designed not only to compensate, but also to discourage unreasonable behaviour by making (in theory) those who are guilty of it pay for it. It can only be because of this second, deterrent function that it provides compensation only for those who are injured by a negligent defendant. It is surely consistent with this deterrent function to penalise the careless plaintiff by depriving him of some of his damages where he too is guilty of unreasonable conduct. Admittedly an unreasonable failure to wear a seat belt, unlike careless driving, is unreasonable conduct of a kind which does not obviously endanger other people; but even if a careless person injures no one but himself, his injury is bound to cause some undesirable social dislocation, and it is therefore a proper object of the law to discourage this sort of carelessness as well. *Froom v Butcher*, therefore, is a decision entirely consistent with the composite notions of policy which underlie fault liability in general and the tort of negligence in particular; and any criticism of the decision because it limits the compensation which the victims of road accidents will receive – though just – is surely criticism which ought to be directed at fault liability as a whole, rather than at one particular decision which is entirely consistent with that concept. Rugger may be a better game than cricket: but if it is, give up cricket and take up rugger; do not try to change cricket by playing it with an oval ball.

Finally, *Froom v Butcher* should be noted as an example of a trend which has developed since 1945 – the resurrection and extension of the concept of contributory negligence. In the very distant past, contributory negligence was probably just a rule of causation, invented to provide a harsh but simple solution in a case where one of the contributory causes of the damage was the plaintiff's own culpable conduct. Because in those days it meant that the plaintiff completely failed, the notion of contributory negligence was later felt to be too harsh, the concept was cut down and qualified, and in the end contributory negligence became so complex that it appeared to be a separate notion, an appendage to – rather than part of – the usual rules of causation. Then the Act of 1945 allowed apportionment for contributory negligence. After that, contributory negligence reappeared as a useful device for solving some of the inextricable problems of causation which arise where the plaintiff's injury is due to several factors. The courts have therefore removed one by one the limitations which earlier courts had put upon it, and have given the concept an ever widening scope. In *Davies v Swan Motor Co. Ltd.* [1949] 2 K.B. 291 they decided that contributory negligence could be invoked even where the plaintiff's negligence did not consist of a breach of a duty owed to the defendant. *In Froom v Butcher*, the Court of Appeal has now decided that there can be contributory negligence (and hence apportionment) where the plaintiff's negligent conduct augmented the damage, although it did not help to cause the accident. And it now remains to be seen whether or not the courts will follow the lead given by Brandon J. in *The Calliope* [1970] P. 172, and will decide that the concept of contributory negligence can be invoked even where the plaintiff's careless conduct occurred *after* the original negligence of the defendant – so enabling them to apportion the loss instead of producing an all-or-nothing result based on a complex discussion of *novus actus*, chains of causation, and all the other mystical metaphors with which at present they have to disguise a test of first impression.

Ask for it, Get it, and Sue for it – Provocation and Contributory Negligence
Murphy v Culhane
CLJ 1977, 36(2) 242–245

If you provoke another to strike you an unlawful blow, can you sue him for damages? Nobody doubts his criminal liability, or the moral justification for it. To preserve peace and good order, society is entitled to require its members to exercise reasonable restraint even in the face of provocation, and may justly punish those who fail to do so. But in civil law it is another matter. Morally, you are as bad as the man you provoked to hit you. Most people would also say that you are the main cause of your own misfortune. Whatever the criminal liability of the man who struck you, it is hard to see any good reason why you should be entitled to his money. Thus when in *Lane v Holloway* [1968] 1 Q.B. 379 the Court of Appeal held that substantial damages could be claimed, the decision was understandably criticised. Now in *Murphy v Culhane* [1977] Q.B. 94 the Court of Appeal has come to the opposite conclusion.

John Culhane, an Irish labourer, deliberately and unlawfully hit Timothy Murphy, another Irish labourer, on the head with a plank and killed him. Mrs. Murphy thereupon sued John Culhane for damages under the Fatal Accidents Acts. A precondition of her claim, of course, was that Timothy Murphy had been killed in circumstances such that he could have sued John Culhane had he been injured rather than killed. Culhane said that Murphy could not have sued him, because "the said assault occurred during and as part of a criminal affray which was initiated by [Murphy] and others who had together come... with the joint criminal intent of assaulting and beating [Culhane]". The case came to the Court of Appeal as an interlocutory appeal as to whether or not these facts, if proved, would amount to a defence to Timothy Murphy's notional – and thus to Mrs. Murphy's actual – claim. In view of *Lane v Holloway*, it looked as if they did not. But the Court of Appeal held otherwise. Lord Denning, who delivered the judgment of the court, said that these facts if proved would afford Culhane the complete defence of *ex turpi causa* and probably *volenti non fit iniuria* as well. He added that as a third string to his bow, Culhane might also have the partial defence of contributory negligence.

It is respectfully submitted that this decision is entirely right and to be welcomed. The case deserves fuller comment, however, because it raises fundamental questions about the nature and scope of several tortious defences.

It is interesting to see *ex turpi causa*, long a neglected defence, making a deserved comeback in recent years. A very long time ago the courts widely applied it, frequently defeating claims by people whose behaviour was *turpis* only in the technical and extended sense that they were breaking the letter of the law. Thus it seems to have been the origin of the rule, now exploded in *Herrington's* case, that a trespasser cannot sue an occupier who negligently injures him. In this wide form, the defence understandably fell into disfavour. But this case shows that there is still room for the defence where the plaintiff's conduct was *turpis* in the narrow and literal sense that it was atrocious or disgusting. It would be outrageous if, thanks to *Herrington's* case, an I.R.A. assassin could sue his intended victim for injuries sustained when he tripped, machine-gun in hand, on the defective carpet which presented a foreseeable danger to the victim's lawful visitors. *Ex turpi causa* is the obvious reason why such a claim should fail, better surely than any mystical exercise about foreseeable and unforeseeable plaintiffs. It would be equally outrageous if Murphy's claim in this case succeeded, the defendant's version of the facts being true. *Ex turpi causa* as so interpreted will not often be needed, because plaintiffs as bad as this do not usually have nerve enough to sue. But *Murphy v Culhane* shows that such cases do sometimes arise in practice, and it is a good thing that the law can still give such a cheeky plaintiff a suitably rough answer. It is also interesting that the Court of Appeal thought that *volenti non fit iniuria* would also be a defence. This is further evidence that the Court of Appeal, although at one time limiting the scope of the defence, is now going back to an extended version of it – a development already noted above.

There is more to be said about the Court of Appeal's suggestion that contributory negligence was also a potential defence here, reducing Murphy's (and hence Mrs. Murphy's) claim if it did not fail entirely because of one of the total defences. This suggestion will raise a few eyebrows. It looks surprising because of the semantic overtones of the words "negligence" and "contributory negligence". Contributory *negligence* suggests the plaintiff's inadvertent conduct as a factor contributing to damage resulting from the defendant's unintentional tort. Is the expression – and the idea enshrined by it – properly applicable in the context of deliberate acts provoking intentional torts? The wording of the Law Reform (Contributory Negligence) Act 1945 provides a possible answer. The scope of the defence is set out in section 1 (1): "Where any person suffers damage as the result partly of his own *fault* and partly of the *fault* of any other person…". "Fault", potentially wider than negligence, is defined by section 4 as including an "act or omission which gives rise to a liability in tort". Lord Denning, sensing the difficulty and seeing this as the way out, said that Murphy's behaviour in this case was probably "fault" within the definition because it might have made him liable in tort. This solution, with all due respect, is unsatisfactorily narrow. It is submitted that on principle it ought to be possible to reduce a plaintiff's damages where he brought the tortious infliction of deliberate harm upon himself by deliberate misconduct towards the defendant, whether or not this misconduct was itself a tort. A plaintiff is equally undeserving of damages where he provokes an assault by threatening behaviour, whether or not this technically amounts to an assault; and he is equally undeserving of a court's sympathy where he provokes an assault by insulting words, whether or not these happen in the circumstances to be actionable as slander. The way is open for a court to reduce the provoking plaintiff's damages even where the provocation was no tort. It could be done by a wide reading of the 1945 Act, which already has a history of broad interpretation whenever the courts have needed a life-belt in a stormy sea (see [1976] C.L.J. 44). Or it could be done by invoking a general principle independent of the 1945 Act, the principle that a person cannot sue for damage which, in law, he has caused himself – a principle which normally abolishes a claim completely, it is true, but which occasionally reduces it in part, one instance being in defamation where the plaintiff's damages are reduced if he provoked the defendant to libel him.

Finally, something must be said about the Court of Appeal's treatment of its own decision in *Lane v Holloway*, a case which it steered around in a manner which some might think not strictly in accordance with the judicial highway code. Lord Denning distinguished the case partly on the unsatisfactory ground that there the plaintiff's provoking behaviour was not a tort, as we have seen. But he also said that *Lane v Holloway* was altogether different because "the conduct of the injured man was trivial – and the conduct of the defendant was savage – entirely out of proportion to the occasion". This is remarkable. This was the case, it will be remembered, where Lane roused Holloway from his bed at night with a challenge to fight, and then called Holloway's wife a "monkey-faced tart" to her face. There the defendant's reaction was out of all proportion, it seems, because he punched the plaintiff in the eye, but here it was another matter, because he only killed him. We get the feeling that the Court of Appeal was rightly unhappy with its earlier decision, and, unable to overrule it, was glad to find any and every way round it. In practical terms, this is usually the judicial equivalent of what John Culhane did to Timothy Murphy with the plank of wood.

Kidnapping – The Crime Backs Down on its Demands
R. v Wellard
CLJ 1979, 38(1) 9–10

Common law offences, being vague, are inclined to swell. Kidnapping is no exception, as the recent case of *Wellard* [1978] 1 W.L.R. 921 shows.

A seventeen-year-old girl was out on Stafford Common with her boyfriend. Wellard came up, introduced himself as a policeman, and said he was taking the girl away. The boyfriend, like Masetto confronted with Don Giovanni, watched open-mouthed as Wellard relieved him of his girlfriend, and then had belated second thoughts. Hailing some friends nearby he went in pursuit, and caught up with Wellard as he was about to drive the girl off in his car parked 100 yards from where he had arrested her. The villain was then unmasked. Wellard was no policeman, but an imposter with a record of sexual offences.

Wellard was prosecuted for abduction contrary to section 19 of the Sexual Offences Act 1956, and, for good measure, kidnapping at common law. The statutory abduction offence requires a sexual motive. As Wellard kept out of the witness-box, and the prosecution had nothing to indicate a sexual motive except for his record which they could hardly use in evidence, Goff J. had to direct an acquittal on this count. However, he told the jury that Wellard's arrest, plus the 100-yard walk to his car, constituted without more the offence of kidnapping. Of this the jury convicted him, and he was sentenced to twelve months' imprisonment. On appeal, Wellard unsuccessfully argued that Goff J. had misdirected the jury on the ingredients of the crime of kidnapping. In a brief judgment delivered by Lawton L.J., the Court of Appeal ruled that he had not.

Kidnapping is supposed to be an aggravated version of the crime (and tort) of false imprisonment: but what, exactly, are the aggravating features? In his essay in honour of Glanville Williams in *Reshaping the Criminal Law* (1978), Dr. B. W. Napier shows that kidnapping originally consisted of capturing people and secretly exporting them for sale as slaves to the American plantations – once a prevalent social evil, and as ghastly an aggravation of false imprisonment as one could want. Over the years, the original aggravating features such as removal abroad have been quietly dropped without replacement, and *Wellard* marks a further stage in this process. It is now apparent that kidnapping needs no violence: it was tacitly accepted in *Wellard* that it can be kidnapping as well as false imprisonment if the victim peacefully submits to an arrest under a mistake induced by fraud. Whatever other aggravating factors may actually have been present in this case, according to the definition of the offence accepted by the Court of Appeal the only aggravating features needed to turn false imprisonment into kidnapping are either concealment of the victim, or carrying him or her away – and for "carrying away" a removal of as little as 100 yards will do.

As so defined, kidnapping now extends to cover most cases of false imprisonment, and its legal requirements bear little resemblance to the popular conception of the offence. For example, in *Brewin* [1976] Crim.L.R. 742 a private citizen, reasonably believing a child to have committed criminal damage, arrested him and took him home to his parents to deal with rather than taking him to the magistrates or the police. A Crown Court judge held this to be false imprisonment. If he held right, this would now be a case of kidnapping as well.

False imprisonment carries the same maximum punishment as kidnapping: life imprisonment and an unlimited fine, both still being virgin common law offences, unspotted by statute. So, apart from the mere untidiness of having two offences covering much the same ground, does the extension of kidnapping to cover most of false imprisonment really matter?

Yes, to some extent it does. Kidnapping is viewed very seriously. "It cannot be too clearly stated that it must be met and will be met with drastic punishment", said Roskill L.J. in *Ogden* (1974) 58 Cr.App.R. 457, where the kidnapper ended up with an eight-year sentence. In *Beagle* (1976) 62 Cr.App.R. 151 an eighteen-year sentence was imposed. Sentencers occasionally tend to punish the same piece of misbehaviour the more heavily merely because it has been charged as the more serious of two offences, the availability of a higher maximum not being the crucial factor. The taste in the mouth, so to speak, is occasionally unduly influenced by what the label on the package says the taste will be. Therefore, when a supposedly serious offence is over-broadly defined, the prosecutor who throws the book at the accused can sometimes make things really bad for him, as well as complicated for the court.

Wellard's behaviour was undoubtedly the crime of false imprisonment. It is a pity that he was not charged with that, so

43

relieving the courts of the temptation to put a broad interpretation on the more serious offence – the requirements of which were admittedly vague – in order to stop a rogue going free. Wellard got his just deserts, but the next man may get rather more.[4]

Tissue Donors: Are they Rescuers, or Merely Volunteers?
Urbanski v Patel
CLJ 1979, 38(1),45–47

Urbanski v Patel (1978) 84 D.L.R. (3d) 650, a decision of Wilson J. in the Supreme Court of Manitoba, is a grisly addition to the "rescuer" cases, and puts a new twist on the "egg-shell skull rule" as well.

Mrs. Firman, hale and hearty, went into hospital to be sterilised. There, the doctor absent-mindedly removed her kidney in mistake for an ovarian cyst. To make matters worse, she was a medical freak and it was her only one – as she and they discovered when she nearly died. They plugged her into a dialysis machine, and her family rallied round to help, including her father, Mr. Ubanski, who donated one of his kidneys for a transplant attempt. Mrs. Firman sued the doctor, and not surprisingly, he admitted liability to her. More surprisingly, her father also claimed damages for the loss of his kidney and for the disruption to his life which this had entailed. Even more surprisingly, perhaps, he got them.

The major obstacle in the way of such a claim as this is the legal rule laid down in *Admiralty Commissioners v S.S. Amerika* [1917] A.C. 38: "no person aggrieved by an injury is by common law entitled to increase his claim for damage by any voluntary act". *A fortiori*, therefore, he cannot claim if it was only by his voluntary act that he became "aggrieved" at all. To take an extreme example, a passer-by who sees a man knocked off his bicycle and stands the shaken man a commiseratory pint of beer cannot sue the negligent

---

[4] The issues this note raises are still topical: the Law Commission is currently engaged on a review of the offence of kidnapping.

motorist for the price of the pint. It was for this reason that a similar kidney-donor's claim had failed in the United States in *Sirianni v Anna*, 285 N.Y.S. (2nd) 709 (1967). Since *Haynes v Harwood* [1935] 1 K.B. 146, however, an exception to this principle has been recognised in favour of the rescuer, who is not regarded as voluntarily causing his own loss. If he gets injured, he wins if his help was urgently needed – provided, of course, his act and injury were reasonably foreseeable, which the courts will always say they were. In the present case the judge held that Urbanksi counted as a rescuer, and his claim on that basis succeeded.

Was this right? Does this mean that any officious Tom, Dick or Harry who gives away his vital organs has the possibility of a lucrative claim provided someone was liable to the donee for his parlous state? With respect, it is suggested that the judge was right, and his ruling on this point does not have these lurid and factually unlikely implications. Urbanski was Mrs. Firman's father. In the rescue cases, the plaintiff is not only highly meritorious, but has acted in an urgent situation which would put any decent person under moral compulsion to act. A father or other close relative might reasonably feel morally compelled to give a kidney whereas anyone else would have a much freer choice in the matter. It is inconceivable that anyone not closely connected with Mrs. Firman would have succeeded in a claim. Perhaps the decision can be seen as part of a general recognition by the courts that members of a family feel morally obliged to do more for each other than they are legally required to do, and a consequential willingness to compensate them, directly or indirectly, when they do it: compare *Donnelly v Joyce* [1974] 1 Q.B. 454.

A second apparent obstacle to this particular claim is the requirement of a foreseeable plaintiff. The doctor negligently removed one kidney from an apparently normal woman. He did not know that she had only one kidney to lose. The unforeseeable extent of *her* loss due to this physical peculiarity was, of course, irrelevant as between the doctor and herself because of the "egg-shell skull rule": you take your plaintiff as you find him. But was it not relevant as between the doctor and her father? As against him, could the defendant not plausibly say that it was unforeseeable that removing a single kidney from an apparently normal patient would set the patient looking for a spare? These difficulties notwithstanding, the judge managed to find as a matter of secondary fact that this harm to the father was reasonably foreseeable, and the obstacle was somehow overcome.

In recent years it has often been said that where the defendant is proved to have acted carelessly in relation to someone, the supposed limitation that harm be foreseeable to this particular plaintiff is a flexible requirement – or in plain English, a bit of a sham. It is said that where the courts feel it moral and right to give damages in an improbable case, they find that the *possibility* of this *general* sort of harm, looking ahead from the *middle* of the story, was reasonably foreseeable; and when in a more probable case the courts feel it would be wrong to give damages, they find that the *probability* of this *particular* sort of harm, looking ahead from the *beginning* of the story, was not. *Urbanski v Patel* certainly bears this out. (So, incidentally, does *Egerton v Home Office* [1978] Crim. L.R. 494 where a judge said that the Home Office was careless in not telling prison officers that a man in association with other prisoners had been convicted of raping little girls; but that his claim failed because experienced prison officers could not reasonably have foreseen that his co-prisoners, a hearty bunch of thieves and murderers, would make such a *spontaneous* attack.)

So what are the unspoken factors in cases such as these which influence judges to find that consequences are or are not reasonably foreseeable? To a large extent, they are how badly the defendant has behaved, and how meritoriously the plaintiff. It is hard to think of a more striking piece of medical negligence than removing a kidney in mistake for an ovarian cyst. And it is hard to think of a more meritorious plaintiff than the altruistic Mr. Urbanski who, in the face of pain, risk and personal inconvenience, volunteered his vital organs in an attempt to repair the mistake.

Blasphemous Libel Resurrected – Gay News and Grim Tidings
R. v Lemon and Gay News Ltd
CLJ 1979, 38(2), 245–251

Woody Allen enthusiasts will remember the scene in "Annie Hall" where the hero and heroine, who have just met, are holding a high-flown conversation which we hear on the sound-track, while their real thoughts appear as subtitles on the screen: "I wonder what she looks like less fully dressed", etc. In the same way there are law cases where what we see is of greater significance than what we hear. In *R. v Lemon and Gay News Ltd.* [1979] A.C. 617 what we heard was mainly an elevated discussion of certain aspects of legal history. What we saw, however, was the resurrection of the crime of blasphemous libel, and its use by a private busybody to punish with fines of £1,500 and untold costs the publication of a poem which, though in appalling taste and annoying to those who have Christian tendencies, had not the smallest chance of doing the slightest harm to anyone. Unfortunately, in this case the subtitles on the screen raise issues too broad to do them justice in a case-note. What follows is therefore a discussion of the soundtrack only.

Lemon and his corporate manifestation Gay News Ltd. published in their newspaper for homosexuals a poem describing, as a sort of allegory of religious experience, "acts of sodomy and fellatio with the body of Christ immediately after the moment of His death". For this, Mrs. Mary Whitehouse privately prosecuted them for the common law offence of blasphemous libel. They were tried at the Old Bailey where the jury convicted by a majority of ten to two. Judge King-Hamilton Q.C. protested when the defendants tried to make the prosecutor prove their involvement in the publication because, Lemon being legally aided, "technical" defences were a misuse of public funds; he publicly commended the jury for their moral courage in convicting, hoping "that by this verdict the pendulum of public opinion is beginning to swing back to a more healthy climate"; and he not only imposed heavy fines, but sentenced Lemon to nine months' imprisonment – though this part of the punishment was set aside on appeal.

The part of the conduct of the trial upon which the defendants based their appeal, however, was the judge's refusal to allow Lemon to give evidence that he did not mean by publishing the poem to vilify Christianity or Christ. The judge so refused because he ruled that in blasphemous libel the intention of the writer is irrelevant. The Court of Appeal upheld this ruling as correct and affirmed the convictions, but certified this as a point of public importance for the House of Lords to consider. After three months' deliberation, the House of Lords agreed with the Court of Appeal and the trial judge by a majority of three to two. So the convictions stand.

Blasphemous libel is one of the four branches of the crime of libel at common law: defamatory libel, seditious libel, obscene libel and blasphemous libel. In the eighteenth century, when libel prosecutions of all sorts were common, the invariable practice was for an indictment for libel to accuse the defendant of acting with the juiciest of evil intentions. It would say "intending to excite and diffuse amongst the subjects of this realm discontents, jealousies, and suspicions of our Lord the King" in a seditious libel prosecution, and "with an intent to vilify and subvert the Christian religion" in one for blasphemous libel. But when criminal libel defendants tried to defend themselves by denying the intentions attributed to them, the judges, like Judge King-Hamilton, refused to allow it on the ground that their intentions were legally irrelevant. The words about intention were "mere words of course, mere inference of law, with which the jury were not to concern themselves . . . just as when it is said in bills of indictment for murder 'instigated by the devil'", said Lord Mansfield C.J. in *Woodfall* (1770) 20 St.Tr. 901. This was one of the sources of discontent with the law of libel which led Parliament to pass Fox's Libel Act of 1792. Nowadays, this Act is remembered as the provision which transferred the question whether or not given words amount to a libel from the judge to the jury. At the time, however, everyone also thought it had made the defendant's intention a relevant issue. The words of the Act do not obviously say this. The Act merely says that in a libel trial the judge must leave the general issue of guilty or not guilty to the jury, and may not direct them to convict merely if they find D published the words in question. In other words, the jury, not the judge, are to decide all the relevant issues. Of course, if D's intention was not a relevant issue before the Act, on the face of it, the words, of the Act do not make it one, and hence do not entitle the jury to consider it. Nevertheless, as Stephen says in his *History of the Criminal Law* (Vol. II, 359), the Act tacitly assumes the defendant's intentions are relevant, "and the law has ever since been administered upon the supposition that they are". Thus from 1792 onwards, judges in libel prosecutions began to tell juries to consider the defendant's intention.

Unfortunately, however, the question of *mens rea* in criminal libel remained to some extent obscure. In the first place, the judges often coupled directions to the jury to consider the defendant's intention with the remark that he was presumed to intend the natural and probable consequences of his words; and although these directions probably turn on rules of evidence set aside by the subjective test of intention imposed by section 8 of the Criminal Justice Act 1967, it is possible to see them as ruling that, notwithstanding Fox's Libel Act, the defendant's intention is still irrelevant. Secondly, after 1792 the courts still blithely continued to hold booksellers criminally liable for libels which, unknown to them, the books they or their servants sold contained – a ruling clearly inconsistent with a *mens rea* requirement – and it took the Libel Act 1843 to stop them.

Confronted with this wilderness of ancient Acts and precedents, Lords Diplock and Edmund-Davies, the dissentients, saw as a beacon to guide them the principle that a person is not to be held guilty of a serious criminal offence unless he intended to commit it. Accordingly they delivered speeches of great clarity, consistency and power in favour of allowing the defendants' appeals, notwithstanding their "strong feelings of revulsion over this deplorable publication".

Unfortunately no such unanimity of principle illuminates the judgments of the majority, which vary widely in content as well as in style. Viscount Dilhorne went patiently through many obscure cases. He doubted the developments from the 1792 Act described by Stephen; if they occurred at all, they were a misconstruction of the Act and the law must be restored to the pristine state in which it left the hands of Lord Mansfield. As a policy reason for this, he added

"If it be accepted, as I think it must, that that which it is sought to prevent is the publication of blasphemous libels, the harm is done by their intentional publication, whether or not the publisher intended to blaspheme" – an argument which also explains why it is theft intentionally to take goods from a shop forgetting to pay for them, and murder to cause death by an intentional act which you did not foresee would kill or hurt.

By contrast, Lord Russell's speech was very short. He upheld the conviction on the basis of common sense and referred to no cases at all. Nor did he refer to any legal principles, although he tacitly condemned the one in *Woolmington v D.P.P.* [1935] A.C. 462 as follows: "Why then should this House, faced with the deliberate publication of that which a jury . . . has held to be a blasphemous libel, consider that it should be for the prosecution to prove, presumably beyond reasonable doubt, that the accused recognised and intended it to be such or regarded it as immaterial whether it was? I see no ground for that."

Lord Scarman's speech was altogether more adventurous. He accepted that the authorities were obscure – so the courts must make a policy decision. In a preamble, he said that modem Britain was "an increasingly plural society", where all religions ought to be protected from attack. The present crime of blasphemy ought to be extended to cover attacks not merely on Christianity, but on all religions. Therefore, he reasoned, we must hold Lemon guilty of the present crime of blasphemy; which protects only Christianity, whether or not he intended to attack it. As "the movement of the law is illustrated by recent statutes", it is permissible, he said, in construing the seventeenth-century offence of blasphemous libel, to look at the Race Relations Act 1976. This makes it a statutory offence to utter words likely to cause racial hatred, even if racial hatred was not intended. Because Parliament thought the law on racist propaganda needed tightening up, therefore, he reasoned, it follows that the courts must for their part tighten up the crime of blasphemy too – presumably because blasphemy ought to have something to do with race hatred and so must be treated as if it did – possibly because both punish people for expressing their opinions, which, in "a plural society", are things one should keep in at one's peril. "All this makes sense", he explained, "in a plural society which recognises the human rights and fundamental freedoms of the European Convention. Article 9 provides that everyone has the right to freedom of religion, and the right to manifest his religion in worship, teaching, practice and observance. By necessary implication the article imposes a duty on all of us to refrain from insulting or outraging the religious feelings of others." In other words, freedom to practise one's religion includes freedom to stop others preaching against it, by having them locked up if need be. For good measure, though not relevant to the issue before him, he added that it is not, as previously thought, an ingredient in blasphemy that the words be likely to cause a breach of the peace. This, presumably, followed from his earlier classification of blasphemy as belonging "to a group of criminal offences designed to safeguard the internal tranquillity of the kingdom".

This is a remarkable judgment. It consists of a series of non-sequiturs. And, although the style and terminology are very different, the spirit is the spirit of *Shaw v D.P.P.* [1962] A.C. 220 all over again: deliberate judicial extension of the criminal law; inflating broad, vague common law offences derived from a society that no longer exists; penalising in generous terms what the judges on the spur of the moment happen to dislike; resulting in criminal law which Parliament would reject if offered it disinfected on the end of a barge-pole.

What are the implications of this decision for the criminal law generally? And what are its implications for the various forms of criminal libel in particular? On the first point, Professor Smith has described the decision as a severe set-back to "the principle of subjective *mens rea* which, since the disaster of *D.P.P. v. Smith* [1961] A.C. 290, has made steady, though not unfaltering, progress in our criminal law" ([1979] *Crim.L.R.* 313). Is it quite as bad as this? The defendants were arguing for intention as an element in a crime of which the actus reus (Bentham help us!) is publishing something which vilifies Christianity in such a way as to outrage and insult the religious feelings of Christians. The House of Lords rejected the requirement of intention. A person is taken to intend a consequence both when he desires to cause it, and also when he knows it is bound to follow from the act which he proposes to do, although he does not desire it. Thus the House rejected a requirement that D should either desire to vilify Christianity so as to outrage and insult believers, or know that his words were such. Absence of *mens rea* usually means ignorance of *primary* facts: D did not know that P was in the room when he shot, or thought that P, a trespasser, was armed when he was not. Mistakes about *secondary* facts, which are evaluations of the primary facts made by the jury rather than the judge, are normally treated as if they were mistakes of law, and avail a defendant nothing. It does D no good to say, for example, that he thought grievous bodily harm was reasonable force with which to remove an unarmed trespasser, or that he believed a bullet in the buttock would not amount to *grievous* bodily harm. Whilst there may be room for argument, the question whether given words vilify badly enough to outrage and insult looks suspiciously like a question of secondary rather than primary fact: a point Lord Russell seems to stumble upon when he says "I see no justification for holding that there is no offence when the publisher is incapable . . . of agreeing with the jury on the true nature of the publication." If this is so, the result at least of the *Gay News* case can be reconciled with the principle of subjective *mens rea*. There are, of course, important exceptional cases – blackmail for example – where it is thought necessary to allow D the benefit of a mistake of secondary fact; and in the interests of free speech, which even in a "plural society" some persons consider valuable, it might have been sensible to add blasphemous libel to the list of cases Where the requirement of *mens rea* so extends. Failure to do so, however, is not a general disaster for the principle of subjective *mens rea*.

What is the effect of the decision on the *mens rea* requirements of the crimes of seditious and defamatory libel, which are historically part of the same thing, and equally governed by Fox's Libel Act of 1792? The House did not discuss the crime of defamatory libel. However, the case obviously suggests that D is guilty where he makes, fully understanding it, a remark about P which he does not regard as defamatory, but others, including the jury, do: if D, for example, being an I.R.A. man, calls P another. The case should not, however, make D guilty in the *Artemus Jones* sort of case, where he says something which, through facts unknown to him, is taken by others as defamatory of P. It might, however, be taken to do so, because unfortunately the Court of Appeal bolstered its arguments with approving references to the law of civil libel, where liability is indeed truly strict, D being liable even where ignorant of the primary facts which make his words defamatory. What about seditious libel? This case indicates that D is now guilty even where he did not intend to stir up discontent and disorder, or know that his words were likely to do so – although the bulk of the modem seditious libel cases, strongly relied on by the dissenting Lords Diplock and Edmund-Davies, say or assume that he is not. Lord Scarman saw this implication and welcomed it, though Viscount Dilhome deliberately left the point open. Thus as regards D's intentions, the legal clock seems to have run backwards to 1792 in all areas of criminal libel. The shades of Lord Mansfield and Lord Ellenborough must rejoice.

Given seditious libel prosecutions are unlikely to be resurrected, however, it is a totally different aspect of the decision which in practical terms is likely to be the major change. Since *Bowman v. Secular Society* [1917] A.C. 406 everyone had thought that to amount to a blasphemous libel the publication must tend to create a breach of the peace. In other words, there must be a good chance that it would lead to blows. Judge King-Hamilton told the jury that such a tendency was needed, and then defined it to include the mere possibility that the publication might arouse anger. Understandably puzzled, the jury returned and asked for the riddle again, and when it was repeated, convicted. There were attempts to argue this aspect of the case at both levels of appeal, but nevertheless it rather sank from sight. The Court of Appeal approved the judge's direction generally, as did the majority of the House of Lords. Two Lords even went so far as to say that there need be no risk of a breach of the peace at all. Thus a secondary effect of this case seems to be to remove, directly or indirectly, a serious limitation from the scope of the offence. If it is now a blasphemous libel to publish words attacking or ridiculing the Christian religion which might possibly make believers angry,

Mrs. Mary Whitehouse's ancient weapon has been ground to a fine edge.[5]

Lies, Damned Lies, and Corroboration
R. v Lucas
CLJ 1982, 41(1) 27–29

Sensibly enough, the criminal courts require certain types of presumptively unreliable evidence to be *corroborated*.[6] Sometimes, as with the unsworn evidence of little children, the requirement for corroboration is absolute. More often, it is less than absolute, and the judge is merely required to warn the jury that it is risky to convict on this type of evidence uncorroborated, but that they may do so if they are absolutely satisfied that the witness is telling the truth. The meaning of "corroboration" was clearly explained in *Baskerville* [1916] 2 K.B. 658:

> ...evidence in corroboration must be independent testimony which affects the accused by connecting or tending to connect him with the crime. In other words, it must be evidence which implicates him, that is, which confirms in some material particular not only the evidence that the crime has been committed, but also that the prisoner committed it.

This statement of principle has long been obscured by a large number of reported decisions which rule, at the lowest possible level of abstraction, that this, that or the other is or is not corroboration. The courts and the reporters have thereby laid a wall-to-wall carpet of eggs, upon one of which any judge who tries to put the matter to the jury in plain terms is almost certain to tread. Lord Lane and his brother judges in the Court of Appeal in *Lucas* [1981] 3 W.L.R.

---

[5] Despite the outrage these proceedings caused, the offences of blasphemy and blasphemous libel proved remarkably durable. They were finally abolished by s.79 of the Criminal Justice and Immigration Act 2008. For a brief account of the steps that led up to their eventual abolition see Francis Bennion, "Farewell to the Blasphemy Laws", (2008) 172 *Justice of the Peace* 448.

[6] Most of the formal corroboration requirements that existed when this note was written have now been abolished. But *Lucas* is still the leading case on the weight that criminal courts are supposed to give to the fact that the defendant can be shown to have told lies.

120 deserve credit for a decision which clears a small egg-free patch for future judges to walk on.

The question at issue was: can the defendant's lies corroborate? Approaching the matter in ignorance of the case law, one would expect the answer to be "yes, sometimes". Being taxed on the disappearance of his wife, Crippen told an elaborate story about her making a trip abroad to see relations, which was disproved, and which he admitted was a lie. Any sane person would take this lie as tending to show Crippen's guilt of murder when her body was found under the cellar floor. On the other hand, if a man is accused of rape, and the only evidence that he did it is the girl's testimony that he raped her, there is clearly a flaw in the reasoning if the judge tells the jury: "Her evidence needs corroboration; his lies can corroborate her story; if you believe her, he is lying; her evidence is then corroborated, and you may safely convict." The answer would seem to be that lies may corroborate provided, first, that they amount to more than a denial of the bare disputed elements of the offence and, secondly, that they are shown to be lies by something other than the evidence of the witness it is sought to corroborate. Needless to say, the case law was more complicated than this. As a result of *Chapman* [1973] Q.B. 774, there appeared to be a distinction between lies told in and out of court. Out-of-court lies could corroborate, subject to approximately the limitations already mentioned. Lies in court could not corroborate at all. In *Lucas*, the Court of Appeal said that *Chapman* decided no such thing. Lies in court can corroborate as much as lies out of court, that is to say, subject to the following safeguards:

> To be capable of amounting to corroboration the lie told… must first of all be deliberate. Secondly, it must relate to a material issue. Thirdly, the motive for the lie must be a realisation of guilt and a fear of the truth… Fourthly, the statement must be clearly shown to be a lie by evidence other than that of the accomplice who is to be corroborated, that is to say by admission or by evidence from an independent witness.

It is possible to pick certain holes in the precise form of this safeguard. A jury can only find a man to have "a realisation of guilt" if they have first decided that he is guilty – and as they are supposed to be looking for corroboration as an aid to deciding that question, this puts the cart before the horse. Better, surely, to have said that "there must be no obvious innocent explanation for the lie", or something to that effect. Also, it would have been useful if the Court of Appeal had said that the lie must consist of something other than a denial of the element of the offence which the tainted or unreliable witness alleges, and which is in dispute because the defendant denies it. Nevertheless, it is generally satisfactory in that it assimilates in-court and out-of-court lies, and is a considerable improvement on the previous law.

Lucas was about the corroboration of accomplices. Although *Lucas* improves one aspect of this, the law on the corroboration of accomplices is in an unsatisfactory state in other respects. This is no reflection on the Court of Appeal in the present case. It is the result of *Davies v D.P.P.* [1954] A.C. 378, a House of Lords decision beyond the Court of Appeal's reforming reach. There, the following propositions were laid down. First, the judge must mouth the formula about the danger of convicting on uncorroborated accomplice evidence, even where the case is bursting at the seams with corroboration, and such a warning is needless; if he fails, he presents the defendant with an unmeritorious ground of appeal. Secondly, it said that "accomplice" means an accessory to the very crime for which the defendant is on trial. The man who admits helping a murder defendant to beat the victim up, but says he was horrified when the defendant produced a gun – and who was thus an accessory to assault but not to murder – does not count as an "accomplice" about whose evidence the jury must be warned; and this, of course, is just the situation where the witness is likely to be lying to save his neck, making a warning really necessary. Technicalities of this sort, which might have been created simply to make juries get the wrong answer, turn corroboration into the Bedlam of the law of evidence. And such it remains, although the Court of Appeal has now managed to cure and release one of its less rational inmates.

Dishonesty: What the Jury Thinks the Defendant Thought the Jury Would Have Thought
R. v Ghosh
CLJ 1982, 41(2) 222–225

A dozen Theft Act offences require the accused to have acted "dishonestly". What does this mean? Section 2 of the Theft Act 1968 says a person is not dishonest for the purposes of theft if he appropriates under a claim of right, in the belief that the owner would consent if he knew, or in the belief that the owner cannot be traced. However, in the crime of theft is this list exclusive, or are there any other cases where the accused, although otherwise guilty, is not dishonest? And what does "dishonestly" mean in other Theft Act offences, where the partial definition in section 2 does not apply?

In *Feely* [1973] Q.B. 530 the Court of Appeal ruled that dishonesty means something which the jury, applying its own standards of right and wrong, regards as dishonest. Therefore when an employee, contrary to orders, "dipped the till" intending to repay, the jury at his trial for theft should have been asked whether they regarded such conduct as dishonest, although this fell outside the cases expressly covered by section 2. Soon after, in *Greenstein* [1975] 1 W.L.R. 1353 the Court of Appeal said that the same goes for dishonesty in the other Theft Act offences. Thus Greenstein's ingenious scheme to buy shares with cheques which he knew might bounce was the crime of obtaining by deception, or not, according to whether the jury in question thought it was dishonest. Writers criticised these decisions as making the criminal law far too uncertain.

Nevertheless, some courts began to say that the accused is dishonest, not where the jury regard his behaviour as dishonest, but where the jury find the accused regarded his own behaviour as dishonest. For example, in *Gilks* [1972] 1 W.L.R. 1341 the Court of Appeal approved a direction to a jury to acquit a man of theft from a bookmaker if they thought the man honestly believed that bookmakers were fair game for theft! Something similar was said in *Boggeln v Williams* [19781 1 W.L.R. 873, and in *Landy* [1981] 1 W.L.R. 355.

Recently, the Court of Appeal noticed the conflict between *Feely* and this line of cases, and in *McIvor* [1982] 1 W.L.R. 409 and in *Ghosh* [1982] Q.B. 53 it tried to resolve it. As *Ghosh* and *McIvor* themselves conflict, its efforts can hardly be called a stupendous success.

McIvor dipped his employer's till to fund a family holiday, and on detection, like Billy Bunter, said he always meant to repay when a cheque from Canada arrived. Therefore, he said, he was not dishonest. The jury were told "the fact that the defendant has told you that he thought there was nothing wrong is neither here nor there. It is what you think that matters". The Court of Appeal, in a judgment delivered by Lawton L.J., said that this direction was in line with *Feely*, and *Feely* was correct. So far, so good. But instead of disposing of the notion that the accused's personal standards are relevant by condemning the cases which support this view as wrong, the Court of Appeal distinguished them and left them to work mischief another day. It distinguished *Landy* – the strongest of them – as conspiracy to defraud rather than theft, and so implied that the defendant's personal standards may be relevant in fraud cases, although they are irrelevant in theft: which is irreconcilable with *Greenstein*, and would be a senseless distinction if it were not.

Three months later, the chickens came home to roost in *Ghosh*. Ghosh, a surgeon, told lies to extract fees from the National Health Service to which he knew he was not entitled. On dishonesty, the trial judge directed the jury to decide whether Ghosh's "fiddle" was dishonest by their standards, and they promptly convicted him of obtaining by deception. Ghosh appealed, saying that in the light of Lawton L.J.'s remarks in *McIvor* about dishonesty in fraud cases, the jury should have been asked whether they thought the fraud was dishonest according to the standards of Mr. Ghosh. As might have been expected, the Court of Appeal ruled that there is no difference between the test of dishonesty in fraud and theft, despite what Lawton L.J. had earlier said. Again, so far, so good. Unfortunately, however, the differently constituted Court of Appeal went on to condemn most of the rest of Lawton L.J.'s judgment in *McIvor* as well, and to substitute its own explanation of dishonesty, which it thought would reconcile all the irreconcilable cases. With respect, the new test is no improvement.

The new version of dishonesty involves giving the defendant the benefit of both the pre-existing tests. "…[A] jury must first of all decide whether according to the ordinary standards of reasonable and honest people what was done was dishonest. If it was not dishonest by those standards, that is the end of the matter and the prosecution fails." Then they must additionally be satisfied that the defendant thought that he was doing wrong. Here, however, the question is not whether he regarded his behaviour as wrong by his own moral standards, but rather whether he felt it was wrong by the standards he knew to be accepted by ordinary people. "For example, Robin Hood or those ardent anti-vivisectionists who remove animals from vivisection laboratories are acting dishonestly, even though they may consider themselves to be morally justified in doing what they do, because they know that ordinary people would consider these actions to be dishonest." In other words, the jury must first decide what they think of the defendant's behaviour, and then decide what the defendant would have thought the jury would think of it, had the matter crossed his mind. Clearly, intelligence tests for juries will soon be needed.

At the root of all this confusion is a failure to recognise an elementary fact: that the concept of dishonesty involves not one question, but two. First, there is the question what the accused thought and intended. Did he really intend to repay the money? Did he really believe that a cheque was coming from Canada to enable him to do so? This is a question of primary fact, properly within the province of the jury, and to this extent dishonesty is obviously a question of the defendant's state of mind. Secondly, there is an evaluative question: given that he so thought and intended, was it honest to do as he did? Here, by contrast, dishonesty is a qualification of the defendant's conduct. This question, surely, must be for the court to decide, applying its own and not the defendant's standards. Such evaluative questions are in essence questions of law, for all we call them questions of "secondary fact" when, as here, juries are made to answer them. It is a case of setting standards of behaviour, and we cannot possibly allow the defendant to set his own, even to the attenuated extent the Court of Appeal in *Ghosh* allows. By letting him say "I'm sorry, I thought society tolerated till dipping, or cheating bookmakers, or fiddling the N.H.S.", we are letting him advance what is in effect a mistake of law as a defence. For the courts to take their criminal law from the man on the Clapham omnibus is one thing; to take it from the man accused of stealing it is quite another.

Failure to appreciate the double aspect of dishonesty also explains the confusing way in which the Court of Appeal in *Ghosh* first asserted that dishonesty describes a state of mind, denying that it characterises a course of conduct; and then pronounced a test of dishonesty, part of which is whether "according to the ordinary standards of reasonable and honest people what was done was dishonest".

Judicial fisticuffs between different Courts of Appeal mean that, sooner or later, the question of dishonesty is bound to make its maiden appearance in the House of Lords. Fortunately, this has power to wipe the slate clean and write the definition of dishonesty completely anew. Before it does so, however, there are some basic questions which it should consider. Do we really need an amorphous concept of dishonesty as a universal escape route in hard cases? If we do, should it really be for the jury rather than the judge to decide whether on given facts the defendant is entitled to escape through it? And if it is for the jury, what measure of control, if any, should the judge have over them? With particular emphasis on the indefinite article, let us pray "to have a right judgment in all things".[7]

---

[7] This prediction has proved false and *Ghosh* still remains the leading case. For the latest state of play, see *Simester and Sullivan's Criminal Law* (5th ed, 2013) 547–550.

Retrials, Reason and the House of Lords
R. v Rose
CLJ 1983, 42(1)18–21

An innocent man is cruelly stabbed to death in a London street. A suspect is charged and tried for murder. After the jury have been considering their verdict for eight hours, the judge despairs of their ever deciding anything, and without telling counsel, sends them a note to say that if they do not reach a verdict in twenty minutes he will discharge them: whereupon they convict. The Court of Appeal condemns the judge's conduct, however well intentioned, as improper pressure on the jury, and quashes the conviction. What happens now? Can the suspect be retried? No, says the House of Lords in *Rose* [1982] A.C. 822. And if he did commit the murder? Too bad: *floreat justitia.*

Whatever the merits or demerits of the case against *Rose*, the rule that there can never be a retrial in such a case as this is, surely, quite appalling. In allowing the appeal, the court is not saying that the appellant is innocent – only that his guilt was not properly determined. If he is truly guilty, then we are literally letting him get away with murder. The aims of the criminal law are frustrated, the good efforts of the police thwarted, and the public reinforced in its belief that the law is an ass.

There is an enormous difference in principle between allowing an appeal on the ground that the appellant is not guilty, and allowing it where, as here, the defendant has not been given due process of law. In the first type of case, there can obviously be no question of retrial. In the second, however, almost every other legal system in the world allows one. So why in England do we not? Does its absence reflect some basic principle of the common law? No. Most other common law systems provide one – Northern Ireland, for example. We lack it through an historical accident, and a fairly recent one at that.

Before 1908 there was generally no right of appeal in criminal cases except over certain technical failures of due process; but where such an appeal succeeded, a retrial was usually possible. Where a conviction was quashed for a procedural defect, this was not regarded as an acquittal barring further trial: the earlier proceedings were treated as never having taken place, and the prosecutor was therefore free to prefer a fresh indictment if he wished. Sometimes, instead of completely quashing the proceedings to date, the appellate court would declare a "mistrial" and prescribe a new trial of the original indictment – a course known as "ordering a *venire de novo*".

The Criminal Appeal Act 1907 set up the scheme of appeal which still operates today. The statute (now the Criminal Appeal Act 1968, s.2) lists various "grounds of appeal", including, among others, "material irregularity in the course of the trial", and says that if the appellant establishes one of these grounds, his conviction must be quashed. There follows the proviso: "Provided that the Court may, notwithstanding that they are of opinion that the point raised in the appeal might be decided in favour of the appellant, dismiss the appeal if they consider that no miscarriage of justice has actually occurred." And finally, it is laid down that a successful appeal under the statute counts as an acquittal – and hence precludes retrial.

The original idea seems to have been that the Court of Criminal Appeal should investigate failures of due process, but should uphold the conviction if it thought that despite the irregularity the appellant was still guilty. Indeed, it seems inconceivable that parliament should have abolished the power to have the appellant retried otherwise. However, from the start the new court took a narrower view of its powers. It steadfastly refused to form its own view of the merits of such a case, and interpreted the proviso as permitting it to uphold the conviction only where it was satisfied that no reasonable jury, properly directed, could have failed to convict. As a result, a failure of due process at the trial continued to guarantee almost automatic reversal of the conviction, only now without the possibility of retrial. This was seen as highly unsatisfactory, and there were calls for the introduction of a statutory power of retrial almost as soon as the Criminal Appeal Act was in force. (See, for example, *Dyson* [1908] 2 K.B. 454.)

It was against this background that in *Crane v D.P.P.* [1921] A.C. 299 the House of Lords contrived to hold that the ancient common law power to order a *venire de novo* had survived the 1907 Act and now belonged to the Court of Criminal Appeal, thereby creating a limited power of retrial by judicial action. The difficulty was: when was the power available? The circumstances which gave rise to a "mistrial" were obscure before 1908, and had become no clearer in the interval. The Court of Criminal Appeal gratefully accepted the new power, however, and invoked it to order a *venire de novo* following a number of bizarre procedural errors: where the appellant pleaded "guilty" by mistake or under pressure; where he was invalidly committed for trial; where (horror!) he was tried on two distinct indictments, instead of on one indictment comprising two counts; where he was denied the right to challenge a juror; where the judge or a juror was not qualified to act; where the judge forgot to get the jury to return a "guilty" verdict when the defendant in a contested trial changed his plea; and where the verdict of the jury was ambiguous. The unifying feature of this heterodox list was said – unconvincingly – to be that these mistakes, unlike others, rendered the trial a total nullity.

The point for decision in *Rose* was whether the concept of mistrial also covered the case where the judge put improper pressure on the jury. The Court of Appeal felt that it should, but was constrained by precedent to hold otherwise. So it certified a point of public importance, with a nudge and a wink to the House of Lords. The Lords, however, refused to take the hint, and applied its own brand of freeze-dry logic to the problem instead. According to Lord Diplock, the irregularities which give rise to a mistrial must either prevent the trial from being validly started, or prevent a trial validly begun from reaching a valid conclusion. The concept of mistrial, therefore, does not extend to an irregularity which, as here, occurs somewhere in the middle. So Rose's conviction could only be quashed, without the possibility of retrial. With this the rest of the House agreed.

The line between when there can and cannot be a retrial is most unsatisfactory. The theory is that there are minor procedural errors, which do not make the trial a nullity, and major ones which do. The minor errors are remedied under the Criminal Appeal Act, where there can be no retrial, whereas the major ones activate the common law power to order a *venire de novo*. This is quite perverse. It means the less serious the appellant's complaint about the trial, the more generously we treat him, and that we go easy on the prosecutor who flouts, and does not merely break, the rules. This paradox matters less than appears, but only because, despite the theory, it is usually the less serious irregularities which are held to make the trial a nullity. But if the line of demarcation is not in practice quite perverse, it is certainly capricious. If the judge browbeats the defendant into a guilty plea, there can be a retrial following appeal, and likewise if he packs a prosecution-minded jury; but if he browbeats a dithering jury into convicting, the conviction is quashed without the possibility of retrial – although if he left them to their indecision and they failed to agree, a new trial would follow as a matter of course.

The absence of a general power of retrial after a failure of due process is one of the most glaring defects in the criminal justice system. It would also be one of the simplest to correct. Will nothing ever be done about it?[8]

Theft – Appropriation and Consent
R. v Morris
CLJ 1984, 43(1), 7–10

The crime of theft requires dishonest "appropriation", which section 3(1) of the Theft Act 1968 vaguely defines as "any assumption by a person of the rights of an owner". Two divergent views have emerged as to what this means. The technical view is that an appropriation requires some invasion of the owner's rights as defined and protected by the civil law – from which it follows that there can usually be no appropriation if the owner consents to what is done. On this view the dishonest shopper who takes goods from the supermarket shelf commits no appropriation (and hence no theft) until he gets past the cash-desk without paying, or does

---

[8] Something was. The Court of Appeal was given a general power to order a retrial by the Criminal Justice Act 1988 and some dozens are now ordered every year.

something else which would make Messrs. Marks and Spencer shout "Hoy!" if they saw it. The non-technical view, on the other hand, is that an appropriation consists of any act which only the owner would normally do to the property. On this view, the dishonest supermarket shopper appropriates (and hence steals) as soon as he picks the article up. Each view has its merits and demerits. The technical view keeps the crime of theft within bounds, but at the expense of complications when owners permit dishonest persons to take property by mistake, through fraud, through duress, or in order to entrap them. The non-technical view avoids these difficulties, but leaves theft almost without limits, bounded only by the vague notion of dishonesty. Which represents the law?

In *Lawrence* [1972] A.C. 626 the House of Lords seemed to accept the non-technical view when it upheld a theft conviction on a London taxi driver who took from a foreign visitor, with his apparent consent, more than the permitted fare. Viscount Dilhorne, in whose speech the rest of the House concurred, said:

> That there was appropriation in this case is clear... Belief or absence of belief that the owner had with... knowledge consented to the appropriation is relevant to the issue of dishonesty, not to the question whether or not there has been an appropriation. That may occur even though the owner has permitted or consented to the property being taken.

Yet there was reluctance to take this decision at face value. Writers sought to explain it away. And in the courts below, two conflicting lines of authority developed. In one, it was assumed that there can be an appropriation although the owner consents, and in the other it was assumed – despite, and usually without reference to *Lawrence* – that there cannot.

Matters came to a head in *Morris* [1984] A.C. 320. In a supermarket Morris stuck the label from a cheap item on a dear one, which the cashier then unwittingly sold him at the cheap price. At that point in the story Morris undoubtedly committed the crime of obtaining by deception contrary to section 15 of the Theft Act 1968, as the Court of Appeal and the House of Lords later agreed. He was convicted of theft, however, and from the theft conviction appealed. The Court of Appeal could have said that whether or not the owner's consent is relevant, the owner did not consent to his goods being relabelled, and Morris had therefore appropriated them on either view of appropriation. But Lord Lane C.J. spurned the easy way out, took the opportunity to examine both lines of cases, and condemned the ones which take a technical view of appropriation as inconsistent with *Lawrence*. Thus Morris appropriated the goods when he relabelled them, but would have appropriated them as soon as he took them from the shelf even if he had not swapped the labels.

In the House of Lords a very different view on the meaning of appropriation was expressed. Morris's theft conviction was again affirmed, but only because he had relabelled the goods, this being an act to which the owner did not consent. In a brief speech in which the rest of the House concurred, Lord Roskill denied that merely removing goods from a supermarket shelf could be appropriation, because

> ... the concept of appropriation in my view involves not an act expressly or impliedly authorised by the owner but an act by way of adverse interference with or usurpation of those rights... It is with the consent of the owners of the supermarket, be that consent express or implied, that the shopper does these acts and thus obtains at least control if not actual possession of the goods...

How did Lord Roskill square this with the result in *Lawrence* – which is difficult – or with Viscount Dilhorne's remarks on appropriation – which is impossible? Although he took Lawrence as his "starting point", Lord Roskill made no attempt to do so, and we must guess whether it is distinguishable, right for the wrong reasons, or impliedly overruled.

And what of the various Court of Appeal decisions which have taken the *Lawrence* approach to appropriation? Lord Roskill told us that *Macpherson* [1973] Crim.L.R. 191 – where a dishonest shopper was held to have stolen a bottle on removing it from the supermarket shelf – was right given that the shopper had hidden the bottle in her own bag, to which the shopkeeper did not consent. But of the rest, like his own decision in *Monaghan* [1979] Crim.L.R. 673, he merely said "those inconsistent with this speech must henceforth be treated as overruled". Again, we have to guess.

Nor were the practical implications of the rival views of appropriation mentioned. Lord Roskill did however say "... these shoplifting cases by switching labels are essentially simple in their facts and their factual simplicity should not be allowed to be obscured by ingenious legal arguments upon the Theft Act which for some time have bedevilled this branch of the criminal law..." – a plea for a simple and non-technical law of theft which comes ill from a House which has just chosen the meaning of appropriation more likely to lead to appeals by defendants who are admittedly dishonest, and which suggests that practical implications were not much thought about either.

Whether one prefers the technical or the non-technical view of appropriation, the decision in *Morris* is depressing. It is the second criminal case in the House of Lords this year which is not even competent in technical respects. In *Seymour* [1983] C.L.J. 187 the House concurred in a single judgment on manslaughter which is internally inconsistent. And now the House has concurred in a single speech which flatly contradicts what the House said in an earlier case, without saying whether the decision is distinguished or overruled. In the brief judgment in *Lawrence* the House of Lords found space to complain that such a case had wasted their time, and in *Morris* the same impatience with the subject matter comes through. But this is no excuse. The House of Lords may find ascertaining the proper limits of a crime for which people can be locked up for ten years a tiresome distraction from really vital matters, but it is their job to attend to it properly, and they deserve criticism for failing to do it.[9]

---

[9] A differently-constituted House of Lords redeemed itself in the later cases of *Gomez* [1993] A.C. 442 and in *Hinks* [2001] 2 A.C. 241 – in which the issues were thoroughly examined, even if the conclusions reached attracted the ire of some distinguished academic commentators.

On Contemplating the Range of Contemplation
Chan Wing-Siu v R
CLJ 1985, 44(1) 8–10

Lam Pui-Yin, a Hong-Kong prostitute, went to the door of her flat expecting to find a customer. Instead there were three Chinese toughs brandishing knives, who burst in and demanded money from her ponce-cum-husband, Cheung Man-Kam. In the resulting scuffle Cheung Man-Kam was stabbed to death and Lam Pui-Yin was stabbed and injured. It was not clear whether all or only some of the attackers took part in the stabbing, and no doubt each hoped the jury would think the others did it. But the judge directed the jury as follows:

> The Crown does not have to prove which accused inflicted the fatal blow. You may convict any accused of murder if you come to the conclusion that he either personally inflicted the fatal wound on the deceased with the intention of causing at least serious bodily injury or that one of his companions inflicted that wound and that the accused contemplated that either of his companions might use a knife to cause serious bodily injury on any one or more of the occupants of the flat.

The jury accordingly convicted all three of murder, and they appealed to the Privy Council. Their complaint was that the jury should have been told to convict a non-stabber of murder only if he thought a stabbing by one of his colleagues was more probable than not: to say he was guilty if he thought it *might* happen was unduly severe. The Privy Council in a judgment delivered by Sir Robin Cooke dismissed the appeals (*Chan Wing-Siu v R.* [1985] A.C. 168.) In such a case as this, he said, accomplices are guilty of all crimes committed which are within their range of contemplation, and a crime may fall within the range of someone's contemplation even if he does not think it will more probably happen than not; the participant in a joint enterprise of this sort escapes conviction only if he does not foresee the risk in question at all, or thinks it is extremely remote. Unfortunately, however, this pronouncement does not seem to have settled the question. If the apparently similar case of *Jubb and Rigby* [1984] Crim.L.R. 616 is correctly reported, the Court of Appeal has considered *Chan Wing-Siu* and deduced from it that the correct direction for the jury is to convict the participant if he foresaw the criminal consequence as "probable". This hardly seems to square with what the Privy Council actually said. On principle and authority, which is correct: the "possible" Privy Council or the "probable" Court of Appeal?

Stripped of its exotic setting the story in *Chan Wing-Siu* is as old as armed robbery, and has spawned reported cases since the seventeenth century. (For example, the *Three Soldiers' Case* in Foster, 353.) The English decisions say the participants are liable for what fell within the range of their contemplation, but usually elaborate no further. A series of decisions from Australia and New Zealand hold the test to be "possible" rather than "probable," however, and these were approved and applied by the Privy Council in *Chan Wing-Siu*. The Privy Council did not discuss it, but the House of Lords decision in *Maxwell* [1978] 1 W.L.R. 1350 also points the same way. Maxwell, it will be remembered, led a group of terrorists to a bar not knowing exactly what they would do when they got there, but believing that they would either blow it up, burn it down or shoot someone in it. It was held that this was enough to make Maxwell guilty as an accessory to the terrorists' attempt to cause an explosion. In the Northern Ireland Court of Appeal Lord Lowry C.J. said:

> The situation has something in common with that of two persons who agree to rob a bank on the understanding... that violence *may* be resorted to. The accomplice knows, not that the principal *will* shoot the cashier, but that he may do so; and, if the principal does shoot him, the accomplice will be guilty of murder.

This judgment was unanimously approved by the House of Lords, one member of which adopted it as his own speech. On authority, the Privy Council with its "possible" is surely right. Furthermore, on principle it is surely sensible that the participant should be guilty even where he does not believe the prohibited consequence to be more probable than not – at any rate where he provides major assistance in the commission of a really serious offence. People have no business to help others rob bank-messengers, or even ponces, and they should be discouraged from taking part in any activity which they know to involve even the remote chance of serious and unlawful personal violence. It does not follow, however, that so strict a rule would necessarily be sensible for those who furnish minor assistance, particularly minor assistance to less serious offences. It would be silly if a jeweller could be prosecuted for selling a ring to someone he suspected might *possibly* be a would-be bigamist, or if a pump attendant could be prosecuted for fuelling up a car which he suspected might *possibly* have no valid M.O.T. certificate, or if a bus company could be prosecuted for putting up a bus-shelter foreseeing that the village exhibitionist might *possibly* use it as a place to display his wares. As Professor Williams warns us, the law of accessoryship constantly threatens to get out of hand, and we must watch lest rules which are necessary to penalise taking a prominent part in serious crimes mechanically extend themselves down the scale to become an unreasonable fetter on normal life.

Precedent and Criminal Cases in the House of Lords
R. v Shivpuri
CLJ 1986, 45(3) 361

The Criminal Attempts Act 1981 was unquestionably meant to replace a tangled mass of barely comprehensible case-law with a simple statutory rule that a person is guilty of attempt where he would have committed the completed offence if the facts had been as he believed them to be. So eyebrows were considerably raised when in *Anderton v Ryan* [1985] A.C. 560 the House of Lords interpreted the Act as preserving most of the case-law, and held that a person could not be convicted of attempting to handle stolen goods when she bought a video recorder believing it to be stolen, but the prosecution could not prove that it actually was. The case was resoundingly attacked, notably by Glanville Williams in a previous edition of the Journal [1986] C.L.J. 33. The next case, *Shivpuri* [1986] 2 W.L.R. 988, [1987] A.C. 1, involved a much more sinister defendant: a man who was caught trying to smuggle heroin, and who was as surprised as the police were to discover that what he was carrying was only snuff. In this case Lord Bridge, who had delivered one of the opinions in *Anderton v Ryan*, now accepted that his views in that case were wrong – and gracefully acknowledged the help which he had received from Glanville Williams's article in reaching this conclusion. The other four Law Lords agreed. So the House overruled *Anderton v Ryan* and upheld Shivpuri's conviction for attempting to smuggle drugs.

The decision is doubly historic. It is both the first time that the House of Lords has overruled one of its recent decisions, and the first time that it has expressly overruled its decision in a criminal case. When the House of Lords announced its willingness to overrule itself in the Practice Statement [1966] 1 W.L.R. 1234, it hinted that criminal cases fell outside the new dispensation by uttering discouraging noises about "the especial need for certainty as to the criminal law". In the years that followed, the House twice refused to consider overruling criminal decisions which had attracted the most bitter criticism: *Shaw v D.P.P.* [1962] A.C. 220, and *D.P.P. v Smith* [1961] A.C. 290. What were the reasons for this reluctance? As the Court of Appeal is *more* willing to reverse itself in a criminal than in a civil case, they need to be looked at with scepticism. The main reason for refusing to overrule decisions which extended the criminal law seems to have been the fact that people might have been convicted under the extended law meanwhile. To borrow the words of Vaughan J. in a nineteenth-century case, "numbers have been improperly executed if it is a defence". This reasoning occurs again and again in *Knuller v D.P.P.* [1973] A.C. 435, where the House of Lords refused to overrule *Shaw*. But this is monstrous, because it amounts to saying that where a person has been unjustly locked up in the past, it is better to lock another person up unjustly than to admit that a mistake was made. Where the decision under attack was favourable to the defence, the main argument against overruling is that this enlarges the criminal law with retrospective effect, and potentially punishes people who reasonably believed that their behaviour was no crime. This, by contrast, is a very respectable objection (although it is not one which has always influenced the House of Lords when minded to extend the criminal law). However, as the House of Lords pointed out in *Shivpuri*, it deserves little weight where, as there, the defendant was actually trying to do something which he knew full well to be illegal.

If the courts too readily refuse to reverse their previous decisions, two consequences result, both of which confirm the citizen in his worst views of lawyers and the judicial process. The first is the unedifying spectacle of the Law Lords saying, as Lord Reid said in *Knuller*, "our previous decision was wrong, but we nevertheless affirm it". "It is a maxim among these lawyers," wrote Jonathan Swift, "that whatever hath been done before, may legally be done again: and therefore they take special care to record all the decisions formerly made against common justice and the general reason of mankind. These, under the name of *precedents*, they produce as authorities to justify the most iniquitous opinions; and the Judges never fail of directing accordingly". The second is the equally unedifying spectacle of the judges distinguishing cases on non-existent grounds when they can and should be overruled. This results in a jumble of distinctions without moral differences, which is exactly what the Man in the Saloon Bar believes the law to consist of, and was the very evil which the Criminal Attempts Act was designed to cure.

So it bodes well for the sensible development of the criminal law in future that the House of Lords, having accepted that *Anderton v Ryan* was a blunder, was prepared to overrule it instead of affirming it unwillingly or distinguishing it in some preposterously complicated way. Their Lordships, and Lord Bridge in particular, are to be congratulated on their courage and intellectual honesty as well as on their excellent good sense.

A Duty of Common Humanity to Bees
Tutton v A. D. Walter Ltd.
CLJ 1986, 45(1) 5–17

In a beehive, as in a university, 95% of the population are busy workers, which support the other 5% – the queen and drones. So if the field of flowers where my worker bees are busy is drenched with insecticide, this will wipe out my whole colony of bees. If my bees were working in your field, and you killed them when you sprayed your crops, do you have to pay for this? Or is it my bad luck because it is your field and you are free to do what you like on your own land? The issue arose in *Tutton v A. D. Walter Ltd.* [1985] 3 W.L.R. 797, where Denis Henry Q.C. (sitting as a deputy High Court judge) held that the crop-spraying farmer was potentially liable in negligence.

There was little doubt that the farmer was negligent. He sprayed a field of oil seed rape when it was in full flower, contrary to advice widely circulated by the Ministry of Agriculture and repeated by the manufacturer of the insecticide, which was to wait until the plants had finished flowering in order to avoid killing bees. The farmer could not say that the damage, though regrettable, was necessary in the cause of good husbandry, because the spray was most effective against the weevils and midges whose holocaust he was plotting if it was applied after petal-fall, its use when the farmer used it being both wasteful and inefficient. Furthermore, he knew his neighbours kept bees which were at risk from spraying because they had complained in previous years; yet he did not warn them in time to move their hives away. So he had to argue that this is a situation where a farmer may be careless without liability.

Although the flowers are full of nectar, oil seed rape is wind pollinated, and the farmer who grows it has no need of bees. Because the bees could buzz off as far as the farmer was concerned, he argued that they were trespassers, to whom he owed no duty of care. The judge rejected this approach. It was foolish, he said, to try to apply the law of occupiers' liability to bees, when the farmer can neither invite them in nor shut them out. The case in hand was a new and original problem for the courts, where – as the House of Lords has repeatedly told us – the correct approach is to assume that a person is potentially liable for his carelessness. The farmer was careless, so for his carelessness he must pay. Alternatively, if the farmer was right and the bees were trespassers, he still owed the "duty of common humanity", the limited duty to avoid carelessly harming trespassers set out by the House of Lords in *Herrington v*

British Railways Board [1972] A.C. 877, and he was liable because he was in breach of that.

The decision is obviously a famous victory for country parsons, village schoolmistresses, and everyone else who indulges in the agreeably dotty pursuit of keeping bees, but it is of wider significance. than this. First, the judge was willing if need be to hold an occupier liable at common law for negligently injuring a trespassing chattel. The Occupiers' Liability Act 1984 attempts to replace the common law governing an occupier's liability to trespassers with a new statutory duty which is expressly limited to cases of personal injury. By a hiccup in the drafting, the Act abolishes liability at common law only in so far as this governs personal injury suffered by a trespasser, and leaves the common law intact in so far as it covers – if it does cover – damage to a trespasser's property. *Tutton v A. D. Walter Ltd.* suggests this is important, because the common law does indeed cover certain injuries to a trespasser's property.

Secondly, there is the judge's willingness to apply the general principle that a person is liable for his negligence to limit an occupier's freedom to do what he likes on his land.

The part of the law of tort which traditionally governs relations between those who are literally neighbours developed long before the recognition of any general principle of liability for negligence. Broadly speaking, it held that an occupier must confine his chattels and his activities to the boundaries of his own land. So he was liable if his livestock strayed, or his fire spread to the house next door, or if his privy or his millpond overflowed and flooded his neighbour out; by analogy, he was also liable for unreasonable emissions of smoke, smell and noise. If what the neighbour complained about was something which the defendant did on his own land without invading his neighbour's territory, the question the courts usually asked was "has the plaintiff got an easement?" If the defendant had done on his land something which interfered with an easement such as a right of way, or support, or a right of light to a window, then the defendant was liable whether he had been careless or not. If no such right existed – as where the defendant spoilt his neighbour's view, or generally darkened his garden, or caused his spring to dry up – then there was no liability, and it was irrelevant whether his behaviour was morally blameworthy or not.

Despite *Donoghue v Stevenson* [1932] A.C. 562 and its successors, in this sort of case the courts still sometimes assume that there can be no liability, however careless the defendant was, unless the plaintiff had a right of some sort over the defendant's land: for example, see *Ray v Fairway Motors (Barnstaple) Ltd.* (1968) 20 P.C.R. 261. In *Tutton v A. D. Walter Ltd.*, however, the judge clearly thought that the *Donoghue v Stevenson* principle trumps all. Some lawyers will welcome this. To others it will be heresy. In the end it all depends on which one regards as more important: magnifying the freedom of occupiers to exploit their land as they like, or – bearing in mind that for every square mile of land in this country there are several hundred inhabitants – encouraging them to avoid harm to others when exploiting it.

Murder in the Dark
R. v Moloney
CLJ 1986, 45(2) 161–165

What is the mental element in murder?

It includes an intention to kill, obviously, and less obviously it also includes an intention to cause grievous bodily harm short of death. Thus many murder convictions result from brutal attacks where the attacker desired to do grave injury, although he may not have intended to kill. But people quite often kill without actually desiring to cause either death or grievous bodily harm, although they know that what they propose to do may cause it. Does murder also cover killing by deliberately exposing the victim to a serious risk? And if it does, where is the line drawn between murder and manslaughter in this sort of case? If it is ever murder, how great a risk of death or grievous bodily harm must be foreseen? Unfortunately nobody knows. The House of Lords has re-written the law of murder five times in the last twenty-five years, and the point is still obscure.

The issue first arose in *D.P.P. v Smith* [1961] A.C. 290, where a criminal seeking to avoid arrest killed a policeman by driving off at speed with him clinging to his car, zigzagging to throw him off. There, the House of Lords held that murder covers killing by risk-taking, and pitched the level of risk required to make it murder very low. They unanimously ruled that Smith had committed murder because death or grievous bodily harm was the "likely" result. For good measure, they also ruled that he was deemed to have foreseen the risk if a reasonable man in his position would have foreseen it, whether or not he actually did so – a ruling which, after the most bitter criticism, was reversed by section 8 of the Criminal Justice Act 1967. But even if the question then became "did Smith himself realize that death or grievous bodily harm was likely?" it left the scope of murder wide.

Then came *Hyam* [1975] A.C. 55, where a woman burnt down the house of her rival in love over her head, incinerating her children. The judge, pitching the level of risk higher than *D.P.P. v Smith* seemed to require, directed the jury to convict Hyam of murder if she knew it was "highly probable" that her act would cause death or grievous bodily harm, and they did so. The House of Lords affirmed the murder conviction by a majority, but unfortunately even the majority could not agree among themselves on the level of foresight required to make it murder. Of the three Law Lords who were in the majority, one agreed with the trial judge that killing by risk-taking is murder only when death or grievous bodily harm is foreseen as "highly probable", one said this was too generous and Hyam was guilty if she foresaw it as no more than "probable", and a third said she was guilty provided she realised there was a "serious risk". To add to the confusion, Lord Hailsham also suggested that a risk-taker was only guilty of murder where his act was "aimed at" his victim – whatever that means – and other Law Lords expressed doubts as to whether murder really extended to the case where the defendant had in mind not death, but only grievous bodily harm. This inevitably led to a further appeal in *Cunningham* [1982] A.C. 566, where, suppressing their earlier doubts, the House of Lords held that *mens rea* as to grievous bodily harm will do.

Hyam left the boundary between murder and manslaughter quite obscure, and the Director of Public Prosecutions seems to have responded by playing safe and prosecuting most risk-taking cases as manslaughter, reserving murder for cases where death or serious injury was clearly desired. But it meant that a risk-taker could still be prosecuted for murder rather than manslaughter if he was thought to be particularly odious. And, of course, a case which initially looked like an intentional killing might easily turn out to be a case of risk-taking when the defence evidence was heard at the trial.

Such a case was *Moloney* [1985] A.C. 905. The prosecution case was that Moloney had deliberately blown his stepfather's head off with a shotgun in the course of a family row. The defence case was that Moloney and his stepfather had got cheerfully drunk together, his stepfather had then challenged him to a race to see who was the quickest to load and fire a shotgun, Moloney won, and his stepfather's head got in the way at the crucial moment. As the shooting took place in the living room of a house, this story raised the possibility that Moloney, although not meaning to kill or injure, had deliberately taken a serious risk. To cover that possibility the judge told the jury that it was murder not only if somebody kills meaning to cause death or serious injury, but also if he "foresees that it will probably happen, whether he desires it or not". After a lengthy retirement, in the course of which they asked for further directions on the necessary mental element, the jury convicted him of murder. On his appeal, which failed in the Court of Appeal but succeeded in the House of Lords, the law of murder was rewritten yet again.

In his speech, Lord Bridge said that murder requires intention; contrary to what was said in *Hyam*, foresight of the high probability of death or grievous bodily harm is not enough – much less is intention to expose the victim to a serious risk. In a risk-taking case, he said, "the probability of the consequence taken to have been foreseen must be little short of overwhelming before it will suffice to establish the necessary intent" – a sentence he later paraphrased by talking of "a moral certainty". Under this new formulation Lord Hailsham's qualification in *Hyam* that the defendant's act be "aimed at" someone was unnecessary and should be discarded. In most murder trials, Lord Bridge added, the facts are such that there is no need to explain to the jury the meaning of intention; but where (as here) the need arises, they should be told that an act counts as intended to cause death or grievous bodily harm where "the defendant foresaw that consequence as being a natural consequence of his act". The rest of the House concurred. Lord Hailsham, the only Law Lord who had also sat in *Hyam*, added a few words to try to show that although almost everything said in Mrs Hyam's case was wrong, her murder conviction was not a miscarriage of justice; and he concluded with the pious hope that the question of murder and risk-taking was now settled forever.

Lord Hailsham's hopes were disappointed, because within a year the House of Lords had to consider the mental element in murder once again in *Hancock and Shankland* [1986] A.C. 455. The facts of this case are notorious: two striking miners dropped lumps of concrete from a bridge onto a taxi taking a "scab" to work, thereby killing the driver. The prosecution case was that the miners desired to kill or cause serious injury, and backed this up with evidence of threats they had earlier made against the intended victim. The defence case was that they only intended to block the road and frighten him, and did not intend to cause him harm. Even if their story was true, however, they can hardly have failed to notice that there was a risk of death or serious injury, and the case surely cried out for a direction to the jury on the meaning of intention. So the judge obediently fed them the form of words prescribed by Lord Bridge in *Moloney*: "Was death or serious injury a natural consequence of what was done? Did a defendant foresee that consequence as a natural consequence?" The jury, having wrestled with this for five hours, asked for further directions on the meaning of intention, and, fortified by second helpings of the same diet, convicted of murder. The miners appealed.

The Court of Appeal, in a judgment delivered by Lord Lane C.J., boldly condemned Lord Bridge's model direction to juries as misleading. The main point of the decision in *Moloney*, he said, was to root out the notion that in murder, knowledge of a risk of death or grievous bodily harm counts as intention to cause it. But to anyone who had not read the rest of Lord Bridge's speech, the question "did the defendant foresee death or grievous bodily harm was a natural consequence?" would mean exactly the same as "did he foresee that it might happen?", the very test the House of Lords wanted to discard. Because it feared the jury might have been misled, the Court of Appeal quashed the murder convictions and substituted convictions for manslaughter, with sentences of eight years' imprisonment. Lord Lane put forward his own much longer model direction to the jury for future use in such cases, an abridged version of which is as follows:

> ... are you sure that the defendant appreciated that what he did was highly likely to cause death or really serious bodily injury?... If your answer is 'yes,' there is evidence before you from which you can infer that the defendant intended to cause death or really serious bodily injury, but you must not find him guilty of murder unless you feel sure that he so intended. If however, you are sure, the fact that he may not have desired that result is irrelevant. Desire and intent are two different things.

The prosecution appealed to the House of Lords, which affirmed the Court of Appeal decision. In a speech by Lord Scarman in which the other Law Lords concurred, the House accepted the Court of Appeal's criticism of Lord Bridge's model "natural consequence" direction in *Moloney*. To make honours even, however, it then condemned the Court of Appeal's proposed model direction in return. Guidelines, said Lord Scarman, should be reserved for "cases of real difficulty" – a category into which he evidently thought this kind of case does not fall. All the judge need do here, he said, was to direct them in general terms that murder requires intention, and emphasise that the probability of the consequence occurring is "only a factor, although it may in some cases be a very significant factor" in determining whether the accused acted with intention.

This is all very unsatisfactory, because we still do not know when killing by risk-taking amounts to murder. The Court of Appeal and the House of Lords have told us that murder needs intention. They have also told us that several things are not the same as intention: that it does not mean desire, because intention is wider than desire, and that it is not the same as foresight of a high probability, because this is only evidence of intention. But although they tell us what it is not, nowhere do they tell us what it actually *is*. If we go back to Lord Bridge's speech in *Moloney* and read between the lines we will get the general impression that intention means, as well as desire, foresight that the prohibited consequence is almost certain to happen. But it would be unwise for a judge to tell a jury this, because in the present state of uncertainty it would guarantee another appeal. The one thing that the appeal judges have been consistent about is that trial judges should generally avoid trying to explain the meaning of intention to the jury. So it seems that the best bet for a judge who wants to keep his wig clean is to tell the jury nothing about the meaning of intention and let them interpret it how they like. But what this means is that whether it is murder or manslaughter depends on what the jury in any given case happens to think is meant by intention. So there is no rule. And this matters. Although a murder conviction no longer means the rope, it still attracts a mandatory sentence of imprisonment for life. For manslaughter the sentence is discretionary, and in practice the sentence would usually be around five years, give or take a year or two each way.

The Law Commission's Draft Criminal Code states that murder requires intention, and makes it plain that a person intends a consequence both where he wants it to happen, and where he is almost certain that it will occur. With such a code, this labyrinthine story of confusion and uncertainty would never have happened, and we should now be able to answer the question with which this note began – "What is the mental element for murder?" But of course the Draft Criminal Code will never be enacted. It would completely destroy the richness, the fullness, and above all the flexibility of the common law.

Murder in the Dark: A Glimmer of Light?
R. v Nedrick
CLJ 1986, 45(3), p. 366–367

In an earlier note (*ante*, p. 75) it was lamented that despite five House of Lords decisions on the subject in the last twenty-five years it was still impossible to say when a person commits murder by deliberately exposing someone to a serious risk of bodily harm. In *Moloney* [1985] A.C. 905 and in *Hancock* [1986] A.C. 455 the House of Lords said that the risk-taker was guilty of murder where he "intended" death or grievous bodily harm, but unfortunately omitted to say what degree of risk must be foreseen by the defendant who does not actually wish to cause death or grievous bodily harm before the law treats him as acting with an intention to kill or seriously injure.

The question recently arose yet again in *Nedrick* [1986] 1 W.L.R. 1025, and in a very welcome decision the Court of Appeal (Lord Lane C.J., aided and abetted by Leggatt and Kennedy JJ.) have largely answered it. The defendant, like the defendant in *Hyam* [1975] A.C. 55, set fire to his enemy's house while she was asleep, with the result that a child was burnt to death. The defendant told the police that he did not mean to kill, but set fire to the house just to "wake her up and frighten her". In such a case, said the Court of Appeal, the jury requires a direction on the meaning of intention, and they should be told:

> ...that they are not entitled to infer the necessary intention unless they feel sure that death or serious bodily harm was a virtual certainty (barring some unforeseen intervention) as a result of the defendant's actions and that the defendant appreciated that such was the case.

Because the trial judge had told the jury to convict if the defendant knew death or serious injury was "highly probable" – a state of mind considerably less positive than being certain or virtually certain that it would happen – his murder conviction was quashed and a conviction for manslaughter was substituted, with a sentence of fifteen years' imprisonment.

The Court of Appeal did not go so far as to say that the trial judge should also direct the jury that if the defendant did foresee death or grievous bodily harm as certain or virtually certain, they must hold him intentional, and therefore guilty of murder. But they encouraged the judge to point them in this general direction:

> Where a man realises that it is for all practical purposes inevitable that his actions will result in death or serious harm, the inference may be irresistible that he intended that result, however little he may have desired or wished it to happen. The decision is one for the jury to be reached upon a consideration of all the evidence.

At last it is becoming possible to give a simple answer to the question "What is the mental element in murder?"

Flooding, Fault and Private Nuisance
Home Brewery v William Davis and Co.
CLJ 1987, 46(2) 205–208

When an occupier complains that his neighbour's activities have interfered with his use and enjoyment of his land, his right to sue in private nuisance depends on the type of interference. Broadly speaking there are three categories. The first consists of causing physical damage to the land or property on it, causing physical encroachments on it, and interfering with easements and natural rights. Where his activities do this the defendant is usually liable without more: there is no need to show malice or absence of reasonable care. The second category is interference with the occupier's comfort and convenience, usually by making noise, smells or dust. For these the defendant is liable if the interference is "unreasonable", a word which stands for a number of things, including that the defendant may be liable for causing a certain level of inconvenience maliciously or negligently when he would not be liable for it if he had been acting with due care and for a legitimate purpose. And thirdly, there is a category of interference for which the tort of nuisance simply provides no remedy at all, leaving the defendant free to be as negligent or malicious as he likes. This category owes its existence to *Bradford v Pickles* [1985] A.C. 587, where the House of Lords held that A may dig trenches on his land which deprive his neighbour B of water percolating underground, and may do so not only where he needs the water himself but even where his sole object is to make life difficult for B. In this category of *damnum sine injuria* are also said to fall spoiling a neighbour's view, depriving his land of light or air (except where there is an easement for a particular window), and depriving his buildings of support (except where he has an easement of support).

Bradford v Pickles radiates an extreme disdain for neighbourliness and an extreme concern for an occupier's freedom to do what he likes with his own, which may have suited the Victorians, but looks very out of place in a country as overcrowded as modern England. So it is not surprising that modern judges tend to minimise the third category of interference, and put new kinds of interference into category two rather than category three when there is any doubt about the matter. Thus in *Bernstein v Skyviews* [1978] Q.B. 479 the judge suggested that interfering with an occupier's privacy might be actionable if it was unreasonable, and in *Tutton v Walter* [1986] Q.B. 61 it was held that an occupier is not free to spray his crops with insecticide in total disregard for the safety of his neighbour's bees which are in them at the time. Now in *Home Brewery Co. Ltd. v William Davis & Co. (Leicester) Ltd.* [1987] Q.B. 339 Piers Ashworth Q.C., sitting as a deputy High Court Judge, has held that an occupier can be liable if he negligently or maliciously interferes with the natural drainage of his neighbour's land.

The case concerned a tract of gently sloping land at the top of which P had a pub. Next to it on the downhill side lay a piece of marsh once used for growing osiers for basket making, and downhill of the osier-bed lay a disused clay pit full of water. Originally, rainwater arriving on P's land used to drain rapidly away through the soil into the osier-bed and thence into the clay pit beyond. D bought both clay pit and osier-bed for development. First he drained the clay pit and filled it in. This slowed down the drainage of water from the osier-bed, which in turn slowed down the drainage of water from P's land. As a result P's pub started to suffer from dampness problems, and he was put to the expense of installing and running a pump. Then D started to develop the osier-bed by piling earth and other material on it. This squeezed it like a sponge and until the process was complete made P's land wetter still. As a result he had to put in two further pumps. P sued first for the permanent dampness resulting from impaired natural drainage, and secondly, for the temporary extra dampness during the "squeezing out".

As to the permanent dampness, P sought to argue that the interference fell into category one. An occupier, he said, has a natural right to have the water on his land soak away across his neighbour's property below, just as he has a right for it to flow away over it where there is a river or stream. There was little authority on this point either way, and after carefully considering such as there was, the judge rejected the plaintiff's argument. For his part, D argued that the interference fell into category three. The problem, he pointed out, was about percolating water, and the relevant case is therefore *Bradford v Pickles*. If Mr. Pickles can cut off the supply of percolating water when the Mayor of Bradford wants to receive it, and can do so in total disregard of his interests, or even on purpose to harm them, the Mayor of Bradford must be equally free to block its outflow when Mr. Pickles wants to get rid of it. But this argument the judge also rejected. For many years, he said, the trend of the law had been to subject a neighbour to liability if he was at fault – a development that culminated in *Leakey v National Trust* [1980] Q.B. 485. Thus whether or not someone may cut off the inflow of percolating water with impunity, he is certainly liable if he negligently or maliciously stops the flow of percolating water out.

So the question the judge had to resolve was whether D's behaviour was negligent or malicious. Of malice there was no question, and the judge held that on the facts there was no question of negligence either. An occupier is not to be regarded as negligent for this sort of harm, even if it is reasonably foreseeable, where it is the inevitable consequence of the reasonable use or development of his own property, and he has taken such precautions (if any) as a reasonable occupier would take. To turn a derelict, dangerous and smelly clay pit into a housing estate is a reasonable use of land by anyone's standards, even if it is done to make a profit. So this part of P's claim failed.

This left the claim for "squeezing out," and this the judge viewed differently. When D's activities forced the water out of the osier-bed and into P's land, this, though indirectly caused rather than directly done, was much the same as pumping it out onto P's property, which would have constituted a clear trespass. Causing something to encroach upon an occupier's property which it would have been a trespass to put there is the classic case of nuisance within category one, and makes the causer liable whether his behaviour was reasonable or not. Thus to this extent P's claim succeeded.

The Evidence of Little Children
R. v Z
CLJ 1990, 49(3) 418–421

In 1885, Parliament first enacted what is now section 38 of the Children and Young Persons Act 1933, which is as follows:

> Where, in any proceedings against any person for any offence, any child of tender years called as a witness does not in the opinion of the court understand the nature of an oath, his evidence may be received though not given on oath, if, in the opinion of the court, he is possessed of sufficient intelligence to justify the reception of the evidence, and understands the duty of speaking the truth.

This provision was intended to bring the law of England into line with the law of Scotland, where little children had always given evidence unsworn, and where the courts were (and still are) willing in principle to listen to the evidence of a child, however young. At first there is no doubt that it had this effect. In *Christie* [1914] A.C. 545 we discover that the principal witness was a boy of 5, and in *Crime and Psychology* (1943) Claud Mullins, a stipendiary magistrate, described how he once took evidence from a child of not quite 3.

In 1958 there was an abrupt change as a result of the decision in *Wallwork* 42 Cr.App.R. 153. In that case the Court of Criminal

Appeal, through the mouth of Lord Goddard C.J., condemned an attempt to call a child of 5 as a witness against her father who was accused of committing incest with her. "The jury could not attach any value to the evidence of a child of 5", he said, "it is ridiculous to suppose they could". This decision rapidly found its way into *Archbold*, and created what was in effect a rule of law that no child could be called as a witness under the age of 6. In 1987 the Court of Appeal raised the age limit by applying *Wallwork* to a little girl who had turned 6 but was not yet 7. After quoting Lord Goddard's words they added: "That was nearly 30 years ago. So far as this court is aware, the validity of, and good sense behind, that proposition has remained untrammelled in the practice of the criminal courts." (*Wright* 90 Cr.App.R. 91).

This was surprising, because for the last 30 years the decision in *Wallwork* has been a disastrous impediment to justice in child abuse prosecutions, where in the nature of things there are usually only two people who saw what happened, one being the person who did it, and the other being the child. A young child comes home and complains that X has beaten or sexually abused her, or describes an attack by a stranger whom she later picks out as X at an identification parade. Medical evidence shows injuries consistent with the assault the child describes. Yet the court refuses to listen to her because she is incompetent as a witness – and because of the hearsay rule also refuses to let any adult repeat what she told them. The result, of course, is usually that a child molester goes unjustly free because of his foresight in picking a victim sufficiently young: but it can also cause the conviction of the innocent. If the child accuses X and the police obtusely charge Y, it means that Y is equally unable to show the court that the child accused a different person of the crime (*Sparks v R.* [1964] A.C. 964).

In recent years these problems have been repeatedly ventilated in the legal press, and in March 1990 the Court of Appeal signalled a very welcome change of direction in a case which the Times reported as *R. v B*, and which now appears in the Weekly Law Reports as *R. v Z* [1990] 2 Q.B. 355. Here a Court of Appeal presided over by Lord Lane C.J. denied that there was any rule that children could not give evidence below a given age. Section

38 of the Children and Young Persons Act, they said, contains no age limit, and therefore the courts have no power to impose one. A judge faced with a witness of "tender years" should use his own discretion to decide whether or not the child satisfies the test of competency that section 38 lays down.

There were two reasons, said Lord Lane, why the Court of Criminal Appeal had earlier tried to impose a minimum age limit in *Wallwork*. One was a humanitarian fear that the experience of giving evidence would be extremely distressing for a little child, and the other was the fear that a young child's evidence was so untrustworthy that to admit it would invariably be bad for justice. Recent changes, however, had rendered both these reasons obsolete. The "live video link" introduced by the Criminal Justice Act 1988 had made the process of giving evidence less stressful for the child. And nowadays there was "an increasing belief that the testimony of young children, when all precautions have been taken, may be just as reliable as that of their elders".

By this decision Court of Appeal has done all it can to improve the situation, but problems will undoubtedly remain. In particular, how is a trial judge supposed to decide whether a given child "is possessed of sufficient intelligence to justify the reception of the evidence", and "understands the duty of speaking the truth"? No guidelines on this are contained in the Act or elsewhere, and as a judge once explained to this writer, "We navigate by common sense and the light of nature." This obviously creates a risk that Judge A will routinely reject children as competent witnesses whom Judge B would unhesitatingly accept.

Jeremy Bentham, writing 175 years ago, said that imposing a competency requirement was a false approach: young witnesses (or insane or mentally handicapped ones) should be allowed to give evidence if they can communicate coherently, and their immaturity or handicap should be a factor in deciding whether to believe their evidence, not whether to hear it at all. Earlier this century *Wigmore* put forward the same idea in his monumental treatise in the USA, where it has now been accepted in legislation in a number of jurisdictions. In England, this approach was recently advocated by the Home Office Advisory Group on Video Evidence (alias the

Pigot Committee) in its Report in December 1989. It is the way in which the evidence of young children is handled in France, Germany, Scandinavia, and many other parts of the world. It is, surely, the way the law of evidence should eventually treat the matter here.[10]

Citizens Arrest – At their Peril
R. v Self
CLJ 1992, 51(3), p. 405–408

Any citizen may arrest without a warrant a person who is, or whom he reasonably believes to be, in the act of committing an arrestable offence. However, when it comes to arresting people who are reasonably believed to have committed an arrestable offence, the powers of the ordinary citizen are less than those of the policeman. The policeman may lawfully arrest without warrant any person whom he reasonably suspects to be guilty of an arrestable offence whether or not he has actually committed it. The private citizen, on the other hand, may lawfully arrest a person whom he reasonably suspects to be guilty only in the case where the arrestable offence in question has really been committed, whether by the person arrested or by someone else. If an ordinary citizen arrests someone on reasonable suspicion of their having committed an arrestable offence, and in fact no arrestable offence has been committed by anyone, his arrest is not a lawful one. This rule, which was laid down by Sir Rufus Isaacs C.J. in *Walters v W.H. Smith and Son Ltd.* [1914] 1 K.B. 595, was later codified in the Criminal Law Act 1967, and is now set out in section 24 of the Police and Criminal Evidence Act 1984. Every first year law student, if not every citizen, knows it: and most people, taking their cue from Parliament, assume it makes good sense.

---

[10] It now does. Section 53(1)of the Youth Justice and Criminal Evidence Act 1999 now provides that "At every stage in criminal proceedings all persons are (whatever their age) competent to give evidence." This provision adopts, in essence, the formula I proposed in "Competency: children and witnesses with learning disabilities", [1998] *New Law Journal* 1472, 1526.

Some writers have criticised the rule: notably Glanville Williams in his *Textbook of Criminal Law*, and the editors of *Salmond on Torts*. The recent Court of Appeal case of *R. v Self* [1992] 1 W.L.R. 687 now shows us plainly how bad a rule it is. A store detective (who is of course in law a private citizen) saw Mr. Self pocket a bar of chocolate and leave the shop without paying for it. When she, together with a shop assistant, challenged him just outside, Self pulled the chocolate out of his pocket, threw it under a car, and fled down the street, looking the very picture of guilt. Reasonably thinking he had committed theft, which is an arrestable offence, they chased him, caught him, and arrested him: but not before he had kicked them and struggled with them in an attempt to get free. For this, Self understandably found himself prosecuted for (a) theft of the chocolate, and (b) assault with intent to resist a lawful arrest. The jury, apparently accepting the evidence of Self (an off-duty detective with 17 years' police service) that he had taken the chocolate innocently, forgotten to pay for it, and then panicked, acquitted him of the theft. However, they still convicted him of the assault. The Court of Appeal quashed the assault conviction. Unimpressed with the prosecution argument that a person running away is still "in the act" of committing an arrestable offence, they said the issue turned on the powers of a private citizen to arrest a person who appears to have previously committed an arrestable offence. As Self had been acquitted on the theft count, no arrestable offence had actually been committed. Therefore the store detective and shop assistant had no power to arrest him, and he was within his rights to use force on them to try and break their grip. (And, the Court might have added, he could also have sued them for damages for assault because they laid hands on him to restrain him, and false imprisonment because they succeeded.)

To state the obvious, the law as illustrated by this case is in an unsatisfactory state. The most glaring defect is that it provides inadequate protection to the public spirited citizen who behaves reasonably on the facts as they appeared to him, and permits him to be hit or sued by someone who, if not actually a criminal, had no more sense than to put on a pantomime of being one. At a more fundamental level, however, the law is bad because it sets out to resolve competing interests, and does so in a senseless manner.

On the one hand, there is the good citizen, who needs some measure of legal protection when he does what appears to be reasonable to help enforce the criminal law. On the other, we have the innocent citizen, who needs protection when he finds himself arrested for something he has not done by a fellow citizen who, from the perspective of the person arrested, is not public spirited but officious. This conflict cannot be resolved to both parties' satisfaction, and a stand on point of principle is needed to decide who loses. The competing principles are two: law enforcement, and personal liberty, and we might expect the law to choose decisively between them. The law would be intelligible if it said "the private citizen who arrests is always in the clear provided he acts on reasonable suspicion". It would also be intelligible if it said "the private citizen arrests at his peril: if the person you arrest did not do it, he can always hit you, and if he sues you, you must pay". But the compromise it makes – under which the answer depends on whether *someone else* has committed the offence for which the citizen arrests the suspect – is explicable according to neither principle, and is largely arbitrary. As the case of *Self* demonstrates plainly, the fact that the arrestable offence for which the citizen arrests another has not actually been committed does not necessarily make the arresting citizen's behaviour any less reasonable. Conversely, the fact that the offence has indeed been committed, but by someone else, does not necessarily make the innocent citizen who is mistakenly arrested for it any less innocent. Furthermore, the rule is inconvenient because neither arrestor nor arrestee may know for certain whether an arrestable offence has actually been committed at the time the arrest takes place. So neither may be able to tell whether he is on the right side of the law when one tries to make the arrest, or the other tries to resist it.

Behind the confused and confusing rules which we have at present, there seems to lurk the germ of a sensible idea. This is that private citizens should be encouraged and protected when they "have a go" at catching criminals red-handed, but discouraged from playing Sherlock Holmes in relation to crimes that are over and done with, this being a job better left to the police. To carry out this policy coherently, therefore, it should apply the "law enforcement" principle to the first case, and the "personal liberty" principle to the second.

In detail, what the law should surely say is this. First – as it already does – that the private citizen may lawfully arrest any person who is, or whom he reasonably believes to be, in the act of committing an arrestable offence, whether or not the offence is actually being committed. Secondly it should say – as it now does not – that the same applies where he reasonably believes the person he arrests is running away after having committed such an offence. Thirdly it should say – again as it now does not – that outside these cases, the private citizen arrests at his peril, in the sense that if the person he arrests turns out not to be guilty, that person can hit him with legal impunity at the time, and sue him for damages at leisure later.

With the Report of the Royal Commission on Criminal Justice on the way, new legislation on criminal procedure cannot be far away. Let us hope that next time Parliament is legislating in this area it takes the opportunity to reform our defective rules on citizen's arrest, instead of blandly confirming them.[11]

Causal Links and Congenital Disabilities
The DES-daughters case
CLJ 1993, 52(2) 206–209
Written with A.J.O. Van Wassaneaer

To establish a causal link between the defendant's wrongful act and the plaintiff's harm the law normally requires the plaintiff to satisfy the "but for" test: can he show, on the balance of probabilities, that he would not have suffered the damage but for the defendant's wrongful act? Exceptions are made where this test would produce results which the courts find absurd or unduly harsh. A well-known

---

[11] Alas it didn't. When Parliament "modernised" (i.e., drastically extended) the powers of the police in relation to summary arrest in 2005, the powers of private citizens were altered too – but not so as to cure the problem identified in this note.

example is that of the North American cases where P was hit by one or other of the bullets fired simultaneously by two negligent sportsmen – both of whom were held liable, although against neither could it be said that on the balance of probabilities he did the damage (e.g. *Oliver v Miles* (1926) 144 Miss. 852). In *Fitzgerald v Lane* [1989] A.C. 328 the English courts seemed to have applied the same reasoning when the plaintiff's back was broken by one or other of two negligently driven cars: though something of a cloud may now hang over the "negligent sportsmen" principle in English law after *Wilsher v Essex Area H.A.* [1988] A.C. 1074. In that case the House of Lords rejected the plaintiff's argument that there should be a new exception to the "but for" test for use in medical negligence cases, and affirmed the basic rule in terms sufficiently strong to make us think again about previous exceptions to it.

The "negligent sportsmen" principle was at issue in a very important case recently decided by the Hoge Raad der Nederlanden (Dutch Supreme Court): HR 9 okt. 1992, Rvdw. 1992, nr 219.

The facts were these. Shortly before World War II a "wonder drug" was discovered, which was thought to have beneficial effects during pregnancy. As diethylstilbestrol (or DES) was never patented, many pharmaceutical companies, both large and small, hastily began to market it. Alas, DES proved less wonderful than its inventors hoped. Some mothers, and some male children, suffered unpleasant ailments as a result of it. The plight of the "DES-daughters", however, was much more serious. At puberty or later, many women whose mothers had taken DES in pregnancy grew up to develop tumours or other cancer related diseases of the genito-urinary tract. In the Netherlands alone, more than 18,000 women are estimated to be suffering from DES-related diseases.

Six of these "DES-daughters" sued ten companies which had been marketing DES around the time of their birth. One of the difficulties which they faced was that the events that gave rise to their sufferings were now such ancient history that none of them could say which defendant's DES her mother had taken: a serious impediment.

The legal debate centred around a rule of Dutch law which is now codified as article 6:99 of the *Burgerlijk Wetboek* (Civil Code):

Where the damage may have resulted from two or more events, for each of which a different person is liable, and where it has been determined that the damage has arisen from at least one of those events, the obligation to repair the damage rests upon each of these persons, unless he proves the damage did not result from the event for which he is responsible.

As the part of the Code in which this article appears only came into force in 1992 it was obviously not directly applicable. Nevertheless the Hoge Raad, affirming the court of first instance and the Amsterdam Court of Appeals, held that it only codified a principle that already existed in Dutch law – a little surprisingly, perhaps, because no previous decision of the Hoge Raad had clearly laid it down.

The issue therefore depended on the scope of the principle. The courts below held against the plaintiffs, ruling that the principle applies only if the plaintiff sues – or at least can identify – all the possible defendants. The Hoge Raad, however, said that it applied even if no complete list of tortfeasors can be produced – and, more surprisingly, even where there is a possibility that some of the other manufacturers may not have acted tortiously: a wide interpretation, good news for plaintiffs, and bad news for defendants – even if tempered by the thought that the greater the number of possible other culprits, the easier a defendant's task of persuading a court that the damage was not caused by him.

The defendants' fall-back position was that, if they had to pay anything at all, the most each could be liable for was something in proportion to his share of the market for the drug. This solution, which has found some support in the United States, the Hoge Raad rejected in favour of holding each defendant jointly liable for the entirety of the damage – although it accepted that the "market share" principle might come into play when apportioning the damages among the defendants. In consequence, each defendant is potentially liable for a very large sum. Including physical injury, medical expenses and loss of earnings, the total damages are said to be in the region of 4.5 billion florins: which means that the insurance market is as worried about the outcome as the pharmaceutical industry.

The appeal was on a preliminary point about causation, and does not finally dispose of the case. In order to succeed, according to the Hoge Raad, the plaintiffs must now show the following: (i) that the defendant put DES into circulation at the relevant time, (ii) that he thereby acted tortiously, (iii) that other producers were similarly engaged in tortious acts, and (iv) that the plaintiff suffered damage as a result of DES. If these matters are established, the defendant can escape liability if he can prove that damage did not result from his act.

Thus the plaintiffs still have to prove that the defendants acted wrongfully. They cannot, of course, make use of the strict liability rules deriving from the EC Directive on Products Liability of 1985 because the events in question took place too long ago. (Furthermore, the Hoge Raad was careful to say that its decision on causation did not extend to claims founded on those rules.) So the plaintiffs must bring their claim under the general principles of tortious liability – onrechtmatige daad – where a relevant matter is whether sufficient care was taken to test whether DES was safe before it was put on the market. This, it will be remembered, was where the English plaintiffs in the thalidomide disaster ran into trouble.

The Hoge Raad said that the purpose behind the rule of causation contained in the crucial article 6:99 is to correct the injustice which would otherwise result in this type of case if the ordinary rule of causation were applied. The Dutch judges thought that what they did was clearly just. How just would it have seemed to common lawyers to evade the normal rule in this case? If the "negligent sportsmen" cases are correct, then surely the DES-daughters solution follows *a fortiori*. If a manufacturer did not make the DES which harmed the plaintiff he must compensate, his not-so-wonder drug probably caused harm to other women, perhaps even to one of the plaintiffs who has won against a different manufacturer. Thus at least some kind of global justice is achieved. But if the negligent sportsman who is forced to pay is in fact the one whose bullet missed, he must compensate although he actually hurt no one at all.

Involuntary Intoxication as a Defence
R. v Kingston
CLJ 1994, 53(1),6–9

What is your criminal liability if someone spikes your drink, or secretly drugs your individual fruit pie, and, "high" on alcohol or other drugs, you then commit what would normally be a crime?

The usual theory is that the person who is involuntarily intoxicated has a defence only if he is so "far gone" that he fails to recognise some fact which a sober man must be aware of before he would incur criminal liability for the offence – or *a fortiori* if he has no idea at all what he is doing. On this view, involuntary intoxication which merely undermines the defendant's inhibitions can mitigate the sentence, but is certainly not a defence to the charge. There is very little authority on the matter, however, and a rival view, less commonly accepted, is that involuntary intoxication is a complete defence if the drink or drugs had the effect of reducing the defendant's self-control. On this view, he would have a defence even if he knew what he was doing, and understood the circumstances making it a crime – provided that he would not have behaved in such a way had he been sober.

In *Kingston* [1994] Q.B. 81, the Court of Appeal (Criminal Division) has come down firmly in favour of the second view. Kingston, who had paedophile tendencies, was invited to a flat by a man called Penn, who hoped to blackmail him, and who there entrapped him into committing an indecent assault on a 15-year-old boy in the presence of a camera and a tape-recorder. Kingston's defence was that he only acted as he did because he had been drugged, without his consent, by Penn. The trial judge ruled that Kingston's involuntary intoxication, if it existed, was only a defence if it stopped him knowing that he was committing an indecent assault. The Court of Appeal thought otherwise. After reviewing the authorities, and finding little guidance in them, it said this:

> In our judgment, the question can be answered by turning to first principles... Having paedophiliac inclinations and desires is not

proscribed: putting them into practice is. If the sole reason why the threshold between the two has been crossed is or may have been that the inhibition which the law requires has been removed by the clandestine act of a third party, the purposes of the criminal law are not served by nevertheless holding that the person performing the act is guilty of an offence. A man is not responsible for the condition produced by "the stratagem or fraud of another" [quoting Park J. in *Pearson* (1835) 2 Lew. C.C. 144]. If therefore drink or a drug, surreptitiously administered, causes a person to lose his self-control and for that reason to form an intent which he would not otherwise have formed, it is consistent with the principle that the law should exculpate him because the operative fault is not his.

Accordingly, Kingston's conviction for indecently assaulting the boy was quashed.

Is this right?

If we turn to first principles, as the Court of Appeal sought to do, the broad rule is that where the defendant knows what he is doing, and that it is wrong, internal bodily malfunctions which merely undermine his inhibitions merely mitigate the sentence – even where the bodily malfunction was something for which he was blameless. To fall within the defence of insanity, for example, the defendant must either have been unaware of the "nature and quality of his act", or if he was aware of it, unaware that his act was wrong. If there is no defence of insanity for a previously law-abiding man who hits or cheats or steals, knowing what he does, and knowing it is wrong – but only choosing to do it because of a personality change caused by a tumour on the brain, there can hardly be one for someone whose personality has been temporarily changed, equally without his fault, by drink or drugs: a point made in the last century by J.F. Stephen in his *History of the Criminal Law* (vol.ii, p.165), and again more recently by Glanville Williams (*The Criminal Law – the General Part*, 2nd. ed., para. 562). This is also the line the courts have taken with hormone problems which sometimes manifest themselves in serious pre-menstrual tension – which the Court of Appeal rejected as a defence in *Sadie Smith* [1982] Crim.L.R. 531. Conditions of this sort are only treated as defences, as opposed to matters in mitigation of sentence, in the two cases where Parliament has passed statutes recognising them as partial defences to murder: post-natal mental disturbances in mothers who kill young children, where the Infanticide Act 1938 reduces murder to infanticide, and "diminished responsibility", for which the Homicide Act 1957 reduces murder to manslaughter. Here – unlike involuntary intoxication after *Kingston* – the defence is only a partial one, making the defendant guilty of a less serious offence rather than leading to his acquittal; and both were created because of the fixed penalty for murder, which makes it necessary to turn the killing into something else before the court can take the offender's disturbed condition into account when deciding on the sentence.

There are practical reasons, too, for limiting any defence of involuntary intoxication to where it prevents the defendant having *mens rea* (in the usual sense of the term). If this were the rule, the question the court would have to address is "was D so drunk or drugged that he failed to foresee the consequence of his act, or failed to appreciate the surrounding facts?" This question is capable, in principle at least, of being answered "yes" or "no". But if involuntary intoxication is a defence where it merely undermined his inhibitions, the question is "was D so drunk or drugged that he committed the offence when he would not otherwise have done so?" This cannot be so clearly answered, because it is hypothetical and speculative. The defendant who knew what he was doing must obviously have had some inclination to commit the offence, and in practice it will be a combination of the drugs and his inclinations which caused him to act as he did. It will surely be impossible to say with any certainty that any defendant's inclinations would have been enough on their own without the added drink or drugs. The burden of proving this beyond reasonable doubt, if it can be proved at all, is on the prosecution. If courts are to do their job with intellectual honesty, what all this means is that they will be obliged to acquit any defendant who was involuntarily intoxicated, however slightly, no matter how loathsome or gruesome the act he did. This means the criminal law is heading for the same sort of difficulty as once afflicted the law of tort when the victim's contributory negligence was treated as a total defence: a lot of people escaping liability, although they were substantially to blame, because something which ought to be a partial defence is treated as a total one.

With involuntary intoxication, furthermore, there is also an obvious risk of abuse. In the magistrates' courts the tale of the "spiked drink" is often told by motorists who have been prosecuted for driving with excess blood-alcohol. Up to now it has only been put forward as a special reason for not disqualifying the driver on conviction, and even in this limited context the higher courts have found it necessary to hedge it about with limitations to prevent abuse (see *D.P.P. v O'Connor* [1992] R.T.R. 66). If *Kingston* is right, is the story that the driver's drink was spiked not potentially a complete defence? Against this, prosecutors would presumably quote the sentence from Lord Taylor's judgment where he said "the law permits a finding that the intent formed was not a criminal intent or, in other words, that the involuntary intoxication negatives *mens rea*", and argue from this that *Kingston* does not apply to offences of strict liability, because for them no *mens rea* is required. But once it is accepted that involuntary intoxication is a defence where it caused the defendant to do what he otherwise would not have done – as against where it prevented him from knowing or foreseeing what he would otherwise have known or foreseen – why is it relevant whether the offence is one that defendants are only guilty of when they knew what they were doing?

Given the grudging attitudes of the courts to general defences in the past, it seems a shame to criticise them for a decision which is insufficiently repressive. Nevertheless, the implications of the rule in *Kingston* are surely dangerous. The House of Lords has given the prosecution leave to appeal ([1994] 1 W.L.R. 146). Let us hope they reverse the decision.[12]

---

[12] It did! See p 102 below.

Freedom to Denounce your Fellow Citizens to the Police
Davidson v CC North Wales
CLJ 1994, 53(3) 433–435

Two important Court of Appeal decisions hold that if one person incorrectly informs the police that another has committed a crime, he is not liable if, acting on this information, the police arrest or prosecute him: and that this is so whether the complaint was made honestly or maliciously.

Davidson v Chief Constable of North Wales [1994] 2 All E.R. 597 turns on the law of false imprisonment (alias wrongful arrest). A store detective, Mrs. Yates, thought she saw Miss Davidson and a friend leaving Woolworths without having paid for a cassette. So she rang the police at once, told them her suspicions, and said that they would catch the suspects in the café over the road. The police arrived, the suspects had the cassette but no receipt, and the police therefore arrested them for shoplifting. Two hours later they were released without charges when the assistant at the cassette counter reported selling the friend the cassette the store detective had accused the pair of stealing.

The plaintiff's claim against the police necessarily failed, because section 24(6) of the Police and Criminal Evidence Act 1984 (PACE) provides that "Where a constable has reasonable grounds for suspecting that an arrestable offence has been committed, he may arrest without warrant anyone whom he has reasonable grounds for suspecting to be guilty of the offence." Against the employers of the store detective, however, the plaintiff looked as if she might have had a chance. They would undoubtedly have been liable if the store detective had done the physical act of arresting, because by section 24(5) of PACE a private citizen – including a store-detective – has no power to arrest someone on suspicion of having earlier committed a theft unless the offence in question has actually been committed. Could it be said, then, that because the police had made the arrest on the information that she gave them, their act of arresting was also hers? If so, she would be liable for the arrest they made (although the police themselves would not be). The trial judge ruled the answer was "no", and the Court of Appeal unanimously affirmed him.

This ruling is hardly surprising. A long line of cases makes it clear that if you tell the police your suspicions and they then arrest someone, you are not liable for their act if (as here) they exercised an independent judgment in the matter. Furthermore, to hold otherwise would have had disastrous consequences. This is because the citizen who arrests someone on suspicion of having earlier committed an arrestable offence is strictly liable where it later turns out that no such offence has actually been committed. To attribute the policeman's arrest to the store detective would have made her liable for it not only when – as arguably here – her behaviour was negligent. If no offence had actually been committed she would have been liable, however reasonable her belief, and however sensible her decision to impart it to the police.

More controversial is *Martin v Watson* [1994] Q.B. 425, which holds that the person who tells the police is free from liability even where he tells a deliberate lie in order to get an innocent person into trouble.

As a move in a long-running dispute between two neighbours, Mrs. W complained to the police, and in consequence Mr. M was arrested and charged that he "did wilfully openly and lewdly expose his person with intent to insult a female contrary to section 4 of the Vagrancy Act 1824". The proceedings ended in his favour when the Crown Prosecution Service offered no evidence at the trial. When Mr. M then sued Mrs. W for malicious prosecution, the judge found that she had deliberately made a false complaint, and that "it was all clearly done to get the plaintiff arrested". He therefore found her liable for malicious prosecution, and awarded Mr. M £3,500 damages.

On appeal, Mrs. W argued that to be liable in malicious prosecution you must have been the prosecutor, and that a person who falsely denounces his neighbour to the police is not the prosecutor if, as he hopes and foresees, they prosecute him. The Court of Appeal, by a majority, accepted this, and reversed the trial judge's decision. The result is to leave the victim of an intentionally false accusation to the police with no effective civil remedy. He might be able to sue for defamation if he was rich enough: but even this avenue is blocked if Ralph Gibson L.J. was right in suggesting that complaints to the police might be covered by absolute privilege.

In reaching its decision the court considered a large number of authorities, which in the end helped little because they were conflicting. It therefore decided the case on principle and policy. The majority – Ralph Gibson L.J. and Hobhouse L.J. – recognised that immunity for the malicious denouncer is hard on the person maliciously denounced, but said that it is necessary in order to protect those who make bona fide complaints to the police from harassment by civil actions. As Hobhouse L.J. said, "... public policy accepts that the protection from civil suit applies to the honest and dishonest alike; the policy is that such matters should be the province of the criminal, not the civil, law."

McCowan L.J. vigorously dissented. On principle, he said, the person who maliciously sets out to harm another by making a false complaint should have to compensate. And he saw "no justification for the view that it would be harmful in the circumstances for such a false accuser to be sued for malicious prosecution".

On the majority's position in this case two comments can be made.

First, if the risk of revenge lawsuits against those who report crimes to the police in good faith really justifies immunity for those who denounce maliciously, the machinery of justice must be singularly inefficient. Not only must genuine villains stand a high chance of escaping justice: the civil courts must also be stupid enough to reason that where a criminal court was not satisfied of a defendant's guilt beyond reasonable doubt, it is more probable than not that the person who denounced him did so maliciously.

Secondly, it would be easier to accept their view about what is necessary to protect those who reasonably provoke criminal justice into action if this area of the law did in fact generally protect the public-spirited from harassment. However, as explained in an earlier note [Citizens Arrest – At their Peril; *R. v Self* [1992] 51 C.L.J. 405 above at p.X), it sometimes directly punishes them. The law on citizen's arrest is peculiar, and a particular oddity is that where one citizen in good faith grabs another who is fool enough to act as if he is running off with something he has stolen, the negligent thief-in-appearance-only can hit the arrester with impunity, and sue him for damages at leisure later. In a law which already penalises the public-spirited, granting immunity to the vicious in the name of protecting the public-spirited looks like an additional fault.

Involuntary Intoxication as a Defence
R. v Kingston
CLJ 1995, 54(1) 12–13

In *R. v Kingston* [1994] Q.B. 81 the Court of Appeal laid down a rule about involuntary intoxication which was surprisingly generous to defendants. It was a defence, they said, not only if it stopped the defendant knowing what he was doing: it was also a defence in the more likely case where he knew full well what he was doing, but the drink or drugs which he had involuntarily taken had released his inhibitions, causing him to lose his self control and for that reason to do what he would not otherwise have done. The decision was criticised-in this journal ([1994] C.L.J. 6, above p. 95) and elsewhere – commentators describing it as contrary to principle, and in practice dangerous.

The House of Lords has now reversed the Court of Appeal ([1994] 3 W.L.R. 519). Approving what the trial judge had said in his direction to the jury, the House ruled that involuntary intoxication is a defence if, and only if, the defendant is so drunk or drugged that he does not know what he is doing, or (presumably, though the House does not expressly say so) if he fails to grasp the surrounding facts which make his act a criminal offence. As the trial judge said, "a drugged intent is still an intent" – even if the drugs were involuntarily taken.

The House of Lords decision consists of a long speech from Lord Mustill, in which his brethren concurred. Here Lord Mustill carefully analysed the three possible arguments which could have supported the more generous rule as stated by the Court of Appeal, and demolished them.

The first was that the "generous rule" flowed naturally from general principles of criminal law, and in particular from the idea that the defendant is not guilty unless he acted with *mens rea*. This was the approach which the Court of Appeal had taken, where Lord Taylor C.J. had said "... the involuntary intoxication negatives the *mens rea*". This was wrong, said Lord Mustill, because in modern English criminal law a defendant has *mens rea* if he carries out the *actus reus* of the offence with whatever degree of foresight of consequences, knowledge of circumstances or intention which the law declares to be a necessary element of the offence. If that mental state is present the defendant acts with *mens rea*. The fact that, blamelessly or otherwise, he has difficulty in controlling himself does not wipe out *mens rea* any more than does the fact that he acted with good motives.

The second argument was that the "generous" rule was already established by authority. After reviewing at length such authority as there is, Lord Mustill found nothing which clearly supported the generous rule. On the contrary: he pointed to a line of modem Scottish cases which allows involuntary intoxication as a defence where it leads "total alienation of reason", but rejects it where it merely causes "inability to exert self-control".

The third argument was this: the fact that the defendant's inhibitions were loosened by drink or drugs ought in fairness to be a defence to criminal liability, and if such a defence does not exist already it is time for the courts to create it.

This raised the important question "Is it open to the courts to create new general defences?" Lord Mustill thought that in principle it was. For the House of Lords to do so, said Lord Mustill, would be "a bold step" – but if it was "both practical and just" they ought to take it. This statement ought to make us stop and think. If the days of "judicial creativity" are over in that the judges now no longer claim the power to extend the criminal law by creating new offences, Lord Mustill's words show that they still feel able to develop it in the opposite direction, if justice requires criminal liability to be limited rather than extended.

However, having stated that the courts could still create new defences, Lord Mustill said that it would be wrong to recognise a new general defence consisting of the fact that the defendant was disinhibited through drink or drugs involuntarily taken. The reasons he gave were the ones which were set out at some length in the note in this journal which criticised the Court of Appeal decision. In the first place, it would be contrary to principle. The law does not recognise irresistible impulse as a defence if it arises from blameless internal causes like brain tumours or hormone imbalance, and thus it can hardly recognise irresistible impulse arising from involuntary intoxication. And secondly, the defence would be open to serious abuse. "My drink must have been spiked" is easy to assert and difficult to disprove; and unless disproved it would usually lead to an acquittal, because the court could never be certain beyond reasonable doubt that even without the "spiked drink" the defendant would still have acted as he did.

In rejecting the idea that the loosening of the defendant's inhibitions by involuntary intoxication should be a general defence, Lord Mustill stressed that it was still relevant as something which could mitigate the sentence. In saying this, Lord Mustill was troubled by the mandatory life sentence for murder, which means that if someone deliberately kills when involuntarily intoxicated the judge cannot take account of the involuntary intoxication even to this limited extent. But the mandatory life sentence for murder, he said, was no good reason for elevating involuntary intoxication to the level of a general defence. It would be wrong, he said, "that the law should be further distorted simply because of this anomalous relic of the history of the criminal law".

Protecting the Mentally Disordered Defendant against Herself
R. v Straw
CLJ 1995, 54(2) 232–235

What happens if the defendant on a murder charge is so deranged that, unlike everyone else, he believes that he is sane – and following the logic of his insanity, forbids his counsel to lead evidence of mental illness, telling him to run some obviously "mad" defence instead?

In England the answer, believe it or not, is that counsel is bound to run the hopeless defence: the court does not hear any evidence of his mental illness; in the absence of such evidence it is unable to reach a verdict of not guilty by reason of insanity, or manslaughter on grounds of diminished responsibility; the defendant therefore gets convicted of murder, although he is not guilty of murder; and gets a mandatory sentence of imprisonment for life, which he clearly ought not to receive.

This surprising result was endorsed by the Court of Appeal some years ago in *R. v Kooken* (1982) 74 Cr.App.R. 30. The defendant, who suffered from paranoid schizophrenia, shot her former friend dead in cold blood because she believed the friend had persuaded a surgeon to "de-womanise" her by carrying out a hysterectomy. At trial, she refused to allow her counsel to run a defence of diminished responsibility, and insisted that her counsel should fight the case on the utterly hopeless basis that she had killed under provocation. No evidence of her mental illness was put before the jury – although it was available in quantities, and although the jury had specifically asked for it – and in the absence of such evidence they convicted her of murder; not manslaughter by reason of diminished responsibility, as they presumably would have done had they heard evidence of her mental illness. In the Court of Appeal it was argued on her behalf that the judge has a discretion to call evidence, and that here he should have exercised it by calling doctors to testify about her mental state. The Court of Appeal said that the judge was right not to call the evidence, and dismissed Mrs. Kooken's appeal.

Mrs. Kooken felt no sense of injustice about this. Her appeal was conducted, against her wishes, by the Official Solicitor, her contribution being to write a letter to the court denouncing his efforts on her behalf, and complaining that the reports which psychiatrists had written about her "might just as well be written in Outer Mongolian hieroglyphics anyway for all the good they are". But a sense of injustice was certainly felt by the convicted defendant in the recent case of *R. v Straw* [1995] 1 All E.R. 187. Here another paranoid schizophrenic, this time accused of murdering her husband, rejected the prosecution's offer to accept her plea of guilty to manslaughter on the ground of diminished responsibility, and insisted on fighting the case by a hopeless defence which had something to do with poltergeists. After this had predictably failed, and she had been convicted of murder, she – unlike Mrs. Kooken – decided that she wanted the Court of Appeal to hear evidence of her mental illness, with a view to substituting a verdict of manslaughter on grounds of diminished responsibility. The Court of Appeal, applying *Kooken*, refused. A defendant who is fit to plead, they said, is fit to choose her defence: and having chosen it she is stuck with it, even if her choice was "mad".

This result, surely, is grotesquely bad. Because the court has not heard evidence which everybody knows exists, and is readily available, a defendant has been convicted of an offence of which she is not guilty. She has, in consequence, received for it a sentence which she ought not to have been given: a sentence of life imprisonment, instead of a hospital order subject to restriction, which is what she ought to have had.

And it is no answer for the Court of Appeal to say, as it said in *Kooken*, that none of this really matters, because the Home Secretary can transfer prisoners who are insane to Broadmoor, so people like Mrs. Kooken and Mrs. Straw always end up in the right place in the end. If you get to Broadmoor because a court made a hospital order, a Mental Health Review Tribunal will set you free if you are cured; but if you get cured in Broadmoor after the Home Secretary "nuts you off" – as your former cellmate will paraphrase the transfer power in section 47 of the Mental Health Act 1983 – you are liable to be transferred back to prison.

The French courts handle this problem better. The ethics of the French bar require a defending lawyer to do what the client's interests require, even if the client does not want it: so the defendant's mental illness would certainly be raised by the defence. And it is part of the philosophy of French criminal procedure that the court has an overriding duty to attempt to find the truth. In a case like this, the *juge d'instruction* would almost certainly obtain psychiatric reports on the defendant during the pre-trial phase, and if he failed to, they would certainly be obtained by the presiding judge at trial. So why can't the same solution be adopted here?

It is no answer for English lawyers to say "well, the French have an inquisitorial system: we have an accusatorial one". Although our system is accusatorial in the sense that it places the primary responsibility for collecting and producing the evidence on the prosecution and the defence, an English criminal court does not shrug off all responsibility in the matter: there are a number of important respects in which an English judge takes active steps to see that the decision of the court is based upon the truth. At the plea stage the judge is expected to intervene if it becomes plain from what the defendant says in mitigation that his guilty plea was based on a mistake of law. At the sentencing stage, the court routinely takes the initiative in ordering medical reports. In a contested case, the judge is expected to direct the jury on defences which are suggested by the evidence, even if the defendant or his counsel have not explicitly relied on them. In addition, the judge has always had a discretionary power to call evidence which neither prosecution nor defence have chosen, or been sufficiently organised, to call. Although most of the modern case law has discouraged judges from exercising this power, the Royal Commission on Criminal Justice thought it was potentially valuable, and wanted its use to be revived. And in the recent case of *R. v Wellingborough Justices, ex p. Francois* (1994) 158 J.P. 813 the Divisional Court resoundingly reaffirmed it. They said that this discretionary power belongs to lay magistrates as well as to professional judges, and that both should exercise it if its use is needed to secure a fair deal for the defence. Thus where the Crown Prosecutor, having another appointment, cut her case short and fled without calling a prosecution witness whom the defence were particularly anxious to cross-examine, the magistrates should have intervened and called the witness themselves.

Is it not an equally obvious case for intervention where the court would otherwise be deprived of evidence of crucial importance to the defence, not because the Crown Prosecutor has double booked herself, but because a mentally disturbed defendant has made a literally insane decision not to call it?

There is of course a further factor in the equation, and that is the question of self-determination. Within limits, even the decisions of mental patients deserve to be respected, if they understand the consequences of them. A compulsory patient, who knows that he will die of gangrene unless his leg is amputated, is entitled to refuse the operation – even if you or I would probably choose to have it (*Re C* [1994] 1 W.L.R. 290): so why should we overrule his choice of defence in criminal proceedings, as long as he knows it is likely to lead to a conviction? But if this is a reason for the Court of Appeal's refusing to intervene in a case like *Kooken*, where the defendant warmly embraces the consequences when they have happened, it surely does not justify its refusal to intervene where the defendant has come bitterly to rue them. A civil court is prepared in principle to set aside a disadvantageous contract which a mental patient has made and now regrets, and does not automatically respond by saying, "You are stuck with the decision which you made". The criminal courts should be even readier to intervene, because they are dealing not with his money, but his liberty.

Seances, and the Secrecy of the Jury-Room
R. v Young
CLJ 1995, 54(3) 519–522

IN *R. v Young (Stephen)* [1995] Q.B. 324 the defendant was tried and convicted for a double murder, allegedly committed for gain. Shortly afterwards, one of the jurors told a solicitor that the jury, when considering their verdict, had tried by occult means to make contact with the spirit of one of the victims. This led the Court of Appeal to ask the Treasury Solicitor to make enquiries, which revealed that in the hotel where the jury had been spending the night together, the foreman and three others – apparently having taken drink – had set up a "ouija board". That is, they sat at a circular table round the edge of which were bits of paper with letters of the alphabet on them, each person with a finger on an upturned glass placed in the middle of the circle, in the hope that the movement of the glass towards one letter or another would reveal a message from beyond the grave. By this means, they got – or thought they got – the message "Stephen Young done it". On hearing about these capers, the Court of Appeal quashed the conviction, and ordered a retrial (at which a second jury, presumably without the help of supernatural means, also convicted).

What is extraordinary about this case is not the fact that the jurors used a ouija board, nor that the Court of Appeal quashed the conviction because they had done so. It is that it was, legally, an uphill task to get the conviction quashed on such a ground. The Crown first argued that the inquiry the Court of Appeal ordered was illegal, and then tried to say that it should not quash the conviction because of the results. And what is more, in so arguing, the Crown seemed to have the law on its side. Section 8(1) of the Contempt of Court Act 1981 provides:

> ... it is a contempt of court to obtain, disclose or solicit any particulars of statements made, opinions expressed, arguments advanced or votes cast by members of a jury in the course of their deliberations in any legal proceedings.

The section goes on to make certain limited exceptions; but, as the Court of Appeal accepted, none of these cover enquiries made or information supplied with a view to overturning the jury's decision because of the illegal or improper way it went about its job. If it is illegal to give this information for this purpose, the Court of Appeal can hardly ask people to give it, or act on it when they do. Thus the Court of Appeal felt able to order the inquiry and then act on the results only because the ouija board incident had taken place, not at the court house, but during their overnight break at the hotel. What went on there, said the Court of Appeal, was not "in the course of their deliberations" for the purposes of section 8 – and could be enquired into and acted on. If, however, the jurors had set up their ouija board in the jury room at the court house, the Court of Appeal could have done nothing whatever about it: even though using a ouija board at court itself would surely have been even worse.

That this situation is an odd one hardly needs saying. How can the law of a supposedly intelligent people produce a result like this?

Section 8 of the Contempt of Court Act 1981 began as a measure aimed at newspapers publishing interviews with jurors; as the *New Statesman* had recently done after the sensational trial and acquittal of the politician Jeremy Thorpe. The provision in the Bill would have permitted questions put anonymously to jurors by social scientists carrying out research on the workings of juries – but even this became prohibited when, in the House of Lords, the measure was toughened up at the instance of legal peers who liked social science research as little as they liked investigative journalism. Since then, the need to amend section 8 to allow social science research on juries has been a theme much harped upon by reformers of the legal system. The Royal Commission on Criminal Justice, indeed, thought it so important that it made it the first of its 352 recommendations. Nobody, however, ever seems to have complained about the much more basic problem: that section 8 also makes it impossible to investigate gross misbehaviour in the jury room of a kind which makes the conviction in the case unsafe.

Compared with the need for this, the supposed need for social science research into how well juries do their job is surely of secondary importance. Indeed, there is even reason to be sceptical about the importance of such research. The basic problem is that there is no such thing as "the jury". A jury is a collection of twelve individual people, press-ganged at random, and with nothing in common but the fact that they were the ones who could not get away. The qualities of any jury will therefore vary, naturally, according to the qualities of the people serving on it. On juries, as in the world generally, there are likely to be four types of person: intelligent and sensible ones, unintelligent and sensible ones, intelligent but silly ones, and – most frightening of all – ones who are both unintelligent and silly. Whether the jury works well, adequately, badly or atrociously must always depend on which of these four groups predominates. The information that such research can produce is therefore likely to be so general as to be of limited use: as, for example, that jury trial usually works quite well, that it sometimes works less well, that jurors only occasionally misunderstand the basic issues, and that bizarre misbehaviour is extremely rare.

Yet if bizarre and irresponsible behaviour by jurors is rare, it certainly does happen, both in the jury room and out of it. Last year, for example, the Court of Appeal also heard an appeal from a conviction in a murder case where one of the defendants complained that a woman juror had spent her time in the jury box falling in love with one of the barristers, with whom she had tried to make a date after the court had risen (*Cambridge Evening News*, 2 July 1994). If such cases are statistically rare, their rarity is no consolation to the hapless defendant in the case, whom the jurors' vagaries, in a murder case, may have landed life imprisonment. When such things do happen, it is obviously vital to be able to do something about them, whether the scene of the jurors' irresponsible behaviour was the hotel, the court room, or the jury room itself.

Civil Liability for Making False Accusations to the Police
Martin v Watson
CLJ 1996, 55(1) 8–9

In *Martin v Watson* [1994] Q.B. 424 the Court of Appeal, by a majority, decided that where A deliberately lies to the police that B has committed an offence, and in consequence they prosecute him, B is unable to sue A for malicious prosecution. A, they said, is not the prosecutor: and the prosecutor is the only person who is liable for malicious prosecution. This decision was criticised in an earlier number of this journal (Freedom to Denounce Your Fellow

Citizens to the Police; *Davidson v CC North Wales* [1994] C.L.J. 433, above n. 99) – where the graphic facts are also stated.

The plaintiff in *Martin v Watson* subsequently appealed to the House of Lords, which allowed the appeal and held that the malicious complainant can indeed be sued: [1996] A.C. 74.

In a speech in which the rest of the House concurred, Lord Keith expressed surprise that this basic question had apparently not been decided by an English court before. There was, however, plenty of authority on the matter from other parts of the common law world, all of it in favour of the plaintiff. Fortified by this, Lord Keith laid down the law of England in the following terms:

> Where an individual falsely and maliciously gives a police officer information indicating that some person is guilty of a criminal offence and states that he is willing to give evidence in court of the matters in question, it is properly to be inferred that he desires and intends that the person he names should be prosecuted. Where the circumstances are such that the facts relating to the alleged offence can be within the knowledge only of the complainant, as was the position here... the proper view of the matter is that the prosecution has been procured by the complainant.

In the House of Lords, as in the Court of Appeal, the defence argued that the law should confer a complete immunity suit on everyone who complains to the police. Otherwise, they said, there is a danger that A will make a genuine complaint about B, B will be wrongly acquitted, and B will then add injury to insult by suing A for malicious prosecution. The result, said the defence, would be to make the public less inclined to cooperate with the police: and in consequence even fewer criminals would be caught and brought to justice than are now. This argument, which impressed a majority of the Court of Appeal, cut no ice at all with any member of the House of Lords. The complainant, they said, is only liable for malicious prosecution where he or she has deliberately lied, and the person complained about can prove it: and this, their Lordships felt, is all the protection that is needed.

This, with respect, is surely right. For the person improperly acquitted to sue his accuser is a risky business. Although acquitted, his innocence is not in law conclusively presumed. Thus if he sues his accuser after the criminal courts have "cleared" him, he runs the risk that his accuser – making use of evidence which would be inadmissible in a criminal court – will defend himself by proving that he really did it after all.

Bugging and Burglary by the Police
R. v Khan
CLJ 1997, 56(1) 6–8

In the famous case of *Entinck v Carrington* (1765) 2 Wils. K.B. 275 it was decided that the Secretary of State has no power to authorise government agents to burgle suspects' houses to search for evidence of crimes. A search so made constitutes the tort of trespass, for which the agent is liable in damages to the suspect whose house he had broken into, the Secretary of State's invalid authorisation being no defence. When professional police forces were established, this case was taken as authority for the principle that a house search by the police was illegal unless carried out under some specific power conferred on them by the common law or statute, or authorised by a search-warrant issued by a magistrate.

Undeterred by this decision, in 1984 the Home Office issued "Guidelines" to the police saying it was in order for policemen to burgle houses and plant listening devices, provided the Chief Constable himself gave permission. In *R. v Khan* [1997] A.C. 558 the police, following the Home Office Guidelines, did exactly this, and thereby obtained tape-recordings of conversations that conclusively showed Khan to have been involved in smuggling heroin with a street value of £100,000. And so it was that, 230 years after *Entink v Carrington*, break-ins by order of the Minister gave rise to another leading case.

This time the legal issues were rather different. Unlike the plaintiff in the earlier case, Khan was not claiming damages, but appealing against his conviction in the criminal courts, which the Crown had secured by using the evidence obtained by the hidden "bug". And the Crown did not even seek to argue that the Home Secretary's

Guidelines made the police break-in to plant it legal; it admitted that this "had involved a civil trespass, and had occasioned some damage to the property". The issue was whether the evidence, being illegally obtained, had been properly admitted at his trial.

In this country the position has long been that illegally obtained evidence is admissible in principle, although the trial judge has a discretion to exclude it – a discretion that exists both at common law, and also under section 78 of the Police and Criminal Evidence Act 1984, which expressly allows the judge to exclude prosecution evidence the use of which would make the trial "unfair". In practice judges usually exercise their discretion so as to admit illegally obtained evidence if it looks convincing and reliable despite the illegality – particularly where the offence for which the defendant is on trial is grave enough to make the unlawful act by which the evidence was obtained look pale by comparison. It is therefore not surprising that in *Khan* both the Court of Appeal and the House of Lords held that the evidence of the tape-recordings had been properly admitted, Lord Nolan concluding that he reached this decision "with relief".

Much more could be written about what the courts said in this case on the subject of admitting illegally obtained evidence, but this commentator proposes to concentrate on a different aspect of the case. This is the broader issue of police powers; a subject on which the decision reveals a state of affairs which is both frightening and depressing.

First, there is the revelation that for the last 12 years the Home Office has been openly inciting the police to commit crimes and torts where this would enable them to get evidence they could not otherwise obtain. In a country which likes to imagine that it invented civil liberties and the Rule of Law, this is astonishing.

Secondly, there is the Government's reaction to the revelation of the fact that the police have been bugging and burgling houses illegally, which is to promote instant legislation legalising these activities when policemen do them. A clause in the Police Bill, currently before Parliament, provides that "No entry or interference with property or with wireless telegraphy shall be unlawful" if the Chief Constable of the force "thinks it necessary ... on the ground that it is likely to be of substantial value in the prevention or detection of serious crime, and is satisfied that what the action seeks to achieve cannot reasonably be achieved by other means".

Lastly, there is the general mess we have now got into over the law regulating the powers of the police to gather evidence.

In a free country which has subscribed to the European Convention on Human Rights it would be reasonable to expect the powers of the police to gather evidence to be carefully graded, with the ones that are particularly invasive, sinister or frightening always needing the prior authorisation of the courts. Instead, look what we have! To search my house openly and above board, the police must indeed obtain a warrant from the justices. To tap my telephone on the other hand, the Interception of Communications Act 1985 allows them to act on the permission of the Home Secretary. And if they want to burgle my house at dead of night, or to plant secret listening devices all over it, the new Police Bill – if passed in its original form[13] – will allow them to do this without the prior authorisation of any external agency at all.

Electronic Eavesdropping and Anomalies in the Law of Evidence
R. v Aujla
CLJ 1999, 58(1), p. 43–45

There is nothing wrong with the Court of Appeal decision in *R. v Aujla* [1998] 2 Cr.App.R. 16. Almost everything is wrong, however, with the law that the court was called on to interpret, and the decision is interesting because it shows this up.

The defendants were awaiting trial for smuggling illegal immigrants from Holland, and a preliminary question arose as to whether the prosecution could use as evidence the tape-recordings of incriminating telephone calls that the defendants had made in Holland. The calls had been intercepted by the Dutch authorities,

---

[13] Fortunately, it was not. As eventually enacted, the Police Act 1997 permits the police to bug and burgle, but only where authorised to do so by a Surveillance Commissioner.

acting legally under local law, and collaborating with the English police.

Where the English police tap telephones in England, the fruits of their eavesdropping are – surprisingly – inadmissible in evidence; and this is so whether they listened in legally or illegally. This is the effect of section 9 of the Interception of Communications Act 1985, which says:

(1) In any proceedings before any court or tribunal no evidence shall be adduced and no question in cross-examination shall be asked which (in either case) tends to suggest
   (a) that an offence [of tapping telephones illegally contrary to s. 1 of the Act] has been or is to be committed by any of the persons mentioned in subsection (2) below; or
   (b) that a warrant [from the Home Secretary authorising a tap under s. 2 of the Act] has been or is to be issued to any of those persons;
(2) The persons referred to in subsection (1) above are-
   (a) any person holding office under the Crown;
   (b) the Post Office and any person engaged in the business of the Post Office; and
   (c) any public telecommunications operator and any person engaged in the running of a public telecommunication system.

Obviously, when the Dutch authorities tap telephones in Holland they act neither under the English legislation on telephone-tapping nor in contravention of it, so there could be no question of the evidence being excluded under section 9 as such. The defence, however, argued that the strict letter of the statutory provision was surrounded by the broader spirit of the common law of evidence, under which all use of evidence obtained by telephone-tapping must be viewed as making trials "unfair" – and hence liable to exclusion under the judge's discretion to exclude such evidence contained in section 78 of the Police and Criminal Evidence Act 1984. Affirming the decision of the court below, the Court of Appeal rejected this argument and said that the Crown could use the Dutch tapes as evidence.

Section 9 is an oddity, and this decision makes it look even odder than it did before.

The basic rule of criminal evidence is that everything is admissible if it is relevant. To this rule section 9 makes a narrow exception, which the courts – apparently disliking it – have interpreted restrictively. In consequence, the total picture as regards the admissibility in evidence of the fruits of electronic eavesdropping is strangely incoherent. Thus: (i) the contents of an officially intercepted telephone conversation are inadmissible; (ii) however, the official records of the telephone company are admissible to show that at a given date and time, the defendant made a call from one number to another; (iii) and the contents of the call itself are admissible if the person at one end of the line knew it was being recorded, even if the other one did not (*Rasool* [1997] 2 Cr. App. R. 190); (iv) and likewise where the police intercepted the call in ignorance of both parties, if instead of tapping the line in the usual way, they intercepted radio-waves winging their electronic way from a portable 'phone to the mechanical part of the system (*Effick* [1995] 1 A.C. 309); (v) and it also looks as if the court can hear the contents of the call if the line was tapped not legally, but illegally – provided the criminal offence of interception was committed not by a State official, but by someone outside the list contained in section 9(2) – a private detective, for example, or an investigative journalist; (vi) and the court can also hear the contents of a private conversation recorded not by tapping the defendant's telephone, but by planting a bug – legally or otherwise – in the wall of his house (*Khan* [1997] A.C. 558). To this extraordinary list of exceptions to an exception, *Aujla* adds a new one; (vii) the fruits of official telephone-tapping are also admissible in evidence, provided it took place abroad.

This astonishing state of affairs provokes the question: what policy underlies the imperfect attempt by section 9 to make evidence of telephone-taps inadmissible, even where they were legally carried out? It is sometimes said that such evidence was inadmissible at common law, and section 9 was simply meant to affirm existing common law. But this explanation is a weak one, because the common law rule (if it existed) evolved when telephone-tapping was a shady business with no legal basis. The purpose of the Interception of Communications Act was to give it one – and this, one might have thought, destroyed the basis for the earlier rule.

It is also said that section 9 was intended to protect the police from defence questioning which might reveal information about their methods that they need to keep secret in order to win their fight against crime. But this too is unconvincing. First, the risk already arises in the situations where section 9 does not apply. Secondly, and more fundamentally, there is no need to protect them against this risk where (as often) it is the police who wish to use the evidence, and the desire to exclude the evidence comes from the defence.

The real explanation for section 9, I believe, lies in the circumstances in which the Interception of Communications Act was enacted. The government of the day was pushed into legislating on telephone-tapping by the *Malone* case (1984) 7 E.H.R.R. 14, hated doing it, and was determined both to keep the power to issue warrants to tap telephones in the hands of the Home Secretary, and to ensure as far as possible that his decisions could not be examined – directly or indirectly – in the ordinary courts. The primary aim of section 9 was to protect the Home Office – and only secondarily the police. The protection of defendants, needless to say, was not part of the scheme at all – although, as with some other ill conceived evidential rules, it is guilty defendants who mainly profit by it.

In the rest of continental Europe, I believe, the rule is simple: the fruits of telephone-tapping are admissible if it was done legally, but inadmissible if it was not. And one does not have to be a europhile, surely, to believe that this should be the rule in England too.[14]

Everybody Out
R. v Richards
CLJ 1999, 58(3) 497–499

The common law tradition strongly favours witnesses giving evidence in public. In the leading case of *Scott v Scott* [1913] A.C. 417, the House of Lords ruled that at common law, even embarrassing

---

[14] In 2008 an official review chaired by Sir John Chilcot reported in favour of lifting the ban on the admissibility of intercept evidence and the Prime Minister of the day, Gordon Brown, announced his conversion to the idea; but to date, no action has been taken.

evidence about sexual impotence in a nullity suit must be so given. Public justice is said to be essential to make sure that judges behave themselves and that witnesses tell the truth. For these two purely altruistic reasons, it is always staunchly defended by the media. In consequence, almost every statute passed to enable the judge to clear the court exempts the representatives of the press.

The continental tradition, by contrast, is much more favourable to allowing witnesses to give evidence in private. It is therefore not surprising that Article 6 of the European Convention on Human Rights, which guarantees public justice, allows exceptions which to common lawyers (and journalists) seem rather wide:

> In the determination of his civil rights and obligations or of any criminal charge against him, everyone is entitled to a fair and public hearing ... Judgment shall be pronounced publicly but the press and public may be excluded from all or part of the trial in the interests of morals, public order or national security in a democratic society, where the interests of juveniles or the protection of the private life of the parties so require, or to the extent strictly necessary in the opinion of the court in special circumstances where publicity would prejudice the interests of justice.

In *Richards* [1999] J.P. 246, the Court of Appeal (Criminal Division) reaffirmed that the judge in a criminal case has a general power at common law to clear the court when witnesses are giving evidence. This power exists, of course, in addition to the various statutory powers.

In this case an 18-year-old girl who was the key witness to a murder refused to testify unless the court was cleared. At first she said she was scared of the defendant's friends and relations, who were thought to be sitting in the public gallery. She later said she "just didn't feel comfortable". No stranger to the dock herself, she said she would go to prison rather than give evidence in public. In equal defiance of the judge and common law traditions, she said "I don't want to give evidence in front of the public gallery so you take it how you want it; if you want to hold me in contempt, you can hold me in contempt; if you want to clear the public gallery, you can clear the public gallery". The judge did clear the court, she gave her evidence, and the defendant was convicted.

On appeal the defendant argued that these circumstances did not justify in law the court's being cleared, in support of which he argued *Scott v Scott* and Article 6 of the Convention. The Court of Appeal said that they did, and affirmed his conviction. In reaching this conclusion they quoted the words of Lord Haldane in *Scott v Scott* who had said that the principle of public justice must occasionally give way to "a yet more fundamental principle that the chief object of courts of justice must be to secure that justice is done".

While this was happening in the Strand, in Westminster the Government was putting the finishing touches to its Youth Justice and Criminal Evidence Bill, which received the Royal Assent this summer. Among much else, this Act empowers the judge in a criminal case to decree a range of "special measures" for the protection of vulnerable witnesses. By section 25, one of these is the power to clear the court while they are giving evidence.

In some respects this new power is broader than the power to clear the court at common law. Thus the new power, unlike the one at common law, applies wherever the witness belongs to one of various stated categories of "eligible witness" and the order would "be likely to improve the quality of the evidence given by the witness" (s.19(2)(a)).

In some respects, however, the new power to clear the court is significantly narrower than the existing one. First, the precondition that the measure should be "likely to improve the quality of the evidence given by the witness" does not, on the face of it at least, cover the even stronger case of the witness who but for the "special measure" would be unable or unwilling to give any evidence at all. Presumably this difficulty was unintended and will be overcome by robust construction. But there is a further and more important limitation: the statutory provision, unlike the common law power, does not enable the judge to order out the press. As it first appeared in the Bill, the new power expressly extended to the media. The Government backed off, however, and in its final form the media are expressly exempted from it. Any order made under this provision must allow at least one representative "of news gathering or reporting organisations" to remain in court. So it looks as if

Parliament, with great song and dance, has contrived to give the judges a significantly weaker power to clear the court than the common law had given them already.

What is the relationship between the new statutory power to clear the court and the existing power at common law? Section 19(6) preserves the court's inherent powers to make orders "(a) in relation to a witness who is not an eligible witness, or (b) in relation to an eligible witness where... the order is made or the leave is given otherwise than by reason of the fact that the witness is an eligible witness". But this itself is less than wholly clear. By section 17, a frightened or intimidated witness is an "eligible witness". If, when a frightened witness testifies, the judge decides to clear the court (of journalists and all) on the ground that this is essential to enable justice to be done – the test for the exercise of the common law power – is the order then made "otherwise than by reason of the fact that the witness is an eligible witness"? Perhaps one day the courts will have to tell us.

Insanity and Mens Rea
AG's Reference No. 3 of 1998
CLJ 2000, 59(1), p. 9–11

Question: "D, who is mentally ill, believes that he is Jesus Christ. He breaks down P's front door and belabours him with a snooker cue, in the deluded belief that P is about to crucify him. Having been subdued by five police officers, D is eventually tried on indictment for aggravated burglary and affray. What is his criminal liability?"

Answer (from any first year undergraduate): "It seems that because of his mental illness, D either did not appreciate the nature and quality of his acts, or did not understand that they were wrong. At the time in question he therefore seems to have been insane under the M'Naghten rules. Thus the jury should find a special verdict of 'not guilty by reason of insanity' as provided for by section 2(1) of the Trial of Lunatics Act 1883. This verdict will enable the judge to make one of the various orders open to him under section 5 of the

Criminal Procedure (Insanity) Act 1964. The most likely disposal in this case will be a hospital order, possibly subject to restriction."

It is therefore astonishing to learn that when this very case did indeed end up in the Crown Court recently, the trial judge accepted the defence submission that the proper verdict was not the special verdict, but a simple acquittal – which produces the result that the accused goes free. The defence position was that the Crown is only entitled to a special verdict where it can show that, but for his insanity, the defendant would be guilty. And this, they said, means that in such a case the prosecution must prove that the defendant not only committed an *actus reus*, but also that he did so with *mens rea*. Where he lacks *mens rea* – even through insanity – he is entitled to an acquittal. This argument, which turns the previous learning on insanity upside down, the trial judge accepted reluctantly, because he thought he was bound to do so by the decision of the Court of Appeal in *Egan* [1998] 1 Cr.App.R.121.

Egan was not a case about the "special verdict" and insanity at the time of the alleged offence. It concerned what happens after the defendant is found "unfit to plead" because of his insanity at the time of trial. Under section 4A of the Criminal Procedure (Insanity) Act 1964, the next step after a finding of "unfit to plead" is a decision by a jury on whether the defendant "did the act or made the omission charged against him as the offence", and if. the answer is "yes", the judge has then the same powers of dealing with the defendant as after a special verdict of "not guilty by reason of insanity". In *Egan*, the Court of Appeal had said that a finding that the defendant "did the act or made the omission charged against him as the offence" involves a finding of *mens rea* as well as *actus reus*. The judge who tried the *soi-disant* Jesus Christ assumed that *Egan* also applied to the special verdict of "not guilty by reason of insanity".

Unsurprisingly, the resulting acquittal in the Jesus Christ case was followed by an Attorney-General's reference to the Court of Appeal, whose decision is reported as *Attorney-General's Reference (No.3 of 1998)* in [2000] Q.B. 401. Still less surprisingly, the Court of Appeal condemned the trial judge's ruling. After a careful review of the history of the verdict of "not guilty by reason of insanity", it said that, in order to obtain a verdict of "not guilty by reason of insanity", the prosecution must prove "the ingredients which constitute the *actus reus* of the crime". If the Crown can do this, it "is not required to prove the *mens rea* of the crime alleged, and apart from insanity, the defendant's state of mind ceases to be relevant". The earlier decision in *Egan*, the Court said, was probably wrong even as regards the ingredients of a finding under section 4A of the Criminal Procedure (Insanity) Act, and even if it were right, it did not decide the point in relation to the special verdict of "not guilty by reason of insanity" under section 2(1) of the charmingly-named Trial of Lunatics Act 1883.

A few weeks later another Court of Appeal – this time with the Lord Chief Justice presiding – cast yet further doubt on *Egan*. In *Antoine* [1992] 2 Cr. App. R. 225 the point at issue was whether, once a defendant on a murder charge has been found "unfit to plead", he can then attempt to raise the defence of diminished responsibility. In other words, when the jury is deciding under section 4A of the Criminal Procedure (Insanity) Act whether the defendant "did the act or made the omission charged", can it be asked to say (in effect) "yes, he did the act charged, in that he killed the victim; but because of his state of diminished responsibility this was the *actus reus* of manslaughter, not murder"? The Court of Appeal ruled that no such invitation could be put to the jury. In the course of reaching this decision the Court once again considered *Egan*. It did not formally overrule it, because it felt that *Egan* was not concerned with the precise issue now before it, but it made it very plain that it thought that it was incorrect.

At one level the *Attorney-General's Reference (No. 3 of 1998)* is an unexciting decision, because it merely reaffirms that the law is as everyone had previously imagined. At a different level, however, it provokes two important reflections. The first is how easy it is for even the Crown Court to get a basic point of criminal law astonishingly wrong. The second reflection is how bizarre it is that, when this happens and causes a visibly dangerous defendant to be wrongly acquitted, the resulting proceedings in the Court of Appeal always leave the improperly obtained acquittal intact. As the law now stands, the most the Court of Appeal can do when hearing an Attorney-General's reference brought following an acquittal is to wring its judicial hands about the error in the court below, and express the hope that the same mistake will not be made again – however obviously wrong the acquittal was, and however dangerous the offender.

Some weeks ago, this rule of criminal procedure was called into question in a public lecture given by Lord Morris, the present Attorney-General. The fact that the defendant in the case the subject of this note "walked free" – with or without his snooker cue – adds strength to Lord Morris's argument that the Court of Appeal should sometimes have the power to set aside an acquittal.

Procedural Anomalies
R. v Stratford JJ ex p. Imbert
CLJ 2000, 59(1) 50–52

For centuries, English criminal procedure regarded the "surprise witness" as a legitimate weapon, for the prosecution as well as the defence. In a case in 1823 Park J. complained that the defendant had seen the depositions in advance of trial. "The prosecutor or his solicitor might have access to them, but not the party accused. For what would be the consequence if the latter had access to them? Why, that he would know everything which was to be produced in evidence against him – an advantage which it was never intended should be extended towards him ..." (J.F. Stephen, *History of the Criminal Law of England* (1883), vol. 1, p. 228).

During the nineteenth century this attitude changed, to the extent that the defendant acquired the right to advance notice of the evidence the prosecution proposed to call against him in cases that were to be tried on indictment. However, this change did not apply to summary trial in the magistrates' courts, where the prosecutor could still spring evidential surprises on him. This mattered little in the days when summary trial was reserved for truly trivial cases, but as the jurisdiction of the magistrates' court was gradually extended, so it began to matter more. During the

1970s and 1980s, there was public pressure to extend "advance disclosure" to summary trial. To this the Government reluctantly gave way, in 1977 promoting legislation that eventually led to the Magistrates' Courts (Advance Information) Rules 1985, which are still in force. These give the magistrates' court defendant some rights, but ones markedly inferior to those he has in trials on indictment. On summary trial, the defendant has a limited right to be informed about the prosecution case where he is accused of an "either-way offence", and if it is a purely summary offence, no right to advance disclosure whatsoever.

Initially the debate about disclosure centred on the duty of the prosecution to inform the defence of the evidence that it proposed to use at trial. In the 1980s, it began to centre around a slightly different matter: the duty (if any) of the prosecution to tell the defence about the material it had gathered in the course of the enquiry, and which it did not intend to use because it suggested that the defendant was innocent. In the case of *Judith Ward* [1993] 1 W.L.R. 619, the Court of Appeal ruled that the prosecution must in principle tell the defence about such "unused material", and give them access to it. This new judge-made rule was codified (and also restricted in certain ways) by the Criminal Procedure and Investigations Act 1996.

The new duty on prosecutors to share "unused material" applies across the board: not only to proceedings on indictment, but also to all shapes and forms of summary trial, including the summary trial of purely summary offences. And this, in combination with the grudging Magistrates' Courts (Advance Information) Rules already mentioned, gives rise to an extraordinary paradox. In summary trials of purely summary offences, the Criminal Procedure and Investigations Act 1996 now requires the prosecutor to share with the defence the evidence that he does not intend to use, but the Magistrates' Courts (Advance Information) Rules still allow him to keep from the defence the evidence he does!

This remarkable anomaly was publicly exposed in *R. v Stratford JJ., ex p. Imbert* [1992] 2 Criminal Appeal Reports 276. The defendant, following an incident in a public lavatory, was prosecuted for offences of threatening behaviour and assault on the police – both of which are summary only. The Crown Prosecution Service, relying on the Magistrates' Courts (Advance Information) Rules, refused to give the defence access to the statements of the prosecution witnesses. In response to this, the defence asked the magistrates to stay the prosecution as an abuse of process, and when the justices refused, sought judicial review of their refusal. Before the Divisional Court, the defence argued that the prosecutor was now obliged to tell the defence the evidence he intends to call in every type of case. This must be so, he said, for two reasons. The first was that the prosecutor's right to refuse to disclose the evidence he intends to call had been in some way overridden by his new duty to disclose "unused material". The second was that his refusal contravened the defendant's right to a "fair trial", as guaranteed by Article 6 of the European Convention on Human Rights.

The Divisional Court rejected both arguments. The first failed because, as the court observed, giving advance notice of the evidence you intend to use is one thing, and sharing the evidence you do not intend to use is another; thus later legislation on the second does not repeal or qualify earlier legislation on the first. The other argument failed because the commodity that Article 6 of the Convention protects is not advance disclosure, but "fair trial". A trial is not a fair one if the defendant is denied the chance to meet the case against him; but even if the prosecution hides the evidence until the day of trial, the court can still ensure the defendant has a fair trial by ordering an adjournment to give him a proper opportunity to meet the case. As Buxton L.J. said, "The case might of course have to be assessed again once the trial had been completed, and its whole conduct fell to be reviewed. But that is a very different matter from saying that the Convention forbids that stage ever being reached."

Although a defeat for this particular defendant, this decision is in a limited sense a victory for defendants generally. Whilst rejecting the defendant's case that he had a right to see the statements, the Divisional Court said that it would be good practice for the CPS to disclose them voluntarily on request – and it hoped that in future it would do so.

If the CPS heeds this sensible advice, the anomaly this case exposes will no longer matter. However, the face of English criminal procedure will still be disfigured by it. And this sort of muddle will continue to be made, I believe, as long as English criminal procedure remains in its present chaotic state of non-codification. If all the major statutory rules on criminal procedure could be just brought together in one single statutory text, as was done in Scotland in 1975, legislative blunders of this sort might be noticed before they are committed.[15]

Protecting the Mentally Disturbed Defendant against Himself
R. v Weekes
CLJ 2000, 59(2) 270–272

A particular problem for English criminal procedure is the defendant on a murder charge who is (to put it crudely) so mad that he believes that he is sane – and instead of running the obvious defences of insanity or diminished responsibility, runs some other defence that seems plausible to him but no one else. In *Weekes* [1999] 2 Cr.App.R. 520 the Court of Appeal departed from its earlier case law on the subject and pointed the law in what this commentator feels to be a sounder direction.

In the earlier cases – notably *Kooken* (1982) 74 Cr.App.R. 30 and *Straw* (1985) [1995] 1 All E.R. 187 (noted [as Protecting the Mentally Disordered Defendant against Herself] [1995] C.L.J. 232 and above at p. 105) – the Court of Appeal took a hard and uncompromising line. Provided the defendant is found fit to plead, it said, he (or she) must live with the consequences of the decisions he has made. The trial judge is under no obligation to pull the defendant's legal chestnuts out of the fire by producing psychiatric

---

[15] Alas, this is still true. The secondary legislation is now codified in the Criminal Procedure Rules, the primary legislation is still a formless jungle. Then after considerable public time and money had been spent on a serious attempt to codify the primary legislation, the project was aborted. For the details, see "Codifying Criminal Procedure – R.I.P.?", [2007] *Criminal Law Review* 331–332.

evidence under his discretionary power to call witnesses, and his failure to do so gives the defendant no arguable grounds for appeal. Nor, it said, does it help the defendant to approach his appeal a different way by asking the Court of Appeal to exercise its own discretionary power to hear fresh evidence under section 23 of the Criminal Appeal Act 1968, with a view to getting it to substitute a different finding for the murder verdict that the jury reached without it. Thus the defendant stays convicted – and though mad, in jail, unless the governor can persuade the Home Secretary to transfer him to a mental hospital.

In *Weekes* the Court of Appeal, having examined these authorities and a number of more recent ones, took a softer line on the question of its power to hear "fresh evidence" from the psychiatrists under section 23. The fact that the defendant had been properly found fit to plead, it said, did not conclude the matter, and despite such a finding, it was still proper for the Court of Appeal to hear from the psychiatrists where his decision not to call them was significantly affected by his mental illness. On this basis it admitted the evidence, and then substituted for the murder verdict a conviction of manslaughter on grounds of diminished responsibility.

So far so good: but it would surely be much better if this particular problem never reached the Court of Appeal and the psychiatrists were always heard at trial. As things stand, however, it is often difficult to ensure the psychiatric evidence is heard at trial, because at trial it often suits neither the prosecution nor the defence to call it. The prosecution claims the defendant is a murderer and does not see it as its job to rebut the case that it has come to court to make. And the defence feels unable to call it, either because defence counsel fears that it will undermine some other plausible and preferable defence, like self-defence or provocation, or (as in the present case) because the defendant has expressly told his counsel that he will not allow it.

The answer, surely, is that the trial judge should be required to call the psychiatrists under his general power to call additional evidence: and that the Court of Appeal needs to rethink what was said in *Straw* and *Kooken* not only in relation to the point about hearing fresh evidence on appeal, but also on the judge's duty (if any) to call such evidence on his own initiative at trial.

It is true that English criminal procedure is basically adversarial, and leaves the parties free to call what evidence they choose with minimum intervention from the court. But it only does so, surely, because it traditionally believes that this is the soundest way of establishing the truth, which is an essential ingredient for doing justice. As Denning L.J. once said, citing Lord Eldon, "truth is best discovered by powerful statements on both sides of the question": *Jones v National Coal Board* [1957] 2 Q.B. 55.

Thus as the law now stands the judge (or magistrates) are already permitted – and sometimes expected – to intervene on their own initiative when this is necessary to prevent normal adversarial practices resulting in inaccurate fact-finding and consequent injustice. So if the defendant tries to plead guilty whilst still protesting his innocence, they must reject his "equivocal plea" and proceed to hear the evidence against him. Where after a guilty plea the prosecution and defence present an "agreed version" of the facts for the judge to sentence on, he can reject it if he thinks it is implausible and have his own investigations made. When directing the jury, the judge is bound to put before them any possible defence that is suggested by the evidence, even if defence counsel – whether for tactical reasons or incompetence – does not expressly rely on it.

Lastly, there are already situations where it seems to be recognised that the court must call witnesses whom neither side has called. In two decisions (*R. v Wellingborough JJ., ex p. Francois* (1994) 158 J.P. 813 and *R. v Haringey Justices, ex p. D.P.P.* [1996] Q.B. 351) the Divisional Court has indicated that the court should intervene to call a witness where the prosecution first says that it will call him, and then at trial tells the defence "We've changed our mind, you call him" – so forcing them, if they want the court to hear him, to call him as their own witness: which means they cannot cross-examine him, although he is probably favourable to the other side.

What lies behind these cases seems to be the principle that the court must intervene to call a witness where his evidence might realistically help to establish a defendant's innocence of the offence of which he stands accused. And it is hard to think of a clearer case for the application of this principle than where a mentally disturbed defendant on a murder charge perversely refuses to call evidence relating to his mental state.

Naming and Shaming Young Offenders
McKerry v Teesdale and Wear Valley JJ
CLJ 2000, 59(3) 466–468

IN the criminal justice system's scheme of unpleasant things, what official part is played by "naming and shaming" the offender? For adults, the unspoken premise seems to be that being named in the newspaper is a part of the sanction, and the risk of public shame is part of the law's system of deterrents. For children and young persons, however, the considerations are different – as the Divisional Court recently reminded us in *McKerry v Teesdale and Wear Valley Justices* (2000) 164 J.P. 355.

The basic rules on naming juvenile defendants are contained in sections 39 and 49 of the Children and Young Persons Act 1933. Between them, these two sections provide that where (exceptionally) juvenile defendants are tried in the Crown Court the media are free to identity them unless the court rules otherwise, but where (as usual) they are tried in the youth court the presumption is the other way round: the media must not reveal their names unless the court expressly says they may.

Section 39 – the Crown Court provision – gives no guidance as to when the courts should order the name of a juvenile to be withheld, leaving them to make up the rules themselves. By contrast section 49 – the youth court provision – does try to guide the courts as to when they should allow the name of the young offender to be published. It originally said this could be done wherever it was "in the interests of justice". In 1969, Parliament substituted a more protective test: henceforth the name could be published only "for the purpose of avoiding injustice to the child or young person". But in 1997 a "law and order" Parliament scrapped this in favour of a new test, similar but not identical to the first one. As section 49 now stands, the youth court can allow the name of the young offender

to be published "if it is satisfied that it is in the public interest to
do so".

But what in this context is meant by "in the public interest"? A
range of possibilities presents itself. At its loosest and widest, "public
interest" could mean that the offence has attracted widespread
attention, so that the public, avid for details, are particularly
keen to know exactly who it was that committed it. Scarcely less
widely, it could mean that the court thinks the young offender was
exceptionally wicked, so that – unlike most juvenile offenders –
he deserves the extra punishment incurred by being "named and
shamed". Or, similarly, it could mean that the court thinks the crime
was exceptionally harmful, so that other potential offenders – even
young ones – need the extra dose of deterrence that stems from
the knowledge that if you get caught you will probably be named
and shamed as well as punished. Or, more narrowly, the "public
interest" could require the naming of the offender because he is
likely to reoffend – so that the public needs to be able to recognise
him in order to avoid him.

In *McKerry v Teesdale and Wear Valley Justices* a sixteen-year-old boy,
with a long record of offending, pled guilty at the local youth court
to taking a vehicle without the owner's consent. At the request of
the local newspaper, and over the objection of the boy's solicitor, the
magistrates made an order permitting his identity to be revealed.
As they explained to the Divisional Court when the boy appealed
against the order by way of case stated: "We announced our view
that the appellant constituted a serious danger to the public and had
shown a complete disregard for the law. These were our reasons for
relaxing the reporting restrictions."

Upholding the magistrates' order, the Divisional Court said
that these reasons were acceptable ones, because "no doubt the
justices had in mind that members of the public, if they knew the
appellant's name, would enjoy a measure of protection if they had
cause to encounter him". The Divisional Court added that the
power to dispense with anonymity "must be exercised with very
great circumspection", and that it will "very rarely be the case"
that the public interest criterion is met. They said that it would
be "wholly wrong for any court to dispense with a juvenile's *prima*

facie right to anonymity as an additional punishment", and that it is "very difficult to see any place for 'naming and shaming'".

This is a more restrictive approach than the courts have taken when interpreting the power of the Crown Court to withhold names under section 39. In the leading case of *Lee* [1993] 1 W.L.R. 103 the Court of Appeal upheld the refusal of a judge to ban the media from identifying a fourteen-year-old boy convicted of robbery and rape because it would involve "no real harm to the applicant, and [be] a powerful deterrent effect on his contemporaries, if the applicant's name and photograph were published".

An important factor that underlay the Divisional Court's more restrictive approach to section 49 was the UK's international obligations – a matter discussed at length in the *McKerry* case, but in *Lee* mentioned not at all. These obligations include the 1989 UN Convention on the Rights of the Child, Article 40 of which guarantees the right of a child defendant "to have his or her privacy fully respected at all stages of the proceedings".

The truth is that many countries take a different view from ours about the proper role of "naming and shaming" as a sanction in the legal system, just as at one time many failed to share our earlier taste for "stripping and whipping". In Holland and in Germany, for example, it is normally thought decent and proper for the media to suppress the names of those whom the courts have convicted, even where they are adults. Against this international background, the rule proclaimed in Article 40 of the UN Convention should cause us no surprise.

Entrapment and the European Convention on Human Rights
Nottingham City Council v Amin
CLJ 2001, 60(1) 30–33

An acutely difficult question of principle arises when a person commits an offence because the police incite him to do so. For the civil libertarian, "undercover agents" (as the prosecution will seek to call them) usually go by another and nastier name: secret police. Even for authoritarians entrapment is of dubious value, because policemen find the crimes they have themselves incited particularly easy to solve – and if we condone entrapment too readily we risk having a police force which expends its energy on committing new crimes instead of solving old ones. But regrettably, the use of entrapment is something effective crime prevention occasionally requires.

In *Nottingham City Council v Amin* [2000] 1 W.L.R. 1071 the courts were asked to look at entrapment in the light of the European Convention on Human Rights in which respect it may well be the first of a series.

Hitherto, the English courts have held that entrapment is no defence in substantive criminal law. However, the fact that the defendant was tricked into committing the offence may be a factor mitigating sentence. And it may also trigger the use of the court's discretionary powers: either to suppress the prosecution as an abuse of process, or (less radically) to exclude the evidence of the undercover agent under section 78 of the Police and Criminal Evidence Act 1984 because its use would make the trial "unfair".

When discussing entrapment in the light of section 78, the higher courts have tried to lay down guidance as to when the use of entrapment (and hence of entrapment evidence) is proper. One factor that is repeatedly mentioned is the degree of police persuasion. Did they actively persuade a truly innocent person to commit an offence, or just team up with a would-be crook who was looking for someone to commit a crime with? Another is the gravity of the offence. The worse the crime, the more sinister the measures that the courts regard as legitimate to counter it.

The resulting law, unfortunately, is less than wholly clear. This is partly because the courts have sometimes invoked other factors. And it is partly because the appeal courts, pointing out that "every case is different", are generally reluctant to second-guess the way first instance courts have exercised the discretion section 78 gives them. Some critics also find parts of it too prosecution-minded – notably *Williams* (1994) 98 Cr.App.R. 209, where the police parked a van in a street with the back door open to reveal what appeared to be cartons of cigarettes, arresting those passers-by who stopped to help themselves – and the Court of Appeal affirmed the resulting convictions.

As for Strasbourg, in *Teixeira de Castro v Portugal* (1998) 28 E.H.R.R. 1 the Strasbourg Court decided that the applicant had been denied a "fair trial" as guaranteed by Article 6 of the Convention in a case where he had been entrapped into obtaining and supplying heroin by the Portuguese police. In so ruling, the Strasbourg Court stated its own list of factors which made the use of entrapment unjustified. One was its use against a person whom the police had no reason to suspect in advance of the "sting". Another was the fact that the police had acted on their own initiative and not "as part of an anti-drug-trafficking operation ordered and supervised by a judge" – a requirement that would cause acute problems if applied literally to England, where the police routinely investigate without any supervision from either public prosecutor or judge. And a third factor was that the entrapment was all that the prosecution could produce against him.

In *Nottingham City Council v Amin*, Mr. Amin was prosecuted for plying his taxi for hire in a place where he was not licensed to operate. The offence occurred when two plain clothes officers saw him driving in the street and flagged him down, just to see if he would stop and pick them up. At trial he relied on *Teixeira de Castro v Portugal* and invited the court to exclude the evidence under section 78 of PACE – stressing in particular the fact that the officers had no reason to suspect him in advance. The stipendiary magistrate excluded the evidence and the prosecution case accordingly collapsed.

The Divisional Court disagreed and sent the case back with a direction to convict. The *de Castro* decision, it said, "has to be understood in the context of the whole argument before the Court on that occasion and on the special facts of the case". The real question, they said, is whether admitting entrapment evidence would deprive the defendant of his right to a fair trial – which in *de Castro's* case it did, but in the present case it did not. (The defence was given leave to appeal to the House of Lords, but has decided to take the case no further.)

Lord Bingharn C.J.'s judgment does not explain in any detail why the present case was distinguishable from *de Castro*. And yet it surely was – and here, if I may respectfully suggest, is why.

What Amin, unlike de Castro, was charged with was a regulatory offence existing (like many others) to control who can sell what, to whom, when, where and how. One characteristic of these offences is that – unlike selling heroin or stealing cigarettes – they attract trivial punishments and comparatively little social stigma. Indeed, English judges traditionally describe such public welfare offences as "not criminal in any real sense". Another characteristic shared by many of them is that random test purchases by plain-clothes agents are the only effective way in which the law can be enforced. Irksome as these laws may seem to those who wish to buy or sell in circumstances where the law forbids it, they are needed to protect people's health and safety, and to save them from being cheated. If they are not enforced, furthermore, honest traders who obey the law are driven out of business by the rogue ones.

Prosecution for these offences after random test purchases is surely far removed from the sort of evils of the police State that the authors of the Convention had in mind when they drafted the Convention against the background of Hitler's Germany and Stalin's Russia. Although in *de Castro* the Strasbourg Court said "The public interest cannot justify the use of evidence obtained as the result of police incitement", to interpret the Convention so as to make these laws practically unenforceable would surely be to devalue it and bring it into disrepute.

"Rape Shields" and the Right to a Fair Trial
R. v A
CLJ 2001, 60(3) 425–455

In *R. v A* (No. 2) [2001] 2 W.L.R. 1546 the House of Lords knocked a dent in the controversial "rape shield" provision, section 41 of the Youth Justice and Criminal Evidence Act 1999 (YJCEA). They did so wielding Article 6 of the European Convention on

Human Rights, given direct effect by another piece of "flagship" legislation, the Human Rights Act 1998. The decision is important for constitutional law as well as for criminal evidence.

In a rape case where the defendant claimed that the complainant had consented, at one time she could always expect to have her sex-life publicly examined in some detail. In an attempt to limit the abuses to which this was put, section 2 of the Sexual Offences (Amendment) Act 1976 forbade questions or evidence about this except where the judge gave leave. But feminists complained that judges gave leave too readily, and in response to this, the government promoted section 41 of the YJCEA. This, like the 1976 provision, imposes a requirement of judicial leave – but sets out in exhaustive detail the circumstances in which it may be given.

Even as amended on its way through Parliament this provision was highly controversial, and it has attracted heavy criticism. It is said to be too narrow, because whilst banning evidence (or questions) about the complainant's sex-life when used to suggest that the complainant actually consented, it allows them without restriction to suggest that the defendant, having heard about her reputation, mistakenly believed she did. And it is said to be too wide, because in banning the use of such evidence to suggest that the complainant did consent, it sometimes prevents the court from hearing information that is highly relevant.

Section 41 allows evidence (or questions) about the complainant's sex-life in support of a defence of consent in three situations only. One is where the prosecution made the running by leading evidence about her sex-life, and the defence wishes to rebut or qualify it (s. 41(5)). Another is where the sexual behaviour to which the evidence relates consists of events that allegedly occurred "at or about the same time as the event which is the subject matter of the charge against the accused" (s. 41(3)(b)). And the third is where the evidence is about incidents which are so similar to the defendant's account of the alleged rape "that the similarity cannot reasonably be explained as a coincidence" (s. 41(3)(c)).

Unlike the 1976 provision, the ban in section 41 even extends to evidence about the complainant's previous sexual behaviour with the defendant. Thus it apparently prevents the defendant from adducing evidence that, at the time of the alleged rape, they had an on-going relationship which included regular consensual sex – unless the last occasion was "at or about the same time" as the alleged rape. As even the most committed feminists presumably accept that a person more readily consents to sex with her regular sexual partner than with others, it seems quite extraordinary that the defendant should not be allowed to show he was one. And yet this seems to be what was actually intended.

The scenario described in the previous paragraph was part of the defence version of events in *R. v A.* Before trial, the judge made a preliminary ruling that the defendant could not lead evidence of any previous sexual relationship between them because of section 41. The Court of Appeal held that he could – but only for the purpose of showing that he believed that she consented, and not to show that she actually did. In the House of Lords, the defence argued that to exclude this evidence contravened his right to a "fair trial" as protected by Article 6 of the European Convention on Human Rights. The defence invited the House to use section 3 of the Human Rights Act – which requires the courts to construe statutes in the light of the Convention – to find a way of reading section 41 to allow the evidence in, or failing this, to make a "declaration of incompatibility" under section 4.

To cut a long story – 55 pages of erudite and closely-reasoned argument – very short, Lords Slynn, Steyn, Clyde and Hutton all agreed that section 41, if read according to the previously accepted principles of construction, would exclude evidence of the sort the defendant wished to admit. They also agreed that in some cases, such evidence would be highly relevant to consent, and that if section 41 then rendered it inadmissible this would indeed contravene his right to a "fair trial". But in such a situation, they said that section 3 of the Human Rights Act now required the courts to abandon traditional principles of construction, and (in effect) to do whatever violence was necessary to the language so that the evidence, if truly relevant, was admissible. On that basis, evidence of the complainant's previous sexual relationship with the defendant could be squeezed within the apparently inelastic wording of section 41(3)(c): behaviour so similar "that the similarity cannot reasonably be explained as coincidence". So there was no need for a declaration of incompatibility. On this basis, they sent the case back to the Crown Court for the judge to reconsider his ruling. (With some of this Lord Hope was most uneasy. Commenting that section 3 "does not entitle the judges to act as legislators", he found it "very difficult" to accept that the courts could read into section 41 a qualification that it could never shut out evidence required to ensure a fair trial under Article 6 of the Convention.)

Much could be said about this case, and the problems with which it grapples. But here there is room for two short comments only.

The first is wonderment at the change that section 3 of the Human Rights Act wrought. Four of the five Law Lords were clear that it gives the courts power to bend an Act to fit the requirements of the Convention, even where the Act is not ambiguous. We may be on the threshold of exciting times!

The second is satisfaction that their Lordships felt able to interpret section 41 in the way they did. For Parliament to pass a law prohibiting a defendant from producing cogent evidence that tends to show his innocence is nothing short of monstrous.

It is monstrous too, of course, that complainants in sex-cases have their sex-lives publicly dissected. But what is wrong here, surely, is not that their sex-lives are examined, but that this happens publicly. The problem should be tackled not by restricting the questions, but by limiting the audience. Complainants should routinely give their evidence with the public and the press excluded: something the "fair trial" requirement in Article 6 undoubtedly permits. And what is also wrong, surely, is that the complainant can be asked if she regularly consents to sex without the defendant having to admit – if such be so – that he has previously forced others to have sex with him without it. In this respect, if in no other, we need to change the rules about evidence of previous misconduct.

Did the Jury Misbehave?
Don't Ask, Because We do not Want to Know.
R. v Quereshi
CLJ 2002, 61(2) 291–293

In *R. v Quereshi* [2002] 1 W.L.R. 518 the defendant, who was Asian, was convicted of arson with intent to endanger life, for which he was sentenced to four years' imprisonment. A few days after the verdict a juror made a series of allegations to the court administrator which the administrator later summarised as follows:

> Despite the usher's warning not to make racist remarks, disparaging remarks were made throughout the trial by some members of the jury about the defendant's appearance, his accent, his poor English, his mannerisms, and his business integrity. It is alleged that the following remarks were made during the trial: "I know his sort, they're all the same"; "I have worked with them in Birmingham. I know what they're like"; "the only reason he's got a clean record is because he's never been caught" and "he would have been better off staying in India." Some members of the jury appeared to have reached a decision at the outset of the trial and did not change their minds. During the trial, newspapers dealing with the trial were brought into the jury retiring room by jurors and shown around. At least three jurors had mobile phones and two of them used them to contact outsiders during the trial and to tell them about the progress of the trial. A juror fell asleep during the evidence. A juror was deaf and could not hear all the evidence. Other members of the jury adopted a bullying attitude.

On hearing this, Quereshi unsurprisingly appealed, asking the Court of Appeal to have the allegations properly investigated.

In the famous case of *Young* [1995] Q.B. 324 some years ago the Court of Appeal did order an investigation when it was alleged that a jury's guilty verdict in a murder trial had been reached with supernatural help provided by a "ouija board", and quashed the conviction when it revealed the allegation to be true [noted above at p. 108 as 'Seances, and the Secrecy of the Jury-Room]'. But in the later case of *Miah* [1997] 2 Cr. App. R. 12 it refused to order an investigation where after trial the juror claimed that the verdict had been influenced by racial bias. In refusing to investigate, the

139

court in *Miah* stressed that the court felt able to intervene in *Young* only because the ouija-board incident allegedly occurred, not in the retiring room, but in the hotel where the jury had all spent the night. Investigating what the jury did at court would require a breach of the secrecy of the retiring room – something which the common law had always regarded as improper, and which section 8 of the Contempt of Court Act 1981 has now elevated to the status of a criminal offence. In *Quereshi* the Court of Appeal followed *Miah*, refused to order an investigation and upheld the resulting conviction.

This decision is, to put it mildly, questionable.

First, is almost certainly incompatible with Article 6 of the European Convention on Human Rights, which guarantees defendants a "fair hearing" before a tribunal that is "independent and impartial". The Court of Appeal got around the difficulties caused by this Article and its attendant case law by quoting passages from the Strasbourg judgments which refer to jury secrecy as "a crucial and legitimate feature of the English trial", and by observing that Miah's attempt to take his case to Strasbourg failed *in limine* when his application was declared inadmissible by the European Commission on Human Rights (which in those days filtered applications). But this is unconvincing. The Commission, it seems, threw out Miah's case mainly because the allegations, unlike those in the present case, were stale and looked extremely flimsy. And irrespective of the dicta they contain, the main thrust of the Strasbourg Court decisions appears to be that, once bias has been plausibly alleged, the courts have a duty to investigate it: as the Strasbourg Court made very plain in *Remli v France* (1996) 22 E.H.R.R. 253, where France was condemned because the French system – by an interesting reversal of the reasoning applied in England – refused to investigate a claim that a juror had publicly boasted of his racism because the boast, if made, was made outside the court room, and not in it.

More fundamentally, the refusal of the legal system to investigate a serious allegation of jury bias or misconduct is objectionable because it amounts to a refusal to intervene where there is a serious risk that the defendant was convicted, not because the jury thought him guilty, but because it did not like him. This point was made by Sir Robin Auld in his recent Review of the Criminal Courts, where he recommends that section 8 of the Contempt of Court Act be amended. "In my view", he said "the effective bar that section 8 puts on an appellate court inquiring into and remedying possible bias or other impropriety in the course of a jury's deliberation is indefensible and capable of causing serious injustice."

The nub of the decision in *Quereshi*, one suspects, is the remark that if the appeal were allowed it might lead "to many such complaints, some perhaps owing their origin to friends or relatives of the defendant". But this simply will not do. The fact that many allegations of this sort are false cannot justify ignoring all of them because, as *Young* so painfully reminds us, some of them regrettably are true.

If juries are composed of twelve people chosen from the electoral role at random, it is inevitable that they will sometimes be dominated by people who are racists, or are irresponsible and silly, and our legal system is gravely deficient if it fails to guard against this obvious danger. To cope with it we have a choice. Either we must allow serious allegations of bias or misconduct to be investigated, and put up with the resulting trouble and expense. Or else – more radically – we must eliminate the problem by abolishing the rule that juries are left to deliberate unsupervised. In France, as is well known, this was done some sixty years ago by radically altering the structure of trial, so that the judges and the jury retire and deliberate together. But it could also be done, with less violence to our traditions, by requiring jury deliberations – like police interviews with suspects – to be tape-recorded. The tape could then be sealed and locked away, to be opened only if plausible allegations of misconduct were later made.

Noted, but not invariably approved

Acquitted: Presumed Innocent, or Deemed Lucky to Have Got Away with it?
Quinland v Governor of Swaleside Prison
R. (Christofides) v Secretary of State for the Home Department
CLJ 2003, 62(1) 50–53

In November, M. Canivet, the First President of the French *Cour de cassation*, gave a public lecture in Cambridge on *la responsabilité du juge*, where he described the recourse that modern French law provides for citizens who find themselves ill served by the legal system. He told us that in France, defendants remanded in custody pending trial now receive automatic compensation if at trial they are acquitted, and that citizens can bring civil claims against the State where they are hurt by the malfunctioning of justice.

Two recent cases show how very different things are in England.

The first is *Quinland v Governor of Swaleside Prison* [2002] EWCA Civ 174, [2003] Q.B. 306. For a package of assorted misdeeds, a judge gave Quinland a package of periods of imprisonment, some concurrent and some consecutive. Unfortunately he added them up wrongly, and described the package as bigger than it was. Nobody noticed, and the excessive period was stated in the warrant for commitment on the basis of which Quinland was then locked up. The error was eventually spotted, and pointed out: but thanks to a further blunder, this time in the Court Service, nothing was done in time to prevent Quinland serving out the period of imprisonment appropriate to the longer sentence – six weeks more "porridge" than he should have eaten. It was only after his release that the Court of Appeal officially varied the sentence. Then, some five years later, Quinland attempted to bring a claim for damages.

He did not even try to sue the judge, because the common law, being judge-made, predictably says that judges are immune from claims in negligence (*Sirros v Moore* [1975] Q.B. 118). So he sued the prison governor for false imprisonment, and the Crown, in the shape of the Lord Chancellor's Department, as liable for the negligence of the nameless official in the Court Service who had

142

blundered. Both claims were struck out by the district judge, whose decision was upheld by the Court of Appeal. The claim against the prison governor failed because he had detained the claimant for the proper period required by the warrant of commitment – which, though based on the judge's poor addition, was valid. The claim against the second defendant failed because section 2(5) of the Crown Proceedings Act 1947 provides that no action shall lie against the Crown in respect of "anything done or omitted to be done by a person whilst discharging or purporting to discharge any responsibilities of a judicial nature vested in him, or any responsibilities which he has in connection with the execution of the judicial process" – a phrase the Court of Appeal thought apt to cover the Court Service blunder. (The court left open the question whether the result would have been the same if the events had occurred after the Human Rights Act.)

Would Quinland have fared any better if, instead of trying to sue for damages, he had sought compensation from the State under section 133 of the Criminal Justice Act 1988, which the marginal note describes as providing "compensation for miscarriages of justice"? That he would not is plain from the second case, *R. (Christofides) v Secretary of State for the Home Department* [2002] EWHC 1083 (Admin), [2002] 1 W.L.R. 2769, which turns on the construction of this provision.

Christofides was convicted of murder in 1992. Nine years later, the Court of Appeal quashed his conviction. For the murder conviction it substituted a conviction for attempted GBH, and for the mandatory life sentence, a sentence of two years' imprisonment. For the seven years in prison which in retrospect he should not have spent there, Christofides applied to the Home Secretary for compensation under section 133, which was refused. Christofides challenged the refusal by way of judicial review, and in the Divisional Court he failed.

Section 133 was enacted to secure compliance with the UK's international obligations towards victims of miscarriages of justice under Article 14 (6) of the UN International Covenant on Civil and Political Rights – but, it seems, as narrowly as possible.

Copying the Convention, section 133 (as amended) first announces a right of compensation where a person "has been convicted of a criminal offence and when subsequently his conviction has been reversed or he has been pardoned on the ground that a new or newly discovered fact shows beyond reasonable doubt that there has been a miscarriage of justice". Then, glossing the Convention, it defines "reversed" narrowly. "Reversed" is taken "as referring to a conviction having been quashed (a) on an appeal out of time; or (b) on a reference (i) under the Criminal Appeal Act 1995 or (ii) under section 263 of the Criminal Procedure (Scotland) Act 1975; or (c) on an appeal under section 7 of the Terrorism Act 2000". Thus there is no right to compensation in a "normal" case, where someone was wrongly convicted at first instance, and the Court of Appeal, acting properly, then quashed the conviction under its usual procedures. Then, as final step to ensure that as far as possible nobody gets anything, it provides that "the question whether there is a right to compensation under this section shall be determined by" – yes, you've guessed! – "the Secretary of State".

Confronted with this singularly mean provision, the Divisional Court construed it in accordance with the spirit in which it was conceived. They held that it only applies where the claimant is eventually cleared of everything, and does not cover the situation where the original conviction was quashed, a conviction being substituted for a lesser offence. Thus the Home Secretary was right to rule that Christofides had no valid claim.

Alongside section 133 the Home Secretary operates what is called "the extra-statutory ex gratia scheme". The Home Office, in other words, will sometimes compensate people even if they fall outside section 133 particularly, one suspects, where the word "Strasbourg" crops up repeatedly in the correspondence. The second string to Christofides' legal bow was an attempt to judicially review the Home Secretary's refusal to make a discretionary payment, on the ground that Christofides had a "legitimate expectation".

This also failed, because the Divisional Court found nothing to found a legitimate expectation in the Home Secretary's pronouncements in relation to the scheme.

In various public statements, the Home Secretary has stressed that he will not pay compensation "simply because at the trial or on appeal the prosecution was unable to sustain the burden of proof beyond a reasonable doubt in relation to the specific charge that was brought". He might pay up, he says, "in certain exceptional cases where the appellant has spent time in custody, for example where there is serious default by a public authority, such as the police, or if an accused person is completely exonerated (whether at trial or on appeal)". None of this applied to Christofides. Christofides had asked the Home Secretary to accept that his case was, in its own way, equally "exceptional", in that his murder conviction had been quashed only after two unsuccessful trips to the Court of Appeal and one successful visit to the Criminal Cases Review Commission, and meanwhile he had spent in prison seven years more than the Court of Appeal eventually thought appropriate for the offence he could be proved to have committed. This invitation the Home Secretary declined – and the Divisional Court refused to interfere. As Sedley L.J. put it, with regret: "The courts are there to ensure that the Home Secretary sticks to what he and his predecessors have promised, but not to enlarge or improve the scheme. That remains a question for government."

For those who were locked up wrongly or unnecessarily, the result of all this is as follows.

First, there is no automatic right to compensation, even if it happened because the criminal justice system grossly and obviously malfunctioned. Second, there is no right if you were imprisoned where it initially malfunctioned, and its own internal processes corrected it. And third, there is – *a fortiori* – no right to compensation if the system functioned properly, but in retrospect too zealously: as where you were remanded in custody where reasonable grounds existed at the time for refusing bail, but in the end you were acquitted.

That this is unsatisfactory surely needs no stressing: particularly when in the rest of Europe, compensation is nowadays more or less automatically given to anyone who was locked up when it turns out they should not have been.

Behind this lies an uncomfortable paradox.

In this country, it is widely believed that a distinguishing feature of our legal system is that it protects the presumption of innocence, whereas in Continental Europe it is set at nought. If anything, the reverse in fact is true. Our version of respecting the presumption of innocence is preserving a range of archaic and irrational rules of procedure and evidence, which ensure that a lot of guilty people are improperly acquitted. And then, uneasily aware of this, we treat everyone who is acquitted as if they really did it.[16]

Spouses as Witnesses: Back to Brighton Rock?
R. v Registrar General of Births, Marriages and Deaths etc.
CLJ 2003, 62(2) 250–252

Graham Greene's *Brighton Rock* is the tragic story of a murderer who marries an innocent girl, with the sole aim of preventing her giving evidence against him. Fact can be as strange as fiction – as the decision in *R. (Crown Prosecution Service) v Registrar General of Births, Deaths and Marriages* [2002] EWCA Civ 1661, [2003] Q.B. 1221 dramatically shows.

Mr. J was the prime suspect for a brutal double murder. Miss B, his long term cohabitee, made statements to the police which gave them crucial information. While J was in prison awaiting the trial in which Miss B was billed as the star prosecution witness, B first tried to retract her statement – and when this failed to persuade the Crown Prosecution Service (CPS) to remove her from the witness list, J and B announced that they were getting married. As under section 80 of the Police and Criminal Evidence Act (PACE) 1984 a wife cannot normally be compelled to give evidence against her husband in criminal proceedings, it looked suspiciously as if the intended union was motivated by this provision. To marry, a prisoner

---

[16] Since this note was written, the situation it complains about has got worse, not better. Those keen to know the details will find them set out in their depressing length in "Compensation for Wrongful Imprisonment", [2010] *Criminal Law Review* 803.

needs a certificate from the Registrar General: a document which the relevant legislation apparently requires this official to issue, provided the prison director raises no objection, which in this case he did not.

Faced with this, the CPS brought judicial review proceedings against the Registrar General, with a view to preventing him issuing the certificate, and the prison director, to encourage him to object. The courts briefly held that the prison director could only object on grounds relating to the suitability of the prison – and the main argument centred on the position of the Registrar.

The CPS argued that although the Registrar's official duties are apparently absolute, this is subject to the implied condition that they should not be carried out so as to enable citizens to commit crimes. Thus although the Registrar has an apparently absolute statutory duty to tell adopted children who their natural parents are, it was held *R. v Registrar General, ex p. Smith* [1991] 2 Q.B. 393 that he could lawfully refuse an application from a would be parricide, currently a resident in Broadmoor (!). In the present case, the CPS argued that by marrying, J and B would commit the offence of perverting the course of justice. Therefore the Registrar should refuse to issue the certificate.

On this argument the CPS won at first instance, but lost in the Court of Appeal. There it was unanimously decided that by exercising their right to marry, even in the present dubious circumstances, J and B would not commit the crime of perverting the course of justice – so the Registrar General had no ground to refuse the certificate.

The result, with respect, is surely correct. The right to marry is a fundamental one. As Waller L.J. pointed out, it "has always been a right recognised by the laws of this country long before the Human Rights Act 1998 came into force". To refuse to allow J and B to exercise it would surely have been a wholly disproportionate reaction to the need for the CPS to solve a problem posed by the peculiarities of the rules of criminal evidence. And there is another point. The evidential rule the CPS wished to stop J and B making use of is commonly justified by the need to avoid putting strain on marriages: which presumably means that the law's official stance on matrimony – unlike Mr. Punch's in his celebrated advice to persons about to get married ("Don't!") – is that marriage is a good thing, and to be encouraged. Thus to prevent people marrying to stop them taking advantage of a rule designed to reinforce the institution of marriage seems strangely perverse.

That said, there is clearly something badly wrong with the law if a double murderer can escape justice by marrying the chief prosecution witness. If courts cannot (and should not) prevent them marrying, then the rules of criminal evidence should obviously be changed so that their marriage does not have this consequence – particularly when contracted in contemplation of the prosecution. This point the Court of Appeal accepted, when it said that section 80 of PACE possibly "needs reconsideration".

The authoritarian solution would be to change the law so that the defendant's spouse is a compellable witness for the prosecution, and hence obliged to testify at trial on the same terms as everyone else: as he or she already is in certain specific situations, set out in section 80 of PACE.

But to force the defendant's spouse to give evidence, on pain of prosecution for contempt of court if he or she refuses and perjury if he or she tells lies or fails to tell the truth, is very harsh; almost as harsh, some would say, as it would be to force the same choice upon the defendant himself. Other legal systems, both in the common law world and in Continental Europe, shrink from this. A rule which put the defendant's spouse in this position could – conceivably – be seen as contrary to Article 8 of the European Convention (respect for family life).

The laws of other countries solve this problem in ways that are less brutal.

In France, the spouse is required to testify, and hence submit to questioning – but does not take the oath, and hence cannot be prosecuted for perjury. In Germany, the spouse is not obliged to testify. However, the spouse is not exempt where (as in the present case) the marriage took place in order to take advantage of the rule. And if an initially co-operative spouse was – as often happens – formally examined by a judge ahead of trial, the trial court can hear the evidence from the mouth of the examining judge if the spouse then declines to testify at trial.

In some parts of the common law world the solution is to provide that, where the spouse takes advantage of the privilege at trial, his or her previous statements become admissible in evidence as an exception to the hearsay rule. This is the position under Rule 804 of the Federal Rules of Evidence in the United States – a provision not limited to spouses, but applicable to the previous statements of any witness who declines to testify on grounds of privilege, and of any witness who without such privilege unlawfully refuses. This solution was proposed for England by the Criminal Law Revision Committee in its Eleventh Report in 1972. But alas, nothing so sensible is to be found in the Home Office's latest proposals to reform the hearsay rule, which at the time of writing are before Parliament in the current Criminal Justice Bill.

This solution would be of limited use, because where (as is the case in England) the defendant has no opportunity to put his questions to the witness ahead of trial, a conviction based exclusively or mainly on such evidence would be contrary to Article 6(3)(d) of the European Convention on Human Rights, which guarantees the defendant the right to "examine or have examined the witnesses against him". However, according to the Strasbourg case law this objection would not obtain in a case where there was substantial other evidence. Nor would it apply if (as in many other countries) we organised our pre-trial phase so that, where a witness is thought likely to retract, he or she can be formally examined at a preliminary hearing at which the defence have the right to participate and put their questions, and at that stage the spouse was prepared to talk.

Civil Liability for Abuse of the Criminal Process: Downstream of Three Rivers
Akenzua v Secretary of State for the Home Office
CLJ 2003, 62(3), 543–545

If the criminal justice system malfunctions and causes someone damage, when can the victim sue the person responsible?

To this question, the traditional answer is "almost never". If the malfunction consists of imprisoning someone who was innocent, or prosecuting them without due cause, there is no civil liability except for acts done in bad faith; liability for merely negligent behaviour is excluded, on grounds of public policy. Where the malfunction consists of failing to catch a criminal who celebrates his continued freedom by causing further damage – or in releasing one with similar effect – the same is true *a fortiori*, because the case is further complicated by issues of causation and *novus actus interveniens*. Thus in *Hill v Chief Constable of West Yorkshire* [1989] A.C. 53 the House of Lords ruled that the Yorkshire police, however negligent, were not liable for their failure to catch the Yorkshire Ripper. Nor was the Home Secretary liable for negligently failing to execute a deportation order against a dangerous criminal – a failure castigated as "utterly lamentable" by a judge when later sentencing him for a further string of terrible offences (*K. v Secretary of State for the Home Office* [2002] EWCA Civ 775).

As result of *Akenzua v Secretary of State for the Home Department* [2002] EWCA Civ 1470, [2003] 1 W.L.R. 741, liability may now be easier to establish than has traditionally been thought.

According to the claimant, the facts were these. One Denton, a Jamaican gangster with a string of murders to his name, arrived in England where he tried unsuccessfully to claim asylum. When his application failed he should have been deported – but the Home Office and the Metropolitan Police did a deal with him under which he was informally allowed to stay, on terms that he acted as a police informer. In pursuance of this arrangement, the Home Office temporarily "lost" his deportation papers, and the police turned a myopic if not blind eye to his criminal activities (including an alleged rape). This cosy arrangement came to a dramatic end when Denton committed a horrendous sexual murder. Outraged, the victim's personal representatives sued the Home Office and the police for damages. They did not base their claim on negligence (when it would certainly have failed) but relied instead upon misuse of public office – a very ancient tort, recently overhauled and re-commissioned by the House of Lords in *Three Rivers District Council v Governor and Company of the Bank of England (No. 3)* [2003] 2 A.C. 1.

Their claim was initially struck out as disclosing no cause of action – but the Court of Appeal reinstated it, ruling that on these alleged facts the claimants had an arguable case.

For 300 years the common law has accepted that, in principle, tortious liability exists for the abusive use of an official power that causes someone damage – but the details were in doubt. Then in *Three Rivers*, the House of Lords was asked to explain in detail what a group of depositors would have to show to hold the Bank of England liable under this principle for failing properly to supervise BCCI, a bank in the collapse of which they had lost their money. Against this background, the House laid down the law as follows. First, liability for misuse of office potentially applies both to acts done in the abusive exercise of official powers, and abusive failures to exercise them. Second, it applies not only where the defendant was actuated by the express aim of causing harm, but also sometimes where the resulting harm was not intended. Third, the defendant is so liable for unintended harm where he both (i) knew his behaviour was improper, or was at least reckless as to whether it might be, and (ii) knew it would cause harm, or was reckless as to whether it might do so. Fourthly and most importantly, liability for unintended harm resulting from misuse of office does not depend on the existence of any kind of "proximity" or "special relationship" between the official and the person harmed. As Lord Steyn put it, "There is no reason why such an action cannot be brought by a particular class of persons, such as depositors at a bank, even if their precise identities were not known to the bank."

Given this, the decision of the Court of Appeal in *Akenzua* hardly comes as a surprise. The main difference between *Three Rivers* and the current case was the nature of the damage – physical injury and death rather than economic loss – but on principle this ought to reinforce the claim, not undermine it. Building on Lord Steyn's reference to "a particular class of persons" quoted above, the defendant tried to argue that liability for misuse of office was limited to those victims who were readily identifiable at the time the allegedly improper act took place. This argument the Court of Appeal rejected. Lord Steyn's reference to a class of persons was, it said, "expansive rather than restrictive". The defendant's argument, if correct, would reintroduce the "proximity" requirement that the House of Lords had expressly rejected.

That the defendant is potentially liable for misuse of office if he was reckless – and, moreover, reckless in the sense that he foresaw the risk of harm to people generally, and not the risk of harm to some identified person – has great practical significance.

By recklessness, the House of Lords in *Three Rivers* said it meant subjective recklessness; that the defendant actually foresaw the risk of harm. This is of course significantly harder for the claimant to show than negligence. However, it is enormously easier for a claimant to establish than intention. It is only because of this that claimants like *Akenzua* can sue with possible success. Thus the decision that recklessness suffices makes this area of the law much more favourable to claimants – and, of course, correspondingly less favourable to defendants.

Obviously this does not mean that a defendant is liable merely because he foresaw a risk of harm. A person is only reckless where the risk he took was one that it was unreasonable in the circumstances for him to take – which is why recklessness is sometimes called "advertent negligence". But if this gives some protection for defendants sued for misuse of office, it is a protection with a sting in its tail. In order to show they were not reckless, official defendants will now sometimes find themselves obliged to justify in court decisions where they had to weigh a choice of evils. And it was partly to protect officials in the criminal justice system from the need to justify such decisions that, in the past, the courts usually ruled that they are immune from being sued in negligence.

Strict Liability and the European Convention
Barnfather v Islington Education Authority and other Cases
CLJ 2004, 63(1)10–13

A basic concept in criminal law is the culpability principle: that people should be punished only for acts or omissions for which they are to blame, in the sense that they committed them intentionally, recklessly or negligently. For prosecutors who (as usual) "know" that every defendant whom they accuse is guilty, the resulting need to prove both the defendant's act and fault is a time consuming and expensive obstacle to justice; and over the years, the concerted efforts of Ministers, Parliament and the courts have done much to relieve them of it by three devices (sometimes alone, and sometimes used in combination). The first is the reverse burden of proof, where the prosecutor only has to prove the *actus reus*, and the defendant then has to persuade the court that he was not at fault. They second and more stringent device is strict liability, where the *actus reus* constitutes the whole offence and the fault element is eliminated altogether. And the third is "situational liability". Here, what would normally be the evidence for the offence is turned into the offence itself; instead of being defined as a blameworthy act or omission, the offence consists of a state of affairs that commonly suggests one – and, where this is proved, the defendant is guilty whether he did anything or not (and let alone whether he was to blame for it). A series of recent cases discuss the compatibility of these devices with the European Convention on Human Rights.

In *Barnfather v Islington Education Authority* [2003] EWHC 418 (Admin), [2003] 1 W.L.R. 2318 the Divisional Court was faced with strict and situational liability. Section 444(1) of the Education Act 1996 provides that "If a child of compulsory school age who is a registered pupil at a school fails to attend regularly at the school, his parent is guilty of an offence". As previously interpreted, this provision imposes strict liability. (The maximum penalty is a fine of £1,000; an aggravated version, added in 2000, now makes the parent liable to imprisonment where he knew of the failure to attend school and negligently failed to do anything about it.) Ms. Barnfather, who had been convicted and fined for the simple offence, appealed to the Divisional Court by way of case stated, claiming that the traditional interpretation of section 444(1) as a strict liability offence is incompatible with the Convention. She based her argument on Article 6(2), which provides that "Everyone charged with a criminal offence shall be presumed innocent until proved guilty according to law". A Divisional Court composed of Maurice Kay and Elias JJ. dismissed her appeal.

Her appeal failed because, in the view of both judges, Article 6(2), like the rest of Article 6, is concerned with procedural fairness, not fairness in substantive law. Article 6 lays down the requirements for a fair trial, for whatever the legislature chooses (however unfairly) to decree to be a criminal offence. Thus it prevents (within limits) contracting States creating offences the elements of which the defendant is required to disprove: but it does not impose any minimum requirements as to what those elements should be. Article 6, in other words, is about "fair trials", not "fair laws", and the courts must not use it to rewrite the underlying substantive law – as Elias J. reminded us, with reference to the decision in *Osman v UK* (1998) 29 E.H.R.R. 245, and the controversy this provoked.

This outcome satisfied Maurice Kay J.'s sense of justice. He went on to say that, if Article 6(2) did in principle strike at strict liability as well as reverse burdens of proof, he would still have reached the same result. In the leading case of *Salabiaku v France* (1988) 13 E.H.R.R. 379 the Strasbourg Court said legislation may contradict the letter of Article 6(2), provided it is limited to petty offences that carry minor penalties. In his view, strict liability for the offence in section 444(1) of the Education Act was consistent both with the spirit of the decision in *Salabiaku*, and the tests that English law has traditionally applied in determining whether an offence carries strict liability.

Elias J., by contrast, was deeply unhappy with it. The standard prosecution arguments that had convinced Maurice Kay J. he thought were seriously inadequate.

> The fact that the prosecution of blameless persons will be rare or that there are other routes for achieving the objectives of the statute seem to me to point strongly against the need for the legislation at all rather than in support of it. Furthermore, it is of no benefit to an innocent parent successfully prosecuted to be told that he or she is something of a rare specimen... The strict liability offence is disproportionate to the objective to be achieved.

Only the existence of binding precedent obliged him to accept that section 444(1) imposes strict liability; had he been free to do so he would have decided the point the other way. He accepted that Article 6(2) was limited to reverse burdens of proof: but he saw a paradox in the fact that the Convention enables the courts to confront the less serious legislative invasions of the culpability principle, whilst leaving them powerless against those that are more drastic.

The *Barnfather* case decides that the excessive use of strict liability is not contrary to Article 6(2) of the Convention. But is it limited by any other part of the European Convention, or its attendant Protocols?

The Court of Appeal decision in *International Transport Roth GmbH and others v Secretary of State for the Home Department* [2002] EWCA Civ 158, [2003] Q.B. 728 suggests that it may be. That case, it will be recalled, arose from one of the Government's attempts to construct in the name of state security a parallel penal universe, in which people are punished by the Home Office rather than the courts.

To deter carriers from importing illegal immigrants, the Government (acting under delegated powers) set up a scheme under which a carrier incurred for every illegal immigrant found on his vehicle an administrative penalty of £2,000 – to be funded, if necessary, by the sale of the vehicle, potentially confiscated pending payment. The carrier could, in theory, escape liability by proving certain facts consistent with due care: but it was the Home Secretary, whose officials imposed the fine, who also had to be satisfied these facts were proved. By a majority, the Court of Appeal found this scheme to be incompatible with the Convention. First, it failed to comply with the "fair trial" requirement of Article 6(1), because it made the Home Secretary the judge in his own cause. Second, the proceedings counted for Convention purposes as "criminal"; thus the additional procedural safeguards contained in the rest of Article 6 had to be respected, which they were not, because the reverse burden of proof was incompatible with Article 6(2).

Third – and here is the point relevant to strict liability – the Court of Appeal said that the blanket fine of £2,000 per head, unvarying with the carrier's fault or absence of it, was contrary to Article 1 of the First Protocol to the Convention, which guarantees security of property. This Article permits the State to confiscate the property of citizens where the "public interest" requires this, but (as the Strasbourg Court said in *James v United Kingdom* (1986) 8 E.H.R.R. 123) there must be "a reasonable relationship of proportionality between the means employed and the aim sought to be realised". This principle is broken, they thought, by fines that bear no relation to the defendant's fault.

But if this is right, it leaves us with another paradox. If the First Protocol prohibits fines that bear no relation to the defendant's fault, what about imprisonment? In *R. v Drew* [2003] UKHL 25, [2003] 1 W.L.R. 1213 and a series of cases that preceded it, attempts were made to use Article 3 (prohibition of torture etc.) and Article 5 (right to liberty and security) against statutes imposing mandatory prison sentences. Although they failed, they did so on the facts – and the courts seemed ready to accept, in principle, that these Articles could apply against prison sentences that are completely disproportionate to fault. As the Criminal Justice Act 2003 has now prescribed mandatory prison sentences for a list of Firearms Act offences that carry strict liability, the day may come when this argument succeeds.

Juries: The Freedom to Act Irresponsibly
R. v Mirza
CLJ 2004, 63(2) 314–316

If the jury that convicted you behaved improperly – reaching its verdict by spinning a coin, for example, or basing it not on the evidence but on the colour of your face – can you appeal? The answer, you might think, is "Yes, of course!" (see this commentator's notes on *Young* [1995] C.L.J. 519 above p. 108 and on *Quereshi* [2002] C.L.J. 291, above p. 139). In *R. v Mirza* [2004] UKHL 2, [2004] 1 A.C. 1118, however, a majority of the House of Lords has ruled that investigating alleged misbehaviour of this sort would break the secrecy of the jury room, a value it is essential to maintain: so the defendant, if convicted wrongly in these circumstances, must put up with it.

The most convincing argument in favour of this position is that, if the jury are to do their job properly, they must know that they are completely free to speak their minds, which they would not be if their remarks could be the subject of public scrutiny by the legal system afterwards (or harassing enquiries by defendants or the lawyers as a preliminary step). It seems to have been this that convinced the majority; but in the course of being convinced by it, they threw in some unconvincing arguments for good measure.

Thus the speeches of the majority also make mention of the need for finality (which if taken to extremes would justify the abolition of all criminal appeals); the risk that such allegations might be manufactured (which surely does not justify ignoring them where they are demonstrably true); the fact that jury misbehaviour is rare (which means, apparently that it can be discounted, like other rare events: explosions at nuclear power stations, for example, and crashing jumbo jets!); that acquittals of the guilty are as serious as convictions of the innocent (wrong!), which means that allegations of jury misbehaviour would have to be investigated at the behest of disappointed prosecutors too (and so they should be – even if perverse acquittals are not as bad as perverse convictions!); and by the fact that the public has faith in juries (as its mediaeval predecessors had, of course, in trial by battle, compurgation and ordeals).

Lord Steyn delivered a powerful dissent. The argument that "the residual possibility of a miscarriage of justice is the necessary price for the preservation and protection of the jury system" he found both morally unacceptable, and contrary to the European Convention on Human Rights.

In my view it would be an astonishing thing for the ECHR to hold, when the point directly arises before it, that a miscarriage of justice may be ignored in the interests of the general efficiency of the jury system. The terms of Article 6(1) of the European Convention, the rights revolution, and 50 years of development of human rights law and practice, would suggest that such a view would be utterly indefensible.

But even if the argument were morally acceptable, he thought that it was false.

The effect of the ruling of the majority will in the long run damage the jury system. Leaving aside the jury, we have reached a position where it is recognised that all actors in the criminal justice system, and notably the judge, prosecuting counsel, defence counsel, police, expert witnesses, as well as lay witnesses, can be the cause of miscarriages of justice. But the consequence of the ruling of the majority is that a major actor, the jury, is immune from such scrutiny on the basis that such immunity is a price worth paying. This restrictive view will gnaw at public confidence in juries. It is a system likely in the long run to increase pressure for reducing the scope of trial by jury. A system which forfeits its moral authority is not likely to survive intact. The question will be whether such a system provides a better quality of justice than trial by professionals.

The majority had the grace to feel uncomfortable with the more startling implications of the uncompromising rule they had laid down, and some sought to mitigate the worst of them. So building on a concession by the Crown that an appeal would lie if a jury in a murder case used a ouija-board to ask the spirit of the murder victim how he really died (cf. the facts of *Young* [1995] Q.B. 324), Lord Hope suggested that an appeal might perhaps also lie if the jury reached their verdict on the toss of a coin. Lord Hope also proposed an extra safeguard that he thought would solve the problem, if there is one: in future, judges should tell jurors that "they are under a duty to inform the court at once of any irregularity which occurs while they are deliberating". This proposal has now been acted on (see the Practice Direction, [2004] 1 W.L.R. 665). But how this will help if all the jurors are involved in the irregularity has yet to be explained; and similarly, how it will prevent miscarriages of justice where those who are not involved in the irregularity are too timid to complain at the time. What underlies the decision of the majority is the practical difficulty of establishing what actually happened in the jury room when an allegation of misbehaviour is made, perhaps a long time afterwards. This problem is a real one, but I believe there is a simple way of solving it. The discussion of the jury should be tape-recorded. If this were done, then when an allegation of improper conduct is made, it would be a relatively simple matter to check whether it is founded. Before this idea is rejected out of hand as likely to inhibit the discussion, we should remember that the same objection was made, a quarter of a century ago, to tape-recording police interviews with suspects, a practice that is now routine, and universally accepted. That tape-recording inhibits the police is undoubted: it inhibits them from threatening and bribing suspects, and inventing confessions they never made. If it inhibited juries from using ouija-boards, tossing coins and expressing racial hatred, so much the better.

Is that a Gun in your Pocket, or Are you Purposively Constructive?
R. v Bentham
CLJ 2004, 63(3) 543–545

In *Bentham* [2003] EWCA Crim 3751, [2004] 1 Cr.App.R. 487 a robber, to intimidate his victim, put his hand inside his pocket to make it look as if he had a gun. For this he was convicted not only of robbery, but also of an offence under section 17(2) of the Firearms Act 1968, which provides that:

> If a person, at the time of his committing or being arrested for an offence specified in Schedule 1 to this Act, has in his possession a firearm or imitation firearm, he shall be guilty of an offence under this subsection unless he shows that he had it in his possession for a lawful object.

The judge held that, so used, Bentham's fingers were an "imitation firearm"; and as he was in possession of them when committing a robbery, which is a Schedule 1 offence, he was guilty of the Firearms Act offence as well. The Court of Appeal – in an unreserved judgment – upheld the conviction. Section 17(2), they said, should be construed purposively. "[T]he protection which the Act seeks to afford is protection to the public who are being put in fear."

This result looks very odd – and there are reasons for thinking that the case is wrongly decided.

First, purposive or otherwise, the construction that the Court of Appeal put on the provision is a strained one. What this defendant did does not look like the behaviour described in the section, which is being in possession of a firearm or an imitation firearm when committing an offence. The Court has read "possessing a pretend firearm" to include "pretending to possess a firearm", a form of misbehaviour that is different, and wider, and to which the words of the section do not naturally apply. If it is permissible for the courts to interpret penal statutes purposively, surely this is only where the reading is one that the words can naturally bear. It does not permit an interpretation to which the reaction, when you hear it, is a sharp intake of breath and the word "Gosh!".

Secondly, it is questionable whether the purpose the Court of Appeal identified is actually the right one. Section 17 was not enacted to deter people from scaring others, but to deter them from going out on criminal purposes "tooled up": that is, having equipped themselves with objects which, if used, are likely to endanger others, or at least to cause them fear. This is clear from the fact that, in order to secure a conviction, it is only necessary to show that the defendant was in possession of the object; it is irrelevant whether or not he tried to use it. The rationale for the section 17 offence is the same as for the offence of possessing an offensive weapon under the Prevention of Crime Act 1953. In that context, the courts have had to deal with the defendant who had an innocent object with him for a proper purpose – a carpenter with a hammer in his tool bag, for example, as in *Ohlson v Hylton* [1975] 1 W.L.R. 724 – which he used as an impromptu weapon in a fight. The courts have refused to apply the Prevention of Crime Act offence in such cases, interpreting it as limited to those who took the object with them intending to use it as a weapon all along.

Third, the Court of Appeal's interpretation of the provision is a harsh one. Offences under section 17 are very serious. The maximum penalty is life imprisonment. And the Court of Appeal has said that where someone is convicted under section 17(2) of possessing a firearm when committing a Schedule I offence, he should receive a separate sentence for the firearm offence, to run consecutively (*R. v McGrath* (1986) 8 Cr. App.R. (S.) 372). So on principle, the offence should be limited to behaviour that is really serious. Furthermore, if fingers count as an "imitation firearm" for the purposes of the section 17(2) offence, they presumably do so for the offence under section 17(1) as well: using or attempting to use a firearm "or imitation firearm" to resist arrest. As resisting arrest carries a maximum penalty of two years, a person who resists arrest by putting his hand in his pocket and saying "Stick 'em up!" instantly converts a two year offence into one that is punishable with life imprisonment. That this is potentially oppressive should be obvious.

This case illustrates a recurrent problem with English criminal law, which is that the courts have no coherent philosophy about the way in which penal statutes are to be interpreted. Repressive political systems like their criminal law to be as wide as possible, and favour the rule that prohibitions in penal statutes are to be read broadly: like Nazi Germany, which in 1935 adopted the rule that "If there is no penal law applying directly to the act it shall be punished under the law whose basic idea best fits it". But political systems that proclaim their adherence to the rule of law and individual liberty usually operate a rule that penal statutes are to be strictly interpreted, and where they are ambiguous the defendant must have the benefit of the doubt. This is so in France, for example, where Article 111–4 of the *Code pénal* provides that "*La loi pénale est d'interprétation stricte*".

What the position is in English law is doubtful. The "strict construction" principle is recognised by writers, and in some of the case law. In practice, the courts oscillate between applying an extreme version of it – as in the celebrated case of *Harris* (1832) 7 C. & P. 446, where they held a "wound" requires a weapon, and so does not cover biting off the victim's nose – and forgetting about it altogether, as they did in *Bentham*.

If this country ever acquires the modern criminal code that the Government has said it wants but does nothing serious about getting, let us hope that the "general part" includes a provision like Article 111–4 of the *Code pénal* in France.[17]

---

[17] The case went to the House of Lords, which – having referred to the comments made in this note and elsewhere – reversed the Court of Appeal decision; see [2005] UKHL 18, [2005] 1 W.L.R. 1057.

Damages for Lost Chances: Lost for Good?
Gregg v Scott
CLJ 2005, 64(2) 282–285

Straight after *Chester v Afshar* [2005] 1 A.C. 134[18] comes another important decision on the liability of doctors: *Gregg v Scott* [2005] UKHL 2, [2005] 2 A.C. 176. This is a big case even in the most literal sense: the Law Lords' speeches, all of the highest quality, extend to 54 printed pages.

The issue was the liability of a doctor who. negligently misdiagnoses a patient suffering from a serious illness (in this case, a rampant type of cancer) for which the chances of successful treatment are already small: and by the time he is correctly diagnosed later, they have shrunk still smaller. In such a case, is the patient entitled to damages for the reduced chance of a successful cure? The orthodox view, as derived from the House of Lords decision in *Hotson v East Berks Area Health Authority* [1987] A.C. 750, is "No". Where the claimant can show that his chances of recovery if treated early were better than even, we say that he has proved his loss on the balance of probabilities and is entitled to full compensation, calculated on the assumption that, but for the defendant's negligence, he would have been cured. But if his initial chance of recovery was only 50 per cent or less, we say that he has failed to prove his loss and so gets nothing. By application of this rule, Mr. Gregg lost at first instance and, by a majority, in the Court of Appeal (see [2003] C.L.J. 253). In the House of Lords his arguments to the contrary convinced Lord Nicholls and Lord Hope, but not Lord Phillips, Baroness Hale or Lord Hoffmann. So by a majority he lost again, and the orthodox position is affirmed.

For Lord Nicholls, dissenting, the main reason for accepting a "lost chance" claim in such a case is the fact that the existing rule produces results that seem so arbitrary:

> The loss of a 45% prospect of recovery is just as much a real loss for a patient as the loss of a 55% prospect of recovery. In both cases the doctor was in breach of his duty to his patient. In both cases the patient

---

[18] The subject of a note by Kumaralingham Amirthalingam at [2005] C..L.J. 32.

was worse off. He has lost something of importance and value. But, it is said, in one case the patient has a remedy, in the other he does not. This would make no sort of sense... It cannot be right to adopt a procedure having the effect that, in law, a patient's prospects of recovery are treated as non-existent whenever they exist but fall short of 50%.

Outside the medical context, he reminded us the law admits claims for loss of less-than-evens chances in many well known situations. To allow such claims in medical cases calculated on a percentage basis derived from medical statistics might do less than perfect justice, because the underlying problem is a causal link that may or may not exist, but which cannot be proved or disproved conclusively. In reality, it might mean that some claimants would get too much because for them the initial failure to treat did not in truth affect the outcome (although we do not know this), whilst others got too little because for them it really did (although we do not know that either). But, said Lord Nicholls, the courts should be prepared to "adapt their process so as to leap an evidentiary gap when overall fairness plainly so requires": as indeed the House of Lords spectacularly did in *Fairchild v Glenhaven Funeral Services Ltd.* [2003] 1 A.C. 32 – the case about negligent exposure to asbestos, and resulting mesothelioma. Similar reasoning was adopted in his long and careful speech by the other dissentient, Lord Hope.

The reasons that moved the majority to reject the claim were more diverse.

For Lord Hoffmann, the key obstacle was the difficulty that Lord Nicholls recognised, but felt that he could live with: the problem of allowing a claim on a percentage basis for a "lost chance" when in reality the doctor's negligence may have caused some claimants to lose everything, but others nothing. In principle, a tortious claimant must show that the cause of his harm was the wrongful conduct of the defendant. If he cannot do this, then in principle his claim must fail: and it is no answer for him to say "but proof here is impossible". Certain exceptions to this are acceptable, but they should be limited, and capable of precise definition. That was so in *Fairchild*, but, said Lord Hoffmann, the exception the claimant wanted here was potentially much wider and clear limits could not be placed upon it.

For Lord Phillips, the main problem was not so much the principle of allowing a lost chance claim based on medical statistics as the practical difficulties of dealing with it. In each case, justice would require the court to make a serious attempt to adjust the statistics to take account of the detailed information that is known about this particular claimant. Here, for example, a problem arose because Mr. Gregg, contrary to the initial prognosis, had bucked the statistical trend and was still alive when his case was heard by the House of Lords – so that, as Lord Phillips put it, "The likelihood seems to be that Dr. Scott's negligence has not prevented Mr. Gregg's cure, but has made that cure more painful." In the light of these difficulties, which Lord Phillips explained in detail and at length, it was better for the law to remain as it is. "A robust test which produces rough justice may be preferable to a test that on occasion will be difficult, if not impossible, to apply with confidence in practice."

For Baroness Hale, a key problem with allowing a "lost chance" claim in cases where the claimant's initial chance of recovery was poor, was the impact she thought this would necessarily have on claims where the initial chance of recovery was good. At present, where the negligent misdiagnosis deprived the patient of a chance of recovery that was 51 per cent or better, he gets full compensation, calculated on the basis that he would have recovered. But a law which allowed the patient to claim full damages where he lost a good chance of recovery, and reduced damages where he lost a bad one, would be both unfair to doctors, and logically inconsistent. In her view, introducing "lost chance" claims where the chance of recovery was low would therefore mean we must stop giving full compensation in "good chance" cases, and reduce the damages in any case where the claimant's initial chance of recovery was less than certain. For this reason, among others, she – unlike Lord Nicholls – embraced Tony Weir's theory that "lost chance" damages are acceptable in the context of claims for financial loss, but not personal injuries.

In closing the door on "lost chance" claims in negligent misdiagnosis cases, two of the majority left it ajar – if only slightly – for claims framed in other ways. Lord Phillips said that a claimant who could not show on the balance of probabilities that if treated in good time he would have recovered might still be able to show, on the balance of probabilities, that the need for painful and invasive treatment would have been avoided: in which case a claim for pain and suffering would succeed. And Baroness Hale said that although Mr. Gregg failed in his claim for a lost chance of a full recovery, he might still have had a modest claim in respect of the "lost years" if he could have shown that his median life expectancy had been reduced.

All this contrasts sharply with *Chester v Afshar* where House of Lords, by a majority, applied the rules of causation very strictly against a surgeon who had failed to warn a patient about the risks inherent in an operation. In doing so, they stressed the need to "vindicate" patients whose doctors failed to treat them with due care. How come this argument, which carried the day in *Chester v Afshar*, failed to do so here? The cases are logically distinguishable, of course – but a different spirit clearly animates the two decisions. The main reason for this, I suspect, is that a claimant-favourable decision in *Gregg v Scott* would have had a far greater practical impact on the working of the law. The facts in *Chester v Afshar* were unusual, and unlikely to recur. But the scenario in *Gregg v Scott*, by contrast, is commonplace, and if Mr. Gregg had won this would have opened the door to very many claims. As Lord Hoffmann said, "It would have enormous consequences for insurance companies and the National Health Service."

Child Witnesses and The European Union
Criminal Proceedings against Pupino
CLJ 2005, 64(3) 569–572

In recent years we have got used to the idea that criminal law and criminal procedure in this country must in principle conform to the European Convention on Human Rights, as interpreted by the Strasbourg Court. But few criminal lawyers, I believe, have ever in their wildest dreams imagined that it must also conform to the law emanating from the Council of Ministers at Brussels, as interpreted by the ECJ at Luxembourg. In the light of this, the recent decision in the *Pupino* case (C-105/3, Grand Chamber, 16 June 2005, [2006] QB 83) will come to many as a surprise, if not a shock.

Signora Pupino was an Italian infant school teacher whose methods of disciplining under fives allegedly included hitting them, refusing to allow them to go to the toilet, and gumming their mouths shut with sticking plaster. For this, unsurprisingly, she found herself prosecuted for offences of cruelty to children. Under Italian criminal procedure, as reformed in 1988, witnesses must usually depose orally at trial, but in certain circumstances their evidence may be taken before a judge ahead of trial by a procedure known as *incidente probatorio*. The public prosecutor asked the court to allow the evidence of the little children to be taken in this way, but the court refused. The Italian Code of Criminal Procedure set out the circumstances in which this could be done, and this was not one of them.

Under the Treaty of European Union (TEU) – the constitutional arrangements agreed at Maastricht in 1992 and modified at Amsterdam in 1997 and Nice in 2000 – the Council of the EU has power to make "Framework Decisions" on a wide range of matters relating to criminal justice. These Framework Decisions are rather like EC Directives.[19] As a matter of EU law, the Member States are bound to amend their internal law to ensure that it complies with them, but as a matter of domestic law they do not take effect within the national system until this has been done. Of these there have been many, the most famous example being the one in 2002 requiring the Member States to replace extradition within Europe by a drastically simplified procedure (the European Arrest Warrant); which the UK Parliament, rather reluctantly, gave effect to in Part I of the Extradition Act 2003. Most Framework Decisions are inspired, like that one, by notions of Law and Order: which is not surprising, since the EU Council that issues them is in effect a club whose members are the Home Secretaries of the Member States. If a Member State fails to amend its law to comply with

---

[19] Under the new constitution regime established by the Lisbon Treaty, Framework Decisions have disappeared and criminal legislation can now be made by Regulations or Directives.

an EU Framework Decision it cannot be hauled before the ECJ in enforcement proceedings to compel it to do so, as where it fails to implement an EC Directive. But the courts of Member States may ask the ECJ for a preliminary ruling on its interpretation of a Framework Decision if they "opt in" to the procedure set out in Article 35 TEU – as Italy and many other Member States have done, although the UK has not.

In 2001, the Council issued a Framework Decision (2001/220/JHA, [2001] O.J. L82/1) setting out a list of guarantees that Member States undertake to provide for the victims of criminal offences. Under Article 3, "Each Member State shall take appropriate measures to ensure that its authorities question victims only insofar as necessary for the purpose of criminal proceedings." And under Article 8 (4), "Each Member State shall ensure that, where there is a need to protect victims – particularly the most vulnerable – from the effects of giving evidence in open court, victims may, by decision taken in open court, be entitled to testify in a manner which will enable this objective to be achieved, by any appropriate means compatible with its basic rights." By Article 17, Member States were required to bring their laws into line with these requirements by 22 March 2002.

The refusal of the judge in the *Pupino* case to allow the children's evidence to be taken in advance of trial led to a discussion about the compatibility of the relevant provisions of the Italian Code of Criminal Procedure with the Framework Decision, and to the judge invoking Article 35 of the TEU to refer the question to the ECJ at Luxembourg. This set alarm bells ringing in Home Offices and Ministries of Justice all over Europe. The governments of several other Member States (including the UK) intervened in the proceedings, in the hope of persuading the Court to say that references under Article 35 are inappropriate in the context of particular cases – and more generally, to try to persuade the ECJ to kill any suggestion that national courts are required to take account of Framework Decisions when interpreting their national laws.

In both of these hopes the national governments were disappointed.

The ECJ said that it was entirely appropriate for references under Article 35 to be made in the course of particular prosecutions. As regards the compatibility of Italian criminal procedure with the Framework Decision on victims, the Court said the instrument "must be interpreted as meaning that the national court must be able to authorise young children, who, as in this case, claim to have been victims of maltreatment, to give their testimony in accordance with arrangements allowing those children to be guaranteed an appropriate level of protection, for example outside the trial and before it takes place". And on the broader issue, it said: "The national court is required to take into consideration all the rules of national law and to interpret them, so far as possible, in the light of the wording and purpose of the Framework Decision."

In reaching the conclusion that national courts must seek to interpret national law in the light of Framework Decisions, the ECJ referred to Article 10 of the EC Treaty [Article 4(3) TEU)] which imposes on Member States what is usually called the duty of "loyal cooperation" in furthering the aims of the European Community. It was this duty that the ECJ invoked long ago to create the rule that Member States must interpret their national law so as to conform with European Community law – i.e., the original body of European law, deriving from the EC Treaty. Though Article 10 EC itself applies only to Community law, a similar duty of loyalty, the ECJ said, applies in relation to the aims of European Union law, deriving from the Treaty of European Union (i.e., Maastricht and its progeny).

The *Pupino* decision is obviously of huge importance for the future of EU law in general. And for English criminal justice it is important too. For this, it has two implications, one narrow and one broad.

The narrow one, of course, concerns the evidence of children. In 1989, the Pigot Committee recommended that the law be changed to allow the evidence of little children (cross-examination and all) to take place out of court ahead of trial. But so far this has not happened, and in contested cases, child witnesses still have to come to court to undergo a live cross-examination. Provisions in the Youth Justice and Criminal Evidence Act 1999 that were intended to implement the Pigot recommendations have been abandoned by the Home Office – rightly, in my view[20] – as over-complex and unworkable. They have not been brought into force, and never will be. The *Pupino* decision suggests that we shall now have to make a further attempt to find a way under which little children can give the whole of their evidence ahead of trial.

The broader and more significant implication is that our criminal courts, when construing the rules of English law in relation to criminal justice, must in future operate not only looking over their left shoulders at the Strasbourg Court and the ECHR, but simultaneously looking over their right ones at the Luxembourg Court and EU Framework Decisions.

At first sight, this looks very worrying. It suggests the image of an unhappy motorist afflicted with not one but two back seat drivers, each with different views about the route the car should take. Fortunately, the ECJ foresaw this problem. The EU, it said, must respect fundamental rights as guaranteed by the ECHR. So when construing Framework Decisions, and trying to interpret national laws to take account of them, courts must always bear in mind the ultimate need to respect the requirements of the ECHR – and in particular the right to a fair trial under Article 6.

Liability for Purely Economic Loss Again: "Small Earthquake in Chile. Not Many Dead"? *London Borough of Islington v UCL Hospital NHS Trust*
CLJ 2006, 65(1) 13–15

As a result of a hospital's negligence, Mrs. J had a stroke which rendered her incapable of looking after herself. Eventually, the hospital financed a structured settlement which provided her with

---

[20] Since writing this note I have changed my mind on this. I advocated the implementation of s.28 of the Youth Justice and Criminal Evidence Act 1999 in chapter 9 of John R Spencer and Michel E Lamb (eds), *Children and Cross-examination – Time to Change the Rules?* (Hart Publishing, 2012).

a specially adapted house where she was cared for by her daughter. But until that happened, the Borough of Islington provided her with residential care, under a statutory obligation imposed on them by the National Assistance Act 1948. This cost the citizens of Islington £81,000, a sum which the Borough sought to reclaim from the hospital by suing it in tort. The claim failed, both at first instance, and on appeal: *London Borough of Islington v University College London Hospital NHS Trust* [2005] EWCA Civ 596, [2005] Lloyd's Rep. Med. 387.

At first sight this decision seems neither particularly important, nor very interesting. The Borough's claim was, of course, a tortious claim in negligence for purely economic loss, resulting from the personal injuries the defendant had inflicted on a third party. As such, it was almost bound to fail. Furthermore, it was a squabble between two pockets of the public purse – like those lawyer-enriching law suits between parishes two hundred years ago, each arguing that the poor law imposed the duty to maintain the pauper on the other.

But in fact the case raises an important point of public policy. In recent years, Parliament has passed a series of Acts enabling the social security system to reclaim what it has spent in looking after accident victims from the tortfeasors who made them incapable of looking after themselves. In 1972, it passed legislation enabling the NHS to reclaim from motorists some of the costs of medical treatment given to those injured in accidents resulting from their negligent driving. In 1989, it passed legislation requiring tortfeasors to reimburse the State for a range of social security payments made to accident victims: an obligation now to be found in the Social Security (Recovery of Payments) Act 1997. Then in 2003, Parliament passed the Health and Social Care (Community Health and Standards) Act, Part 3 of which requires tortfeasors of all types to reimburse the NHS for all the costs involved in hospital treatment for their victims. To ensure that tortfeasors pay up as legally required, a muscular organization, called the Compensation Recovery Unit, has been set up.

This statutory structure protects the parts of the social security system that are run centrally from Whitehall, but does nothing for the parts that are administered and financed locally: that is, the parts for which the Government is not directly responsible, and upon which it is therefore willing to impose duties without worrying too much about whether they have the funds necessary to fulfil them. Unsurprisingly, local authorities do not savour this discrimination: like Shylock, they say "If you prick us, do we not bleed?" It was against this background that Islington Borough Council tried "direct action" in the courts.

Since *Caparo v Dickman* [1990] 2 A.C. 605, the claimant who seeks damages in negligence for purely economic loss in a new situation must satisfy a three-fold test: first, "reasonable foreseeability"; secondly, "proximity"; and thirdly, that the imposition of liability would be "fair, just and reasonable". And in applying these tests the courts are supposed to have respect for "incrementalism": the notion that the common law should move by little steps, like centipedes and corgis, not leaps and bounds, like kangaroos.

In the Court of Appeal, where Buxton L.J. gave the leading judgment, the claimant was held to have cleared the first hurdle, foreseeability. Buxton L.J. then wrestled manfully with the second test, "proximity", and with the concept of incrementalism. Like many commentators, and most law students, Buxton L.J. found neither concept particularly meaningful, and suggested both were really different ways of asking "was the harm reasonably foreseeable?", or "is it fair, just and reasonable for liability to be imposed?" Having reached what he described as a "somewhat inconclusive outcome" on these issues, Buxton L.J. then turned his attention to the third limb of the *Caparo* test, and held that on this point the claimant clearly failed. In shorter judgments, Clarke L.J. and Ousely J. agreed.

In a broad sense, said Buxton L.J. and his brethren, it would be "fair, just and reasonable" to make the defendant pay. The defendant was at fault, and the loss was one for which the defendant would have had to compensate Mrs. J herself had she been richer, and hence able to pay for her temporary sheltered housing out of her own pocket, instead of having to ask Islington to provide it for her out of "public money". But the "fair, just and reasonable" test, they said, must be answered by looking at the bigger picture. This was an area in which Parliament has been active, creating specific statutory duties to reimburse against a legal background which it had evidently assumed to be the absence of any general liability in negligence. To upset a cart with so many legal apples balanced on it is not a matter to be undertaken lightly, wantonly or unadvisedly. Further reform in this area, they said, is a job for Parliament, and not the courts.

With this conclusion it is hard to disagree. But it is equally hard to disagree with Buxton L.J. when he also said that "Islington's basic case attracts a good deal of sympathy". If it is right that the NHS and the part of the social security system that operates from Whitehall should be able to recoup its money from the tortfeasor, there is no intelligible reason why local authorities should not be able to do the same. There are other supporters of the injured who are in a similar position, too: including employers, whom the law requires to give "statutory sick-pay" to employees if they are injured, even by third parties – for only part of which the State reimburses them, and none of which they can recover from the tortfeasor. This is, I believe, an area at which Parliament should look again. And next time, it should look beyond Whitehall when it does so.

Drunken Defence
R. v Hatton
CLJ 2006, 65(2), 267–269

It is black-letter law that a defendant who kills or maims in self-defence is entitled to be judged on the facts as he believed them to be. And it is also well established that the crucial question in such a case is whether the defendant's belief in those facts was honest, not whether it was reasonable. If the defendant honestly but unreasonably believed himself to be under attack, he is entitled (in effect) to the benefit of his unreasonable mistake. This rule was laid down by the Court of Appeal in *Williams* (1984) 78 Cr.App.R. 276 and affirmed by the Privy Council in *Beckford v R.* [1988] A.C. 130.

But what if he was drunk? Here the Court of Appeal in *O'Grady* [1987] 1 Q.B. 995 and *O'Connor* [1991] Crim. L.R. 135 said the rule is different: a defendant who unreasonably believes he is being attacked because his understanding is dimmed by alcohol or drugs (or both) is to be judged on the facts as they were, and not as he erroneously imagined them. It follows, said the court in these two cases, that if he kills his supposed attacker by acts intended to kill or cause grievous bodily harm, he is guilty of a murder. In neither of these cases was this harsh rule actually applied, because both defendants ended up with manslaughter convictions for other, unconnected reasons. But in *Hatton* [2005] EWCA Crim 2951, [2006] 1 Cr.App.R. 16 (247) the Court of Appeal has now reaffirmed the rule, and actually applied it.

Hatton, although not gay, was seen "camping it up" in a bar before he invited Pashley, the future victim, back to his flat. Pashley was a homophobe who claimed to belong to the SAS, and he was also a manic-depressive, in a manic mood; before being picked up by Hatton he had been "behaving in a strange fashion" and "striking martial arts poses" in the pub. Back at the flat a fight broke out which Hatton won conclusively, by slaying Pashley with a sledgehammer. Hatton, who had drunk some 20 pints of beer, claimed to remember nothing: but he said "I must have believed that I was under attack". The trial judge told the jury to acquit Hatton of murder if they believed he might have acted in the honest belief that Pashley was attacking him – but, following *O'Grady* and *O'Connor*, omitted to tell them, when considering this, to bear in mind that Hatton was extremely drunk. The jury convicted him of murder – and the Court of Appeal, approving the direction, upheld the conviction.

It is understandable that the courts dislike defendants who support their claim to have acted under a mistake by evidence that they were drunk: the excuse itself consists of the inexcusable. But where a person kills another person in the genuine belief (however unreasonable) that the other was about to kill or maim him, to convict him of the offence of murder, with its mandatory life sentence, is remarkably severe. And it is also strangely inconsistent, too, with the rest of the law in relation to drunken mistakes. If

Hamlet, high on drugs, kills Polonius because he honestly but unreasonably believes the shape behind the arras is a rat, he has the benefit of his mistake and his crime is manslaughter at most: see *Lipman* [1970] 1 Q.B. 152. But if he does the same thing in the equally honest but unreasonable belief that Polonius is an assassin lurking there to kill him, his crime, as we have seen, is murder.

This harsh and inconsistent rule is clearly not required to prevent those who kill or maim under the influence of drink or drugs from "walking free".

First, the issue here is only whether drunks should be allowed the benefit of their unreasonable mistakes *as to the underlying facts*. There is no question of allowing a defendant who understands the basic facts to be judged by his own drink or drug-warped perception of what it is reasonable to do in response to them. What is "reasonable" in this sense is an objective question, on which defendants (drunk or sober) disagree with juries at their peril, as the Court of Appeal recently reminded us in the case of "Saint" Tony Martin, the farmer who put the bullet in the back of the retreating burglar: *Martin* [2003] 2 Q.B. 1.

Second, there is no question, even where the issue is the defendant's drunken mistake as to the underlying facts, of allowing him to escape punishment completely. Where drunken mistakes are concerned the law, on policy grounds, divides criminal offences into two groups: "crimes of specific intent", which carry the most severe penalties, and "crimes of basic intent", which are the rest. According to the leading case, the House of Lords decision in *Majewski* [1977] A.C. 443, a person may use his intoxicated state as evidence that he lacked *mens rea* when tried for offences in the first group, but not the second. It was on this basis that *Lipman*, who had strangled his girlfriend on an LSD trip when he thought he was fighting snakes in the centre of the earth, was acquitted of murder, but convicted of manslaughter. If this is how the law treats intoxicated mistakes which deprive the defendant of the *mens rea* for the offence, it is also how it could – and surely should – treat intoxicated mistakes as to external facts which, if true, would support a general defence.

In *Hatton* the Court of Appeal affirmed the conviction without much examination of the underlying issues, because it believed that it was bound by a clear line of authority. It did certify a point of public importance, but it also refused leave to appeal. This, I believe, was unfortunate. *O'Grady*, the case this story starts from, was an unreserved judgment, in which the issues were not thoroughly examined, as writers then and since have pointed out; and so too was *O'Connor*. With all due respect to a court that does its commendable best in the face of a gross excess of work, it could be said that this "clear line of authority" has evolved by a process reminiscent of Fougasse's cartoon about the spread of news in wartime: "two lies = one rumour; two rumours = one good authority...". The issues in this case are important ones, and it is high time they were considered by the House of Lords.[21]

The Evidential Status of Previous Inconsistent Statements
R. v Joyce and Joyce
CLJ 2006, 65(3) 518–520

For many years, the common law rule about the evidential status of a witness's previous inconsistent statements was the *pons asinorum* for students of the law of evidence. As those who crossed it will recall, it was as follows. A witness who had earlier told a different tale could have his earlier inconsistent statement "put to him" in cross-examination; if in response he then "adopted" it – i.e. agreed that he had made it and admitted it was true – the earlier statement then became admissible as evidence of the matters it contained. But if he refused to adopt it, the earlier statement was not in law evidence of any facts asserted in it, although the tribunal of fact could treat it as bearing on the credibility of the witness's oral testimony in court. So if the witness told the police "the answer is a lemon", but later told the court "the answer is an orange", there

---

[21] Before this could happen, the Criminal Justice and Immigration Act 2008 was enacted – section 76 of which (alas!) has set the rule criticised in this note in legislative concrete.

would be no legally admissible evidence before the court that the answer was a lemon: but there would be evidence that the answer was an orange, plus a good reason for disbelieving it.

No tears were shed when this abstruse rule was abolished in civil proceedings by the Civil Evidence Act 1968, which provided that where a previous inconsistent statement is put to a witness, the contents count as evidence on which the court may act if it believes the earlier statement, rather than the later one. In criminal proceedings, however, the old rule lived on: where, if it continued to hinder law students, it continued to help those defendants who (or whose muscular friends) could persuade the prosecution witnesses to retract their initial statements to the police. In 1997 the Law Commission said that the old rule should be abolished in criminal proceedings too, and six years later section 119 of the Criminal Justice Act 2003 achieved this. Section 119 came into force in April 2005, and two months later the Court of Appeal considered it for the first time in *Joyce and Joyce* [2005] EWCA Crim 1785. This case shows us that the change, technical as it may appear, has important practical implications.

Following a shooting carried out in broad daylight in the streets of Liverpool, three people who had seen it gave statements to the police identifying the defendants, who were known to them, as the assailants. At trial, all three witnesses retracted their statements, and produced implausible explanations as to why their initial identifications had been wrong. "*Nulla so: nulla vidi, e se c'ero, dormivo*", as they say in Sicily: "I know nothing: I saw nothing, and if I was there, I was asleep". At the end of the prosecution case the trial judge rejected a defence submission of "no case to answer" and left the evidence to the jury, which convicted, evidently because it believed what the witnesses had originally said to the police and not what they had told the court in evidence – and heavy sentences were imposed.

Upholding the convictions, the Court of Appeal said:

> In the light of the new statutory provisions in relation to hearsay, in our judgment it would have been an affront to the administration of justice, on a trial for offences based on this terrifying conduct, if the jury had not been permitted by the judge to evaluate, separately and

together, the quality of the three witnesses' oral evidence and to rely, if they thought fit, on the terms of their original statements...

Under the earlier law, the defence submission of "no case" would have succeeded, and acquittals would undoubtedly have followed; and this change provokes a number of related thoughts.

First, the change can be seen in wider context as a part of a series of moves to modify the traditional rules of criminal evidence to cope with the practical (and horrifying) difficulties of witness intimidation in violent crime. Thus in *Sellick* [2005] EWCA Crim 651, [2005] 1 W.L.R. 3257, the Court of Appeal, after an extensive survey of both the Strasbourg and the English case law, had earlier decided that a conviction could in certain circumstances be based upon the initial statements given to the police by witnesses who, through fear, failed even to appear at the eventual trial. And in *Davis, and Ellis and others* [2006] EWCA Crim 1155 the Court of Appeal, after a similar survey, and a reference to statistics about gun related crime, has now ruled that in certain circumstances a conviction can properly be based on the evidence of witnesses who testify at trial anonymously.

Secondly, *Joyce* and the other cases also mark a decisive move away from the traditional common law position, according to which the only form of evidence on which it is acceptable to found a conviction in a criminal case is oral testimony given live at trial – on oath, in the presence of the defendant, and subject to cross-examination. Behind this change there lurks an unspoken change of attitude towards traditional ideas: including rising scepticism about the value of the oath, and a growing acceptance that, contrary to the traditional view, what a witness said in private immediately after a traumatic incident is quite as likely to be true as what he says in public, in the presence of the defendant, ages later. And there is also an acceptance that, in principle, defendants can be adequately protected by other safeguards than the right to cross-examine: for example, full disclosure of the evidence in advance, and the right to call evidence to challenge or rebut.

(Such notions have, of course, been long accepted in the inquisitorial tradition on the Continent; and here it is interesting to see that in 2001, as part of a conscious attempt to reform their criminal procedure on "Anglo-Saxon" lines, the Italians solemnly enacted the very rule about the status of a witness's previous inconsistent statements that we have just abolished. If the first principle of comparative law is that the grass on the other side of the fence is always greener, the second seems to be that we borrow our neighbours' legal tools only after they have decided to put them in the bin!)

The most obvious effect of *Joyce* and the related case law is to enhance the evidential status of the statements potential witnesses give to the police. This raises important questions about the way in which the police obtain such statements and record them. At present, this is a matter about which there are scarcely any rules, and the law leaves the police to their own devices. A similar situation formerly existed as regards police interviews with suspects: the fruits of which, unlike witness statements, were generally admissible in evidence as "confessions". After years of complaints (both true and false) about police misconduct and ineptitude when interviewing suspects, the English legal system faced this problem with the Police and Criminal Evidence Act 1984, which (inter alia) provides that such interviews must be tape-recorded. If witness statements are to be more widely admissible in evidence, then surely similar precautions are needed here as well.

Acquitting the Innocent and Convicting the Guilty – Whatever will They Think of Next!
R. (D.P.P.) v Chorley Justices and Forrest
CLJ 2007, 66(1) 27–30

Until now, one aspect of our criminal justice system has been what might be called the "penalty shoot-out theory" of the trial. To win the match, the prosecution are allowed one shot at goal; and if their striker misses, however unluckily, they do not get another chance. Traditionally, this has been so even where the reason the prosecution fail to score is that the defence, having carefully "kept its powder dry" until the trial, points out some technical deficiency in the procedure which, if noticed earlier, could easily have been corrected. When in consequence of this some obviously guilty person goes unmeritoriously free, lay people traditionally complain and say "We thought criminal justice was about acquitting the innocent and convicting the guilty". To this complaint, common lawyers traditionally reply that it is based on a misunderstanding of the adversarial tradition, which, unlike the inquisitorial tradition, is not concerned with establishing what continental lawyers call "material truth". The recent decision of the Divisional Court in *R. (D.P.P.) v Chorley Justices and Forrest* [2006] EWHC 1795 (Admin) shows us that, in this respect, English criminal procedure has recently undergone a most dramatic change.

By way of an exception to the normal rule that all evidence must be given orally, the Road Traffic Act 1988 allows the prosecution in a drink-driving case to prove the blood alcohol level in the defendant's blood by producing a written certificate from the analyst. But in order to do this, they must formally serve the certificate on the defendant at least seven days before the trial. When Mr. Forrest was prosecuted for driving with excess blood-alcohol, he pled not guilty and, at the pre-trial case management hearing, "reserved his defence". At the eventual trial, at which the prosecution produced the analyst's certificate rather than the analyst, Forrest submitted that the certificate was not admissible in evidence because it had not been served on him in strict compliance with the formalities the law requires. The justices accepted his submission, and dismissed the case. When the CPS, which thought the certificate had been served with due formality, asked them to state a case, they refused. Against this refusal the CPS went to the Divisional Court, which ordered the justices to state a case: and for good measure, it ordered Mr. Forrest – who had resisted the application – to pay the costs. In so deciding, the Divisional Court took the occasion to criticise in blunt terms the conduct of the case below, making it plain that the "penalty shoot-out theory" is now dead:

[24] In April 2005 the Criminal Procedure Rules came into effect... They have effected a sea change in the way in which cases should

be conducted, but it appears that not everyone has appreciated the fundamental change to the conduct of cases in the magistrates' courts that has been brought about by the Rules. The Rules make it clear that the overriding objective is that criminal cases be dealt with justly; that includes acquitting the innocent and convicting the guilty, dealing with the prosecution and defence fairly, respecting the interests of witnesses, dealing with the case efficiently and expeditiously, and also, of great importance, dealing with the case in a way that takes into account the gravity of the offence, the complexity of what is in issue, the severity of the consequences to the defendant and others affected and the needs of others. Rule 1.2 imposes upon the participants in a criminal case a duty to prepare and conduct the case in accordance with the overriding objective, to comply with the rules and, importantly, to inform the court and all parties of any significant failure, whether or not the participant is responsible for that failure, to take any procedural step required by the Rules.

[25] Rule 3.2 imposes upon the court a duty to further that overriding objective by actively managing cases.

In the light of this, they said, Mr. Forrest should have revealed his proposed defence at the case-management conference. And when, having "kept his powder dry", he had ambushed the prosecution at the trial, Chorley justices, instead of throwing out the case, should have granted an adjournment, so enabling the CPS to serve the certificate with the formalities which Mr. Forrest claimed they had neglected.

By now, the non-specialist reader will probably be wondering where this revolution has come from. Who wrote the Criminal Procedure Rules? And who decided they should proclaim an "over-riding objective" which turns previously treasured notions of the accusatorial tradition upside down?

In 2001, as part of his Review of the Criminal Courts, Sir Robin Auld recommended that the rules of criminal procedure be codified. In 2003, as a step in this direction, Parliament enacted Part 7 of the Courts Act, which set up a new and single Criminal Procedure Rule Committee, empowered to rewrite the existing jumble of secondary legislation on criminal procedure in the form of one single code. Under the energetic leadership of Lord Woolf, then Lord Chief Justice, this body carried out the initial codification exercise very quickly; and it also decided that these new Rules should, like the Civil Procedure Rules, begin with a statement of aims and objects, entitled "overriding objective". Of this, the key elements are paraphrased in the extract from the judgment quoted earlier in this note: in particular, the general aim that "criminal cases be dealt with justly" and, at the head of the list of what this means in concrete terms, "acquitting the innocent and convicting the guilty".

These moves attracted scant attention at the time, despite the Committee's attempts to publicise what it was planning. And if practitioners noticed them at all, most seem to have assumed that all this was fine words likely to make little difference, and in the courts it would be "business as before". But from the Chorley Justices case, and others too, it is now clear that Lord Woolf's "overriding objective" is making fundamental changes in the way that business in the criminal courts is conducted. Although many groups and agencies are represented on it, the Criminal Procedure Rule Committee is dominated by the judiciary, and the "overriding objective" is their own attempt to reform criminal procedure so that it aligns more closely with the instincts of ordinary citizens as to what is just and fair. And, unlike the loudly-trumpeted attempts of our headline-hungry politicians to "rebalance justice", it looks as if this reform might actually achieve its authors' aim.

Arrest for Questioning
R. (C) v Chief Constable of A, and A Magistrates' Court
CLJ 2007, 66(2) 282–284

On 24 May 2006, in the early morning, the police arrived at C's house and arrested him on suspicion of downloading indecent images of children. Armed with a search warrant, they searched his house and seized his computers. And, although (as he later claimed) he was prepared to answer their questions voluntarily, they carried him off, still under arrest, for custodial interrogation. All this was because, in 2002 – four years before – the US authorities had told the UK police that, in 1999, C's credit card had apparently been used, on two occasions, to access a website dealing in child pornography. When questioned, C denied the offences, and when the police searched his computers no indecent images of children could be found. Despite this failure to find corroborating evidence the police were not prepared to let the matter drop and, at the end of his custodial interrogation, C was released on "police bail" to reappear at the police-station in six months' time.

Feeling ill-treated, C brought judicial review proceedings to challenge his arrest, the issue of a search warrant and the decision by the police to keep the investigation open. In all three challenges he failed: *R. (C) v Chief Constable of A, and A Magistrates' Court* [2006] EWHC 2353 (Admin). On all three issues the judgment of the Administrative Court is interesting. For reasons of space, however, this note will deal with the first one only: namely, whether, on these facts, the police were justified in arresting C and taking him to the police station for questioning.

The police arrested C summarily, without a warrant, under powers conferred by the Police and Criminal Evidence Act 1984, section 24 ("PACE"). When first enacted this provision was limited to "arrestable offences", which meant those punishable with five years' imprisonment or more. But under the Serious Organised Crime and Police Act, enacted in 2005 at the instance of the Government and the Home Office, the provision has now been "modernised", to give the police a power of summary arrest for all offences, irrespective of their gravity. This major change, which was steam-rollered through Parliament just before the general election, was opposed by civil libertarians, who thought it undesirable that the police should have the power of summary arrest for all criminal offences, no matter how trivial, and irrespective of how old. In response, the Government said that section 24 in its new form would only operate where one of a closed list of six conditions, set out in the section, was present; and in the light of this, the risk of its oppressive use was nil. But as one of these six conditions is that the arrest would "allow the prompt and effective investigation of the offence or conduct of the person in question", libertarian critics were unconvinced.

Predictably, it was this condition that the police relied upon to justify their arrest of C here. Arresting C for questioning was necessary, they said, for "the prompt and efficient investigation" of the case against him (a case which, incidentally, had been gathering dust in police in-trays for the previous four years). To this, C replied that, as he had been prepared to go to the police station for questioning voluntarily, a "prompt and efficient investigation" did not necessitate his arrest: and so the condition on which the police sought to justify arresting him had not been met. This point the judge discussed – but he was not prepared to make a ruling on it. It only arose for decision, he said, if it was clearly established that C would in fact have gone to the police station voluntarily, and this was a factual issue which had not been properly explored. As C's point was an important one, this absence of a judicial ruling on it is regrettable. In my view, C's point was an obviously good one – and our courts should be prepared to say so loud and clear.[22]

In any circumstances, an arrest is a serious invasion of the arrested person's liberty. One made under section 24 of PACE is particularly invasive, because it triggers off a series of other even more invasive powers: in particular, the power to detain the arrested person for questioning for what could be as long as 96 hours, and the power, without obtaining a search-warrant, to search the arrested person's property. Arrests also carry the grave risk of injuring the arrested person's reputation. In our system the identity of suspects is not legally protected, and if the press discover the fact that a given person has been "nicked", this is likely to be given the same sort of publicity as if he had been convicted. And an arrest is potentially damaging in other ways as well. Some countries even more contemptuous of the presumption of innocence than we are here – like the USA – ask would-be visitors, "Have you ever been arrested?", and if the answer is "yes", refuse to let them in.

You would therefore think that, as an instrument for investigating past offences rather than a means of stopping current crimes

---

[22] On this, see the note on *Richardson v Chief Constable of West Midlands*, p. 217 below.

from happening here and now, the power of the police to arrest a suspect without warrant would be limited to serious crimes. That two years ago Parliament was willing, at a nod from the Home Secretary, to extend it to even the most trivial of offences, seems utterly astonishing. It brings to mind a recent cartoon in *Private Eye* in which one uniformed figure is saying to another: "Actually, establishing a tyranny turned out to be quite a lot easier than we expected."

Given that this extension has now happened, it surely behoves the courts to interpret the restrictions that Parliament has imposed on it – feeble as they are – with strictness.

If a suspect is willing to be questioned voluntarily, arresting him for questioning cannot possibly be necessary for the "prompt and efficient investigation of the offence". The real reason why the police like to arrest co-operative suspects is, I suspect, that it enables them to tell the press that they have "arrested X for questioning" – and so to give the world the impression that they are acting promptly and efficiently, even if the truth is that they are not.

Three New Cases on Consent
R. v B, R. v Bree and R. v Jheeta
CLJ 2007, 66(3) 490–493

In London, they say – or said before "Red Ken" – that you wait for ever for a bus, and then along come three at once. As with buses, so occasionally with cases. The Court of Appeal has recently delivered not one but three important judgments on the meaning of consent to sexual acts: *B* [2006] EWCA Crim 2945, [2007] 1 W.L.R. 1567; *Bree* [2007] EWCA Crim 256, [2008] QB 131; and *Jheeta* [2007] EWCA Crim 1699.

In *Bree* the issue was capacity to consent, the prosecution case being that D had intercourse with V when she was drunk. Section 75(2)(d) of the Sexual Offences Act (SOA) 2003 creates an "evidential presumption" that the complainant did not consent where he or she "was asleep or otherwise unconscious at the time of the relevant act". But what about the situation where, as in the case in hand, the woman was extremely drunk, though conscious and aware of what was happening? In a case in Swansea in 2005, the prosecution had offered no further evidence when the complainant admitted she had been so drunk as to be unable to remember afterwards whether she had consented or not. The publicity this case aroused had led to the popular belief that, if a man has intercourse with a drunken woman who is not actually unconscious, he cannot in law be prosecuted. But this, said the Court of Appeal in *Bree*, is wrong. The indelicate saying "drunken consent is still consent" is broadly true: but not entirely so. Section 74 of the SOA 2003, which defines consent, provides that "... a person consents if he agrees by choice, and has the freedom and capacity to make that choice". The traveller on the road to alcoholic oblivion, the judges said, may reach the point where that "freedom and capacity" is lost. And in order to dispel the false impression that the Swansea case had created, they added, significantly: "We should perhaps underline that, as a matter of practical reality, capacity to consent may evaporate well before a complainant becomes unconscious."

In *B* and *Jheeta*, the issue was when the apparent consent of someone who does have capacity is vitiated.

As every lawyer knows, consent in any legal context may in principle be vitiated by force, fraud or mistake. But what this means in concrete terms varies from one legal situation to another. In the case of sexual acts, the rule at common law was that mistake as to the identity of the other person vitiated consent; but mistake about other matters only did so if the complainant failed to appreciate the sexual nature of the act: i.e., that the other party's purpose was to gratify his sexual desires. So V's consent to D's intimately touching her was vitiated by her mistaken belief that he was carrying out a medical examination (*Tabassum* [2000] 2 Cr.App.R. 328); but not by her mistaken belief, fraudulently induced by D, that he meant to pay her for her sexual services (*Linekar* [1995] 2 Cr.App.R. 49).

Under the SOA 2003 there is now a statutory test. By section 76 "it is to be conclusively presumed" that the complainant did not consent to a sexual act where

(2)... (a) the defendant intentionally deceived the complainant as to the nature or purpose of the relevant act; [or]

(b) the defendant intentionally induced the complainant to consent to the relevant act by impersonating a person known personally to the complainant.

This test was widely assumed to codify the position as it was at common law; and that is how the Court of Appeal has now interpreted it.

In *B*, C alleged that D had raped her using force, but D claimed that she had consented. D was HIV positive; and so the judge directed the jury that, if they were not convinced that D had forced C to have sex with him, they could still convict him on the basis that her apparent consent was vitiated because, had she known of his medical condition, she would not have had unprotected sex with him. The Court of Appeal accepted that, had D infected her, he might have been guilty of maliciously inflicting grievous bodily harm under section 20 of the Offences Against the Person Act 1861, because C had not consented to the risk of infection. But in the light of the wording of section 76(2)(a) of the SOA, C's ignorance of the risk of infection did not vitiate her consent to the sexual act. So D's conviction was quashed, and a retrial ordered.

In *Jheeta*, D, afraid that his relationship with C was about to end, carried out a bizarre and complicated fraud. In the course of this he sent C messages which purported to come from the police, telling her that he was suicidal, and warning her that in order to prevent him killing himself she must continue to have sex with him: and that if she refused, she would be fined. Astonishingly she was taken in, and on this basis unwillingly allowed their sexual relationship to continue. When the truth came out, D was prosecuted; and on legal advice that his fraud and her mistake had vitiated her consent, he pled guilty, inter alia, to rape contrary to the SOA 2003. The Court of Appeal said that, in the light of section 76(2)(a), this advice was incorrect. However, the court felt able to uphold the rape convictions, on the basis that, on D's own admission to the police, there had been at least some occasions "on which the complainant was not truly consenting".

On both *B* and *Jheeta* there is much to say, but room here for brief comments only.

The decision in *B*, it is suggested, is correct. As a matter of policy, it is debatable whether someone who merely exposes an unknowing sexual partner to the risk of serious infection should be guilty of a criminal offence. But if he should, the need for "fair labelling" suggests that his offence should not be rape. It is one thing to say that D is guilty of recklessly infecting his partner, where his partner was ignorant of the risk of infection. It is quite another thing to say that her ignorance of this risk turns the act of consensual sex into a rape – even where the risk did not materialise and she escaped infection. If criminal liability is really needed here, Parliament should create a special offence of reckless endangerment; and unlike rape, it should not carry imprisonment for life.

The decision in *Jheeta*, I believe, is also correct in its understanding of when consent to sexual acts is vitiated by fraud or by mistake. But unlike B, the gap in the law that it reveals is glaring and obvious. It is most reprehensible to procure a sexual act by fraud, whether or not the fraud vitiates consent and turns the act into a rape; just as it is most reprehensible to obtain property by false pretences, whether or not the obtaining also constitutes a theft. With that in mind, section 3 of the SOA 1956 intelligently provided a specific offence of procuring a woman to have intercourse by false pretences: of which Jheeta was convicted, incidentally, in respect of what he had done while the old Act was still in force. But the new Act, though hitting with the heaviest of hands all forms of sexual naughtiness, from teenage petting, via "homosexual incest" to necrophilia, fails to deal with this type of misbehaviour. Its framers in the Home Office apparently thought that this was covered by the new offence in section 4 of "causing a person to engage in sexual activity without consent"; which shows, alas, how little they understood about consent, or fraud, or mistake – or indeed any other basic concept of the criminal law.[23]

---

[23] For further discussion of this point, see J.R. Spencer "Sex by Deception", [2013] 9 *Archbold Review*, 6–9.

Curbing Speed and Limiting the Right of Silence
O'Halloran and Francis v United Kingdom
CLJ 2007, 66(3) 531–533

In Agrigento, on the southern coast of Sicily, there stand the ruins of a row of huge Greek temples, which are said to be bigger than any ever built in Greece. The same tendency to outsize growth is sometimes found in other forms of cultural transplant too, including legal ones. The right to silence, when first consecrated as a human right at Strasbourg, was bigger than it had ever been in its native territory, the common law, and threatened for a time to dominate the local legal landscape. Later decisions of the ECtHR have cut it down to size: most recently *O'Halloran and Francis v United Kingdom* (2008) E.H.R.R. 21, which is the subject of this note.

In its first case on the topic, *Funke v France* (1993) 16 E.H.R.R. 297, the ECtHR held that the right of silence was infringed (and Article 6 of the Convention, which impliedly protects it, broken) by a French law requiring persons suspected of exchange control offences to produce their bank statements to the investigators on request. In the common law world, whence the right to silence originated, the right of silence was thought to be concerned with protecting suspects against compulsory interrogations, not against official orders to produce specific documents, which (as in England, with its "production orders") are a common feature of criminal procedure. The consternation *Funke* caused died down a little when, in *Saunders v UK* (1997) 23 E.H.R.R. 313, the ECtHR then declared that

> The right not to incriminate oneself is primarily concerned.., with respecting the will of an accused person to remain silent ... it does not extend to the use in criminal proceedings of material which may be obtained from the accused through the use of compulsory powers...
> [69]

In the common law world it was also generally assumed that the right to silence was not infringed by laws which allow the authorities to require the citizen to give them, if requested, a specific piece of information which might incriminate him. But in *Heaney and*

McGuiness v Ireland (2001) E.H.R.R. 264 the ECtHR held that legislation of this sort infringed the right to silence too: in this case, an Irish statute which, in the context of terrorist investigations, required citizens to give the authorities, if requested, an account of their movements at a given time. In answer to the argument that terrorism poses an extreme threat to the security or the state, and that the state can properly require some degree of co-operation from its citizens in fighting it, the Court said:

> ... the security and public order concerns relied on by the government cannot justify a provision which extinguishes the very essence of the applicant's rights to silence and against self-incrimination." [58]

This decision appeared, by implication, to pronounce anathema on section 172 of the Road Traffic Act (RTA) 1988, which requires the keeper of a motor vehicle whose driver is suspected of an offence to tell the police, if requested, who was driving it at the given time. The UK courts, however, refused to accept this. Led by Lord Bingham in *Brown v Stott* [2003] 1 A.C. 681 they accepted that the broader interests of the community in general, and the need to maintain road safety in particular, could justify a limited infringement of the right to silence of this sort.

This was the legal background against which O'Halloran and Francis, supported by Liberty, sought to challenge in Strasbourg their convictions from the English courts. In each case, a car belonging to the applicant had been snapped by a roadside camera when speeding. O'Halloran, with reluctance, had complied with section 172 by telling the police that he was driving, and on this information had been convicted of exceeding the speed limit (by 29 miles an hour). And Francis, who had refused to give the information, relying on his right to silence, had been convicted and fined £750 for his refusal.

Their applications were rejected by the Grand Chamber, by a majority of 15 votes to 2. In a lengthy judgment, in which the majority did its best to pick its way across the apparently impenetrable minefield laid by the Court's earlier uncompromising dicta and decisions, the Court decided (in effect) that Lord Bingham in *Brown v Stott* had got it right. The right to remain silent, and the right not to incriminate oneself, it said, are not absolute, and certain derogations from them are permissible without infringing Article 6 of the Convention. The derogation imposed by section 172 of the RTA was justified for two reasons. The first was its limited context. The duty to provide information it imposes was created as part of a scheme for regulating an activity which for citizens is optional. Because motor cars are potentially dangerous, the state is justified in making laws to regulate their use; and "[t]hose who choose to keep and drive motor cars can be taken to have accepted certain responsibilities and obligations as part of the regulatory regime relating to motor vehicles." [57] Secondly, there was the "limited nature of the inquiry". To require a suspect to engage in a compulsory interview with the police is one thing; but to require him to provide a single, specific piece of information is another. [58]

The practical importance of this decision is obvious, and needs no further explanation.

But an interesting footnote to the decision concerns one of the applicants, Mr. Idris Francis, who is a well-known figure. When not campaigning, with the vigour of Peter Simple's mythical J. Bonnington Jagworth, against speed cameras – which he and his supporters claim to make the roads more dangerous – he campaigns with equal verve against "the European super-state". This decision, one imagines, is unlikely to change his views on either subject.

Tort Law Bows to the Human Rights Act
Van Colle v Chief Constable of Hertfordshire Police
2008 CLJ, 67(1) 15–17

Heineken, according to its advertisers, refreshes the parts that other beers cannot reach; and from the recent Court of Appeal decision in *Van Colle v Chief Constable of Hertfordshire Police* [2007] EWCA Civ 325, [2007] 1 W.L.R. 1821, it looks as if sections 6 to 8 of the Human Rights Act 1998, which impose civil liability on public bodies that fail to respect "Convention Rights", may prove to be the legal equivalent.

Giles Van Colle was murdered by a man at whose trial for theft he was the principal witness, in order to stop him giving evidence. The murderer, an Iranian criminal called Ali Amelzadeh and known to the police to be a "nasty piece of work", had earlier threatened Giles, tried to bribe other witnesses, and also organised mafia-style arson attacks against their property. Giles, very frightened, had reported the threats to the detective in charge of the case: who, in the style of *Private Eye's* fictitious Neasden Police Log, did nothing. For this failure he was eventually disciplined – but it seems that he was not the only one at fault. Though doubtless communicated upwards to the Home Office, the force's official policy statement on taking witness intimidation seriously had not been communicated downwards to its officers, and the detective was unaware of it. Had the police been even half efficient, Amelzadeh would have been in prison pending trial and in no position to commit a murder.

Outraged, Giles's family sought redress against the police. In tort their claim would have been extremely difficult because a long line of authority, going back to *Hill v Chief Constable of West Yorkshire* [1989] A.C. 53, holds that on grounds of public policy the police are not liable in tort for negligently failing to stop crimes. So they based their claim on section 6 of the Human Rights Act, which makes it unlawful for a public authority to "act in a way which is incompatible with a Convention right", and section 8, which empowers the courts to award damages against them if they do. The "Convention right" on which they based their claim was the right to life, guaranteed by Article 2(1) of the ECHR, which provides that "Everyone's right to life shall be protected by law. No one shall be deprived of his life intentionally save in execution of a sentence of a court following his conviction of a crime for which this penalty is provided by law."

When considering whether a claimant's "Convention rights" were broken, section 2 of the Human Rights Act requires our courts to read the Convention as interpreted by the court at Strasbourg. A body of Strasbourg case-law (a large slice of which consists, alas, of cases brought successfully against the UK) affirms that Article 2 is infringed not only where agents of the state kill its citizens improperly, but also where they fail to take reasonable steps to protect them against being killed by others. In *Osman v UK* (1998) 29 E.H.R.R. [116] the Strasbourg court had said that Article 2 would be broken in this way where

> ... the authorities knew or ought to have known at the time of the existence of a real and immediate risk to life of an identified individual or individuals from the criminal acts of a third party and ... they failed to take measures within the scope of their powers which, judged reasonably, might have been expected to avoid that risk.

At trial, the first issue was whether the failure by the police to protect Giles was bad enough to satisfy this test, and if so, the second was whether an award of damages was "necessary to afford just satisfaction" – which by section 8 of the Human Rights Act is the precondition for a damages award. On both points the claimants resoundingly succeeded, both at trial and on appeal.

In concluding that a damages award was necessary, and in determining its size, the Court of Appeal examined a series of similar cases where the Strasbourg court had made awards in similar situations. But in upholding the award the Court of Appeal did reduce the size of it: from £50,000 (£15,000 to the deceased's estate, and £17,500 to each of his parents) at first instance, to £25,000 (£10,000 to the estate and £7,500 to each parent). These sums, it should be noted, were not calculated according to the rules applicable in tort. As Giles was a single man without dependants, in tort his estate could have claimed funeral expenses only.

As analysed by the Court of Appeal in its long and careful judgment, the Strasbourg case-law made the result virtually inevitable; and so the Appeal Committee of the House of Lords thought too, presumably, when – as reported in [2007] 1 W.L.R. 2021 – it refused leave to appeal.[24] But the case raises so many important issues that it seems a pity that they will not be considered further by the highest court. At the most basic level, the decision has important financial consequences for the police; a number of law-suits, the Court of Appeal told us, were waiting on its outcome. At a theoretical level, it means that an important House of Lords decision, though not formally overruled, has for most practical

---

[24] But see next note.

purposes been gutted. In future, the issue in this sort of case will be whether the police could reasonably have stopped the crime, not whether they can be sued for failure if they could; but as the basis of the decision was Article 2 of the Convention and the right to life, it remains to be seen what the courts will do when the crime not prevented is something other than a homicide – an attempted murder, for example, or a knee-capping, or kidnapping for which a huge ransom is paid and spirited away to South America.

The case also raises interesting issues of distributive justice. Put simply, the basis of the claim here is that the state has a duty to protect the lives of its citizens, and having failed, must pay damages as "just satisfaction" for its failure. But many years ago, it seems to have been similar reasoning (though the Government denied it) which led to the creation of what is currently called the Criminal Injuries Compensation Authority, by which the state pays automatic compensation to the victims of crimes of violence (including the relatives of murder victims). The incompetence of the police in this case was breath-taking: but as the state already pays compensation for such failures from another pocket of the public purse, it is also a little surprising that money is payable from this pocket too.

Suing the Police for Negligence: Orthodoxy Restored
Ashley v Chief Constable of Sussex
Van Colle v Chief Constable of Hertfordshire
CLJ 2009, 68(1) 25–27

Contrary to what was stated in the Weekly Law Reports, and reflected in an earlier case-note on the Court of Appeal Decision ([2008] C.L.J. 15 above p. 190), the defendant in *Van Colle v Chief Constable of Hertfordshire Police* was given leave to appeal; and last July the House of Lords reversed the decisions of the courts below, acquitting the police of liability. In the process they reinserted in the bottle the genie that the Court of Appeal had seemingly allowed to escape from it, and pushed the cork down firmly on top of him as well: see [2008] UKHL 50, [2009] 1 A.C. 225.

To remind us, this was the case in which a criminal first tried to intimidate the key prosecution witness by a series of mafia-style threats and attacks, and when these tactics failed, silenced him for ever with a bullet. Outraged by what they saw as the culpable failure of the Hertfordshire police to protect their son, the witness's bereaved parents sued the Chief Constable of Hertfordshire for damages under sections 6 and 7 of the Human Rights Act 1998, claiming that the negligence of the police had violated their son's rights under Article 2 of the European Convention on Human Rights (the right to life). At first instance and in the Court of Appeal their claim succeeded: so demonstrating, apparently, that the Human Rights Act might provide a remedy in a situation where, 20 years ago, courts had ruled out claims based on the tort of negligence on grounds of public policy.

In reversing the Court of Appeal decision the House of Lords accepted – as it had to, in the light of the Strasbourg case-law – that the negligent failure of the police to protect its citizens against dangerous criminals can in principle result in the State being in breach of its obligations under Article 2 and hence liable to compensate their bereaved relatives. Indeed, in *Osman v UK* (1998) 29 E.H.R.R. the Strasbourg Court had said that this obligation arises where

> …the authorities knew or ought to have known at the time of the existence of a real and immediate risk to the life of an identified individual or individuals from the criminal acts of a third party and that they failed to take measures within the scope of their powers which, judged reasonably, might have been expected to avoid that risk.

To the untutored eye, this test looks much like the sort of test the English courts would apply in deciding if the police were negligent, assuming liability in the tort of negligence existed; and as a police disciplinary panel had found that the detective in charge of the case in which Van Colle junior was the key witness had "failed to perform his duties conscientiously and diligently", one might also have thought – as the trial judge and the Court of Appeal had thought – that in this case the Van Colle parents were bound to win. But the House of Lords thought otherwise. By implication, though without saying so expressly, they interpreted the *Osman* test as being considerably more stringent than one of simple negligence; and having done so, then decided that the various bungles committed by the Hertfordshire police did not put them on the wrong side of it. And so, despite having won at first instance and before a unanimous Court of Appeal, in the end the Van Colle parents lost.

This outcome prompts two thoughts. The first is how different the same story can sound when different people tell it. As recounted by the Court of Appeal the facts of the *Van Colle* case shrieked negligence, but as reinterpreted by the House of Lords, the mistakes of the police emerge as relatively minor. (Lord Bingham's speech, it must be said, reminds one of the ancient joke: "Yes, I did have a love-child once, but it was only a very small one!") The second thought is that if a Human Rights Act claim failed in the *Van Colle* case, such claims are likely to fail in most other cases too.

The House of Lords heard the *Van Colle* case together with a defence appeal in *Smith v Chief Constable of Sussex* [2008] EWCA Civ 29 ([2008] C.L.J. 239). In this case, the facts of which were rather similar, the victim, who survived, had sued the police not for damages under the Human Rights Act but in the tort of negligence. His claim was initially struck out as showing no cause of action, but the Court of Appeal, with an approving nod towards their earlier decision in the *Van Colle* case, had reinstated it. In their view, *Hill v Chief Constable of Sussex* [1989] A.C. 53 and the rest of the well-known case-law that rules out negligence claims in cases of this type on grounds of public policy now fell to be reinterpreted in the light of the Human Rights Act. But this line of reasoning the House of Lords, by a majority, rejected. The policy grounds identified in those cases, said the majority, remain valid; and so the Court of Appeal decision in *Smith v Chief Constable of Sussex* fell to be reversed as well.

As victims of crimes of violence already receive payment from the public purse via the Criminal Injuries Compensation Commission the outcome in these two cases may be justified in terms of "distributional justice". But is it for money that people like the Van Colles sue the police in cases of this type? Their real motive, one suspects, is the desire for a proper investigation into what went wrong, with the possibility of a public condemnation at the end. That the law of tort in this area fulfils a "vindicatory function" was recently affirmed by the House of Lords in *Ashley v Chief Constable of Sussex* [2008] UKHL 25, [2008] 2 A.C. 962, where it held that the relatives of man whom the police had shot in mistake for a dangerous criminal could sue them on behalf of his estate for damages in the tort of battery, even though the police were prepared to settle the family's claim for financial loss out of court. The tension between that decision and the present one is obvious.

Criminal Liability for Accidental Death: Back to the Middle Ages?
R. v Chargot Ltd. (t/a Contract Services)
CLJ 2009, 68(2) 263–265

From time to time the courts decide important cases without noticing their broader implications, and thereby set the law off in the wrong direction. Such a case, I fear, is *R. v Chargot Ltd. and others* [2008] UKHL 73, [2009] 1 W.L.R. 1.

This arose from a fatal accident at a construction site, in which the driver of a dump-truck managed to tip it over and bury himself under the load of soil that it was carrying. This resulted in the prosecution of three persons – two legal and one natural – for offences under the Health and Safety at Work Act 1974. D1, the driver's employer, was prosecuted for failure to perform its duty under section 2, which is "to ensure, so far as is reasonably practicable, the health, safety and welfare at work" of his employees. D2, the contractor in charge of the site, was prosecuted for failure to perform its duty under section 3, which is "to conduct his undertaking in such a way as to ensure, so far as reasonably practicable, that persons not in his employment who may be affected thereby are not thereby exposed to risks to their health and safety". And D3, a director of D2, was prosecuted under section 37, which says that where a legal person commits an offence against the Act, a director is guilty too if it was committed with his "consent or connivance", or was attributable to his "neglect". All three defendants were convicted, and all three appealed.

The question for the House of Lords was this: what exactly does the prosecution have to prove in order to establish, in a case like this, that defendants such as these are criminally liable?

According to the prosecution, the answer to this question should be "very little". The mere fact of an accident at work raises a presumption that the employer has failed to comply with his duties under sections 2 and 3 of the Act, and he is therefore guilty unless the accident was one that it was not "reasonably practicable" for him to prevent; and because section 40 then says that "it is for the accused to prove" that something was "not reasonably practicable", on this issue it is the prosecution and not the defendant who gets the benefit of the doubt. So in other words, wherever an industrial accident occurs the employer is guilty unless he can talk his way out of it.

The defence, of course, did not accept this. According to them, the prosecutor in such a case bears an initial burden of identifying, in concrete terms, something that the employer did when he should not have done, or failed to do when he should. As the prosecutor in the present case had not put forward any explanation as to how the accident was caused by the negligent behaviour of any of the defendants, they should all have been acquitted. Insofar as section 40 comes into the picture, they said, this only operates to impose on the defendant an *evidential* burden, and does not deprive him of the benefit of the doubt. In other words, if defendants in this type of case are legally obliged to show they took due care, this only means they must produce an explanation for the accident that is consistent with due care: which, in order to secure a conviction, the prosecution must then demolish.

In a speech delivered by Lord Hope, in which his colleagues all concurred, the House of Lords accepted the prosecutor's arguments in their entirety. "In cases such as the present, where a person sustains injury at work, the facts will speak for themselves. Prima facie, his employer, or the person by whose undertaking he was liable to be affected, has failed to ensure his health and safety. Otherwise there would have been no accident." In the light of the purpose of the Act, which Lord Hope identified as "both social and economic", section 40 must be interpreted as requiring the defendant to prove his innocence. And on the facts D3, the director, was rightly convicted too, because when a company is guilty of an offence under the Act "it will be a relatively short step for the inference to be drawn that there was connivance or neglect on [a director's] part if the circumstances under the risk arose were under the direction or control of the officer." *Res ipsa loquitur* .

All of this would have made perfect sense if the context had been a civil claim, brought by the victim of the accident or his family, in search of compensation. Many well-known civil cases, like *Grant v Australian Knitting* Mills [1936] A.C. 85 – the case of the irritant underpants – proceed according to just this type of reasoning. But is it just to apply it in a criminal case?

Criminal liability is not about providing compensation for the innocent: it is about punishing the guilty. The aim of criminal proceedings, in other words, is to inflict a hurt upon someone who is perceived to have done wrong. And this it does. A prosecution in the criminal courts, particularly in the Crown Court as in this case, is stressful and expensive; and the resulting conviction, if it happens, is – and is intended to be – stigmatic and potentially painful. Two of the defendants in the present case, including the director, were fined £75,000, and the director was also ordered to pay £103,000 in costs. And for good measure, Parliament has just added to the potential pain of a conviction for these offences by making them all punishable with imprisonment as well as fines: a fact which Lord Hope mentioned in his speech, but only to say that it did not cause him to alter his conclusions.

The practical effect of this decision is to turn an important group of offences of negligent behaviour into offences of "situational liability". What is punished is no longer negligent conduct in the running of your business, but the fact of being an employer or director in an organisation where an industrial accident has happened; in which situation, should you find yourself, you are now liable to two years' imprisonment as well as massive fines, unless you can identify an innocent explanation and persuade the court that it is probably the truth.

All this is no doubt deeply satisfying to the tabloid cast of mind, which believes that for every accident there is Somebody To Blame, who must be identified and punished, preferably by putting him in prison. But it takes our criminal law back to the harsh days of the early common law, when criminal liability for causing death was strict, and (as Pollock and Maitland put it) "The man who commits homicide by misadventure or in self-defence deserves but needs a pardon."

Assisted Suicide and the Discretion to Prosecute
R. (Purdy) v *Director of Public Prosecutions*
CLJ 2009, 68(3) 493–495

The decision of the judicial House of Lords in *R. (Purdy)* v *Director of Public Prosecutions* [2009] UKHL 45, [2010] 1 A.C. 345 was its last. Fittingly, perhaps, it was also one of its most sensational: the case where Ms Debbie Purdy, who is slowly dying from motor neurone disease, persuaded the House of Lords to tell the DPP to publish a policy-statement saying when he will and will not prosecute those who help others to travel to Switzerland for the purpose of assisted suicide.

The first issue in the case was whether the conduct in question is a crime at all. On this three views are possible. The first is that the offence of complicity in suicide created by the Suicide Act 1961 only applies to suicides in England and Wales, and helping people to commit suicide abroad is therefore legal. The second is that it applies where the *act of assisting or encouraging* takes place in England and Wales, irrespective of where the suicide occurs. The third is that this behaviour constitutes not the offence under the Suicide Act, but complicity in murder at common law, because this would have been the situation before the 1961, when suicide was treated as "self-murder", the abrogation of that rule only operates within England and Wales and murders by British citizens are triable in England, even when carried out abroad.

The House rejected the first analysis, but then failed to make up its collective mind between the second and the third. Reading between the lines, it may have trailed the possibility of liability for murder to show how urgently further legislation in this area is needed. But the loose end it left untied is important, because murder prosecutions, unlike those for complicity in suicide, do not require the DPP's consent; and if the third analysis is right, a "right to life" enthusiast could bring a private prosecution in this sort of case, even if the DPP decided not to proceed.

Assuming the conduct in question is a crime, Ms Purdy's argument that the DPP must issue a "prosecution policy" was as follows. (1) Decisions about whether and when to commit suicide engage the decision-maker's right to "respect for his private and family life", which is protected by Article 8(1) of the European Convention. (2) This right may be interfered with only for the purposes enumerated in Article 8(2), and even then, only when the interference is "in accordance with the law". (3) The present arrangements in England and Wales, whereby assisted suicide is in theory prohibited but in practice widely tolerated by the authorities, do not qualify as an interference "in accordance with the law". (4) To cure this deficiency the DPP must therefore publish guidelines as to when assisted suicide will be prosecuted, and when not.

Ms Purdy's case had fallen at the first hurdle in the courts below, because these were bound by the earlier ruling of the House of Lords in *R. (Pretty)* v *DPP* [2001] UKHL 62, [2002] A.C. 800 that decisions about when to die do not engage the decision-maker's rights under Article 8. However, the Strasbourg Court had later held that Article 8 is indeed engaged: *Pretty* v *UK* (2002) 35 E.H.R.R. 1 – albeit also saying that a legal ban on assisted suicide was potentially justified as necessary "for the protection of the rights of others", a condition for permissible infringements with the right to private life that is mentioned in Article 8(2). In Ms Purdy's case the House accepted correction from the Strasbourg Court and, reversing its earlier stance in *Pretty*, held that Article 8 is indeed engaged.

Naturally, the DPP's response to the second step in Ms Purdy's argument was that the Suicide Act – a statute which explicitly forbids assisted suicide – constitutes a "law" for the purposes of

Article 8, even if it is not invariably enforced. And, he added, even if a criminal statute does not constitute a "law" where the offence is subject to a discretion to prosecute that is open-ended, the discretion is not open-ended here: because in England and Wales the discretion to prosecute is regulated by the official CPS Code, a public document which sets out – admittedly at a high level of abstraction and without specific reference to this offence – the principles on which the discretion is exercised. But the House of Lords rejected this response. A statute that says "it is a criminal offence to do X", coupled with an unstated policy that it is not to be prosecuted unless certain extra factors are present too, is not, their Lordships said, a "law" for the purposes of Article 8(2). And so to put the matter right, the DPP must "promulgate an offence-specific policy identifying the facts and circumstances which he will take into account in deciding, in a case such as that which Ms Purdy's case exemplifies, whether or not to consent to a prosecution under section 2(1) of the 1961 Act".

The main significance of this case is that it marks a step along the road towards making assisted suicide legal – a destination which many people, including the writer of this note, believe to be desirable. But the reasoning it contains has wider implications for the criminal law that are disquieting.

In the first place, the argument that succeeded in this case is equally applicable to other criminal offences in which Article 8 is also engaged; and indeed to offences that engage Articles 9, 10 and 11 as well, because these too specify that any interference with the rights that they protect must be "in accordance with the law". Complicity in suicide could be the first of many broad but rarely-prosecuted offences which the DPP must cut down to size by issuing an "offence-specific" prosecution policy.

But behind this lies a second and more basic issue. Is it really compatible with the rule of law that, when an Act of Parliament makes a certain form of behaviour a criminal offence, the DPP should in effect decriminalise it, in whole or in part, by saying when it will and will not be prosecuted? The orthodox answer, forcibly expressed by the Court of Appeal in the judgment which the House of Lords reversed, is "no": once Parliament has created an offence, only Parliament has the authority to redraw its boundaries so that it catches fewer people in its net. For any other organ of the State to attempt to do so is to infringe the first rule of the constitution, which is the supremacy of Parliament.

That the highest court should rebel against the orthodox view is, in a sense, quite understandable. In recent years Parliament, driven by the executive, has got into the habit of expanding criminal liability in all directions with little or no thought, and almost completely out of the habit of contracting it. And when authority is over-used like this, respect for it is dented. As the revolutionaries said about the authority of the French ruling classes before 1789: "*Vous l'avez perdu en abusant.*"

Legislate in Haste, Repent in Leisure
Adorian v Metropolitan Police Commissioner
CLJ 2010, 69(1) 19–21

An unhappy practice of our present Government is to reform the law in demagogic dialogue with the tabloids. In response to Monday's "scandal" comes Tuesday's ministerial "pledge", and on Wednesday this is followed by an instant Bill, rushed through Parliament with inadequate debate. That legislation made like this is often unsatisfactory should need no demonstration. If it does, however, *Adorian v Metropolitan Police Commissioner* [2009] EWCA Civ 18, [2009] 1 W.L.R. 1859 provides it.

When the Norfolk farmer Tony Martin was jailed for shooting down two fleeing burglars, killing one and injuring the other, he was canonised by sections of the popular press, which thought that he deserved not prison but a medal. When later it emerged that the surviving burglar, on his own release from gaol, planned to sue the farmer for damages, tabloid fury was redoubled – not abating even when the burglar decided, on reflection, to drop his claim. Responding to pressure from the Conservatives – responding in their turn to pressure from the media – the Government promptly added to their current by-now-annual Bill to "rebalance" criminal justice a new clause designed to make law-suits of this type more difficult.

In due (or undue!) course, this became law as section 329 of the Criminal Justice Act 2003. In 455 words of convoluted legislative prose, this provides that where a claimant brings an action for trespass to the person, and "the claimant has been convicted of an imprisonable offence ... committed on the same occasion as that on which the act is alleged to have been done", his action shall not proceed without judicial leave. It then provides that leave shall be given only in one or other of two situations: first, where there is evidence suggesting that the defendant did not believe his act of injuring the claimant was necessary to stop the crime or catch the criminal; or alternatively, where there is evidence suggesting that "the defendant's act was grossly disproportionate". And finally, it provides that if the claim proceeds, the defendant wins if it is shown at trial that, when he acted, he believed honestly – if unreasonably – that what he did was necessary; unless his act was "grossly disproportionate".

Though intended to protect householders, section 329 applies no less to the police. And it is the police, it seems, and not the disciples of "St. Tony", who are now using it. It has been regularly invoked by the police to defeat claims by convicted persons who allege that, in the early stages of proceedings that led to their conviction, truncheon-happy constables illegally detained them, strip-searched them, or beat them up to make them show respect. A case of this type was *Adorian v Metropolitan Police Commissioner*. And it is in Sedley L.J.'s judgment in that case that this disquieting development is revealed.

In August 2004 Adorian was arrested for disorderly behaviour and then charged with obstructing the police, an offence for which he ultimately received a conditional discharge. From the police station where he was taken on arrest he was hastily removed to hospital, where he was found to be suffering from multiple fractures to his leg and hip: injuries the orthopaedic surgeon called "appalling". He complained about mistreatment to the Independent Police Complaints Authority: in whose bureaucracy, three years later, his complaint was still enmired. So on the eve of the third anniversary of the incident, on which his claim became time-barred, he instituted a civil claim against the Metropolitan Police. In answer, the Commissioner pleaded section 329. First, he said, there was here "no evidence" that the force used by his officers arresting Adorian was "grossly disproportionate". Secondly, and more fundamentally, he said that even if there was, the requirement for prior leave was mandatory, not directory, and so its absence could not be cured by the court giving retrospective leave. In such a situation, proceedings started without leave are simply null and void. In law, all this meant that Adorian had failed to institute proceedings within the limitation period, and his claim was now time-barred.

These arguments the Court of Appeal resoundingly rejected. Of grossly disproportionate force, they said, there was ample evidence before them in the papers in the case: such evidence could be circumstantial, and need not be direct. And dealing with the second and more crucial point, they held, after a long and careful examination of the case-law on similar provisions, that section 329 is merely directory. Hence where (as here) a claimant has failed to get leave ahead of issuing a claim, a court can grant it retrospectively.

In reaching this conclusion, the Court of Appeal was mainly motivated by the inconvenience and injustice that, in its view, would result from interpreting the leave requirement in section 329 as imposing a total bar. But in construing it narrowly, the Court was also influenced by the fact that, as an unintended consequence of the way the provision has been drafted, its main beneficiaries are not householders but the police. As Sedley L.J. put it:

> In place of the principle painstakingly established in the course of two centuries and more, and fundamental to the civil rights enjoyed by the people of this country – that an arrest must be objectively justified and that no more force may be used in effecting it than is reasonably necessary – the section gives immunity from civil suits, not confined to those involving personal injury, to constables who make arrests on entirely unreasonable grounds, and accords them impunity for all but grossly unreasonable force in doing so.

Since 1965 there has existed in this country the Law Commission; a body which, unlike headline-hungry politicians, thinks calmly about thorny legal issues, and consults with those who understand them, before formulating a response. It was to the Law Commission that the Government should have referred the problem to which it produced section 329, like a rabbit from a hat, as an instant answer. And it is to the Law Commission that the Government now should refer the mess it has, all too predictably, created.

Fair Trials and the European Arrest Warrant
Symeou v *Public Prosecutor's Office, Patras*
CLJ 2010, 69(2) 225–228

In July 2007 a fight broke out among a group of British youths at a night club in a Greek resort when one of them urinated on the floor. The fight had fatal consequences for one of them, who fell and struck his head. Eleven months later, long after the survivors had gone home, the Greek prosecutor issued a European Arrest Warrant to retrieve Andrew Symeou, whom he accused of the Greek equivalent of involuntary manslaughter.

Symeou resisted surrender, claiming that he had been "fitted up". The evidence against him, he said, consisted of false statements beaten out of his fellow Britons by the Greek police: an allegation which the young men concerned confirmed. When, despite this, the judge at Westminster Magistrates' Court ordered his surrender, Symeou appealed, inviting the Divisional Court to halt the extradition proceedings as "an abuse of process", or alternatively, on the ground that extraditing him to Greece to face proceedings based on tainted evidence would breach his right to a "fair trial" under Article 6 of the European Convention on Human Rights. These arguments the Divisional Court rejected. In the context of extradition, it said, the "abuse of process" argument was in principle available, but only if there was bad faith by the Greek prosecutor, rather than antecedent misbehaviour by the Greek police. And, it said, extraditing him to Greece would not infringe Symeou's rights under Article 6 of the Convention unless he could show that his allegations of a "fit up" were something the Greek courts would refuse to investigate or act upon, which he could not. The gist of the judgment, put colloquially, is that the case against a wanted person may smell bad; but if it does, that is a matter for the courts of the requesting State to worry about when he gets there: *Symeou v Public Prosecutor's Office, Patras* [2009] EWHC 897, [2009] 1 W.L.R. 2384. Having failed to secure leave to appeal further, off to Greece he went. And there, as this note is written, he is currently in gaol awaiting trial.[25]

The decision has produced a barrage of criticism. From the section of the British press that habitually complains that our own legal system is unduly soft towards defendants, the main theme – paradoxically – is the inherent injustice of handing one of our people over to other criminal justice systems which, unlike ours, fails to respect defendants' human rights. For Europhobes, the villain of the piece is said to be the European Arrest Warrant, which is said to mean that prosecutors from continental Europe no longer have to persuade our courts, by means of legally admissible evidence, that the wanted person is truly guilty before they bundle him off to face a form of justice which, by definition, is inferior to our own.

In saying this, the Eurosceptic press has (as usual) got hold of the wrong end of the legal stick. Even in its most protective past, UK extradition law did not require a foreign prosecutor to demonstrate before a British court the wanted person's guilt. He only had to show a "prima facie case", which here clearly existed against Symeou, irrespective of how the evidence against him had been obtained. And even the exiguous requirement of a prima facie case had been abolished over 20 years ago as regards most extradition requests emanating from within Europe, by section 9 of the Extradition Act of 1989. So what exactly has the European Arrest Warrant – implemented here by Part I of the Extradition Act 2003 – done to change things?

---

[25] He was eventually acquitted: but only after a two-year delay, during much of which he had been held, quite needlessly, in prison. If not an indictment of European Arrest Warrants, it is certainly an indictment of the quality of Greek criminal justice, at least in the pre-trial phase.

The key change is that, under the new law, extradition within Europe is now entirely judicial. Previously, after our courts had given the green light to the request, the Home Secretary had to "sign it off". So the wanted person who claimed that it was "all a fix" could ask the Home Secretary to refuse permission, and if he would not listen, he could attack the Home Secretary's refusal in the courts by a series of manœuvres which, if played with skill, could delay his removal for many years (and, incidentally, cost the taxpayer a vast amount of money). It was this situation that the European Arrest Warrant was designed to end, as regards extradition within Europe. And the change was made on the assumption that the EU Member States are all democratic countries which take their obligations under the European Convention on Human Rights seriously. So if, as is inevitable, mistakes are made, the courts of the requesting State can be expected to correct them; and the courts of the requested state are not the proper place for this to be done.

Regrettably, reality is not always in line with the assumption. In practice there are still, alas, some Member States whose criminal procedure, particularly during the investigative phase, puts possibly innocent suspects at grave risk. Points of particular concern include legal advice and legal representation that is poor or non-existent, incompetent interpreters, and oppressive police practices when dealing with suspects and witnesses. These matters are of legitimate concern to all of us. (Though the British should think twice about preaching loudly on this subject to their neighbours, given our own *schreckliche Vergangenheit* in matters of this sort – the cases of Mattan, Kisko, Judith Ward, Paris, the Birmingham Six, Barry George and many others come unhappily to mind.)

Mindful of this problem, seven years ago the European Commission instituted moves designed to raise the standards of criminal justice in those Member States where at present they appear to be deficient. But in 2006, progress towards a new Framework Decision on Defence Rights was abruptly halted when, to its shame, the British government, initially in favour, used its political muscle to block it. For this change of mind no coherent reason was ever given. But the reason was probably that the government had just published a White Paper announcing its intention of "Rebalancing the criminal justice system in favour of the law-abiding majority", which it feared would lose its impact with the electorate if it appeared alongside headlines saying "Brussels Gives UK Criminals Yet More Human Rights."

Three years later the British government has changed its mind again, and at the time this note is written it is actively backing a Brussels "roadmap" with a series of proposed EU instruments designed to improve the protection of defendants in the pre-trial phase of criminal proceedings. But what the UK's policy will be when, on the other side of a general election, this note appears in print, is at present anybody's guess.

Policemen Behaving Badly – The Abuse of Misconduct in Office
R v W
CLJ 2010, 69(3) 423–425

In *R*. v *W* [2010] EWCA Crim 372, [2010] Q.B. 787, a detective in the Metropolitan Police was accused of fiddling his expenses to the tune of £12,500. For this he was at first successfully prosecuted for the common law offence of misconduct in public office. However, the Court of Appeal then quashed his conviction and ordered a retrial because, in their view, the judge should have told the jury, as he would have done in a trial for theft or fraud, that the detective was not guilty unless he was "dishonest". Because "dishonesty" (they said) is an ingredient of the offence of misconduct in public office when committed in such circumstances as these, the detective would not be guilty if he genuinely believed that there was nothing wrong in what he did because it accorded with "the culture in the office at the time", which tolerated false expenses claims, provided the till-dipper intended at some future point to pay the money back.

The decision has been criticised as adding a new and unnecessary complication to the offence of misconduct in public office (Richardson, [2010] *Criminal Law Week*, 11, §5). But what lay behind the Court of Appeal's decision, surely, was a sense of unease that the policeman had been prosecuted for misconduct in public office rather than for a simple fraud or theft. And their unease was understandable, because it is arguable the offence of misconduct in public office should not cover what the detective did, even if "dishonesty" was present.

The essence of the crime of misconduct of public office is either wilfully neglecting to carry out the public duty entrusted to you, or wilfully abusing it for some improper end. On principle, surely, it ought not to cover the incidental commission of another crime in the course of performing it. Here the policeman's behaviour was just a simple expenses fraud, as might be committed by any dishonest employee. His status as a policeman might be thought to aggravate the sentence for the fraud offence. (In France, indeed, it would do so explicitly, because article 313–2 of the *Code pénal* raises the maximum penalty for fraud (*escroquerie*) from five years' imprisonment to seven if the person committing it was a *dépositaire de l'autorité publique*; a provision not required in England, where the maximum penalty even for the basic crime is ten!) But, surely, by fiddling his expenses the policeman in *W* no more wilfully abused his public office than he would have done if, during working hours, he had driven his patrol car dangerously, or groped an unconsenting WPC.

The point at issue here, surely, is the same as the one that recently arose in a different context in the high-profile case of *Chaytor and others* [2010] EWCA Crim 1910, [2010] 2 Cr. App. R. 34, where four MPs accused of false accounting in respect of fraudulent expenses claims tried to argue that they were immune from prosecution because their submission of expenses claims was protected by Parliamentary privilege. In rejecting their arguments, the Court of Appeal said:

> If the allegations are proved … then those against whom they are proved will have committed ordinary crimes. Even stretching language to its limits we are unable to envisage how dishonest claims by Members of Parliament for their expenses or allowances begin to involve the legislative or core functions of the relevant House, or the proper performance of their public duties.

However, it is difficult to say exactly what behaviour the crime of misconduct in public office does cover because it is a common law offence and – like that of its "civil partner" the tort of misfeasance in public office – its definition is uncertain. And so, like other common law offences, it has a tendency, like ground-elder in a garden, to spread in all directions; and, unless it is kept carefully in check, it will take over anything and everything.

In *AG's Reference (No. 3 of 2003)* [2005] Q.B. 73 the offence of misconduct in public office was invoked against two police officers who, it was alleged, had neglected a prisoner who died in the cells at the police station, whose life would have been saved if he had received medical attention: a proper case, one would have thought, for a prosecution for manslaughter by gross negligence. In upholding the trial judge's decision to direct the jury to acquit, the Court of Appeal, having wrestled with a body of case-law dating back to 1599, summarised the ingredients of the offence of misconduct in public office thus: (i) a public officer acting as such; (ii) wilfully neglects to perform his duty and/or wilfully misconducts himself; (iii) to such a degree as to amount to an abuse of the public's trust in the office holder; (iv) without reasonable excuse.

This judicial definition is an improvement on the uncertainty that preceded it, but the resulting offence is still distinctly vague. In particular, this formula does not limit the active form of the offence, as I believe it should be limited, to the improper exercise of the public function, so that it does not extend to behaviour merely incidental to it, like making fraudulent expenses claims.

At the risk of stating the profoundly obvious, the case of *W* is yet another demonstration of the need for English criminal law to be reduced to a comprehensive statutory code. In the twenty-first century there is surely no room in the criminal justice system of a civilised country for common law offences, the scope of which is vague and ill-defined. But to add another obvious but pessimistic point, unless common law offences are codified carefully and thoughtfully, they are better left alone. When confronted with the new statutory definition of the previously common law offence of conspiracy created by section one of the Criminal Law Act 1977, the late Professor Glanville Williams was heard to say: "I've spent my academic life campaigning for codification – but when I look at this I wondered why I bothered!"

Strasbourg and Defendants' Rights in Criminal Procedure
Cadder v HM Advocate, Salduz v Turkey and Taxquet v Belgium
CLJ 2011, 70(1) 14–17

An uneasy relationship exists between the European Court of Human Rights and the UK Supreme Court over criminal procedure. Like many UK politicians, the Supreme Court resents what it sees as "Strasbourg interference" in this area. And so it was that in *Horncastle* [2009] UKSC 14, [2010] 2 A.C. 373 the Supreme Court spectacularly refused to accept a ruling of the Fourth Section of the Strasbourg court which, if applied, would have curtailed the power of UK courts to convict on hearsay evidence. But when faced with a decision of the Grand Chamber (rather than a Section) the Supreme Court is usually prepared to knuckle under; as it did recently in *Cadder v H.M. Advocate* [2010] UKSC 43, [2010] 1 W.L.R. 2601.

The issue there was the rule of Scots law that then denied the suspect the right to legal advice when detained by police for questioning. In *Salduz v Turkey* (2008) 49 E.H.R.R. 421 the Grand Chamber had stated in uncompromising terms that the suspect's general right to a fair trial under Article 6 of the ECHR carries with it the right to legal advice when being interrogated by the police, and that if exceptions to this are sometimes justified, these do not justify the use of incriminating statements obtained at interviews where legal assistance has been denied, as prosecution evidence at trial. On the basis of this, Cadder argued that the Lord Advocate – the Scottish public prosecutor – could not properly use against him an incriminating statement he had made when interviewed under the prevailing Scottish rules. Having failed in Scotland, Cadder took the point as a "devolution issue" to the Supreme Court, where a panel of seven – led by the two Scottish justices – held unanimously in his favour and sent the case back to the High Court of Justiciary in Edinburgh for further consideration.

The effect of this was to undo the Scottish part of a deal reached in the 1980s whereby Parliament resolved an issue of major importance in different ways on different sides of the Border. South of the Tweed, the Police and Criminal Evidence Act 1984 gave the English police the power to detain suspects for questioning for long periods – 24 hours, extensible to 36 on the authority of a senior officer, and extensible to 96 on the authority of a magistrate – but subject to the suspect's right to a solicitor. North of the Tweed, the Criminal Justice (Scotland) Act 1980 gave the Scots police the equivalent power for six hours only, but with no obligation to allow the suspect access to a lawyer. With this apparently unfavourable deal the Scots police were well content: as was accepted by Lord Rodger in his judgment in *Cadder*, where he recognised that the effect of the decision would be "to tilt the balance, to some degree, against the police and prosecution". In reaction to this, the Scottish legislature has already rushed though a piece of legislation which guarantees the Scottish suspect's right to a solicitor, but in return now gives the Scots police the power to detain suspects for 12 hours, extensible by order of a senior officer to 24.

While all this was going on, judicial nails were being bitten to the quick about a case pending before the Grand Chamber which threatened to upset the rule, hallowed this time on both sides of the Border, to the effect that jury verdicts are delivered without reasons. In a line of cases dating back to the early 1990s the Strasbourg Court had held that the general right to a fair trial enshrined in Article 6 includes a specific right to a decision for which the reasons are identified, and in January 2009 the Second Section of the Strasbourg Court applied this so as to condemn Belgium in respect of a conviction returned by a *Cour d'assises* where, as was then the practice, a Belgian jury had convicted a defendant without giving reasons (*Taxquet* v *Belgium*, case 926/05, 13 January 2009). At the instance of the Belgian government the case was referred to the Grand Chamber, and the UK, Ireland and France – all countries where juries give unreasoned verdicts – were given leave to intervene.

On 16 November 2010 the Grand Chamber reaffirmed the condemnation of Belgium ((2012) 54 E.H.R.R. 26), but in terms which presumably left the intervenants with feelings of relief. Whilst stating that the need for reasoned decisions applies even with lay juries, the Grand Chamber accepted that it could be met in other ways than by requiring the jury to provide a reasoned judgment in the same way as a professional judge. One possible way, it said, was by giving the jury a set of "precise, unequivocal questions" to answer, so providing "a framework on which the verdict is based". In France this already happens, at least in some cases, but this had not been done in Belgium in the case in hand. Another way, it said, was by "directions or guidance provided by the presiding judge to the jurors on the legal issues arising or the evidence adduced", which is of course what happens in the UK and in Ireland.

In those two countries the likely reaction will be to say "Hooray! Strasbourg is off our backs, jury trial in its present form is fine, and we can carry on as we have always done!" But this is not a view this commentator shares.

A reasoned decision, surely, is indeed a vital safeguard, in particular for innocent defendants. And even if the Grand Chamber were prepared to say that the combination of a judicial direction and the utterance by the foreman of the jury of the words "Guilty" or "Not Guilty" is equivalent to one, in reality it is not. If the first place, there is no means of telling whether the jury have understood what the judge in his direction told them: a serious matter, since a substantial body of research suggests that juries frequently do not. And secondly, there is no guarantee that, assuming they did understand it, they followed it – and based their conviction on the direction and the evidence, and not by reasoning (for example) that the defendant must have done something bad or he would not be there, or that he is untrustworthy because his eyes are set too close together.

It was with this in mind that, in his *Review of the Criminal Courts*, Sir Robin Auld proposed a reform under which judges should give juries a written questionnaire in which the intellectual route to a conviction or acquittal would be spelt out step by step, and their eventual verdict would have to be based upon it, and consistent with

it: a revival, in effect, of the "special verdict", which was common
once upon a time, but in recent years has fallen quietly into disuse.

The objection that is usually made to this is that the unreasoned
verdict is "all part of the deal" of jury trial; a viewpoint put in florid
language by the Irish government in its submission to the Grand
Chamber, where it claimed "the system of jury trial in Ireland was
the unanimous choice of accused persons and of human rights
advocates", and added that "to require juries to give reasons for
their decisions would alter the nature and the very essence of jury
trial as operated in Ireland."

The underlying fear here is that requiring juries to give reasons
would put an end to "jury equity": the present ability of a jury to
acquit a defendant in the teeth of the judge's direction because
they are sorry for him, or disapprove of the law the prosecution
was intended to enforce – the *locus classicus* of which is the case
of Henriette Caillaut, acquitted in 1914 by a French jury of
murdering, in the coldest of cold blood, the editor of *Le Figaro*, to
stop him waging a disgraceful vendetta against her husband, the
Minister of Finance.

But if this "jury equity" is truly a blessing rather than a bane,
it should surely be a one-way street. If it is right for juries to be
able to acquit guilty defendants who attract their sympathy, they
should not be free to convict innocent ones who attract their hatred
or disgust, despite the fact that the evidence against them did not
convince them. And this, at present, they are just as free to do,
thanks to the unreasoned verdict. Surely the Auld proposal should
be implemented, at least to the extent of requiring guilty verdicts
to be justified by a chain of reasoning, even if the jury's right to
pronounce an acquittal without reasons were retained.

Both the *Salduz* and *Taxquet* cases, and their legal aftermaths in
the UK, are developments that are helpful to defendants; but in
truth it is only guilty ones who stand to profit from the second.

Libel Tourist Ordered to Pay 8,000 Euros
Ministère public c/ Weiler
CLJ 2011, 70(2) 317–319

It is unusual for this journal to carry a note on a first instance case at all, let alone a French one. But the facts of *Ministère public c/ Weiler* are so astonishing, and the underlying issues so important, that a note on the judgment of the 17th Chamber of the *Tribunal correctionnel de Paris* of 3 March 2011 (case 078523043) seems fully justified.

Joseph Weiler is a professor at Harvard, where he edits the European Journal of International Law, which is published on the internet. In 2007 this carried a review by Professor Thomas Weigend, of Cologne, of a book about the International Criminal Court. The review, though expressed in moderate language, was unfavourable. The book, said the reviewer, was heavy on description and light on analysis. This "exercise in rehashing the existing legal set-up", he said, was "particularly unproductive since a large part of the volume consists in a reprint of the ICC Statute and its Rules of Procedure (the Court's Regulations are consistently ignored)." He also criticised the book as being sloppily edited, uncorrected errors including a reference to "the trail (sic) process". By implication, at a price of $155 he did not see it as the bargain of the month.

The author of the book, one Karine Calvo-Goller, took exception to this review, and wrote to Weiler, demanding that he remove it from his journal's website. Weiler, who thought the review was fair, refused to suppress it, but told the author that, if she wished to write a riposte, he would publish it. Instead of accepting this offer, however, Dr. Calvo-Goller instituted proceedings against Weiler in France for defamation. As Dr. Calvo-Goller was an Israeli academic, Weiler an American, the reviewer German, the publisher Dutch and the language of the alleged libel English, the choice of France looked, to put it mildly, a little odd. The venue occurred to her, however, because she holds French as well as Israeli nationality, and had at some point studied law in France.

In France, defamation is criminal as well as civil, and it was the criminal route that Dr. Calvo-Goller chose, constituting herself

215

a *partie civile,* and so putting in train the French equivalent of a private prosecution. In consequence Weiler was summoned to appear before a *juge d'instruction* in Paris, and – after a long series of adjournments – in January 2011 he eventually stood trial before the 17th Division of the *Tribunal correctionnel de Paris,* a criminal court composed of three professional judges, who specialise in defamation cases, and sit without a jury.

Two months later this court dismissed the case.

The central ground for the decision was that the French courts had no jurisdiction. For a French court to be competent in such a case the defamation must have been published in France, and to prove publication it was not enough to show that someone could have accessed the publication there, but an identifiable person must be shown to have done so: a fact which Dr. Calvo-Goller had failed to prove. Though the *Code pénal* gives the French criminal courts extra-territorial jurisdiction in certain situations, one of which is where the victim of the offence is a French national, this only applies where the offence in question is *un crime.* In France, *crimes* are offences of the utmost gravity, a category into which the crime of libel does not fall.

Having let Weiler out of the dock on this account, the *Tribunal correctionnel* then (in effect) put Dr. Calvo-Goller into it. Under French law, a *partie civile* who has made abusive use of her right to start a prosecution is liable in damages at the suit of the acquitted defendant, and by article 472 of the *Code de procédure pénal* these can be awarded by the criminal court before which the prosecution failed. Accepting Weiler's argument that he had been the victim of an abusive prosecution, the court ordered Calvo-Goller to pay him 8,000 euros in compensation.

The proceedings were abusive, it said, for two reasons. First, the complainant had in her evidence "accepted that she had practised what it is convenient to call *forum-shopping*" : searching the world for the legal system that she thought would put her in the strongest position, and her adversary in the weakest one, even though it had no genuine connection with the case. And secondly, she had tried to prosecute for a statement which manifestly failed to satisfy the test of defamation in French law, because the review "... contains nothing that is harmful to her honour or her reputation and only expresses, in moderate language, a scientific opinion on the book, without exceeding the limits of free criticism to which every author of a work is exposed."

What would have happened if Dr. Calvo-Goller had tried to use the English courts to suppress her book's unfavourable review?

The criminal courts would have been closed to her, because criminal libel, long in a vegetative state, was quietly put out of its misery by section 73 of the Coroners and Justice Act 2009. To sue civilly she would have had to show, as in France, that someone had actually accessed the review. Though our courts presume that newspapers are read, they do not make the same assumption about publications on the internet. But had she overcome this hurdle, her case would almost certainly have been dismissed without a hearing. The defence of fair comment would have been so obviously applicable that Weiler would probably have persuaded the court to give him summary judgment.

The judgment would have come together with an award of costs, but the English court would not have awarded Weiler damages. Though abuse of civil process is a tort, at least in theory, it is subject to the same stringent limitations as its more famous cousin, malicious prosecution: limitations which normally ensure that claimants lose. So although Weiler would have won, his victory, when it came, would have been rather less dramatic.

Dramatic or otherwise, Weiler's victory is one at which all academics should rejoice – whether they write honest book reviews, or smart under them.

Arrest for Questioning
Richardson v Chief Constable of West Midlands
CLJ 2011, 70(3) 492–494

If they wish to question a person they suspect of committing an offence, are the police completely free to arrest him for this purpose? Or may they do so only if he refuses to talk to them voluntarily?

Last year this important issue was examined by Mrs. Justice Slade in *Richardson v Chief Constable of West Midlands* [2011] EWHC 773, [2011] 2 Cr. App. R 1 – a decision which attracted much attention.

In 2005, the Labour government persuaded Parliament to "modernise" – i.e. drastically extend – police powers by giving English police officers what are probably the widest powers of summary arrest existing anywhere in Western Europe. Previously the police could, in principle, only arrest without warrant those whom they reasonably suspected of "arrestable offences": which as defined by section 24 of the Police and Criminal Evidence Act 1984 meant, broadly speaking, those that carried a maximum of five years' imprisonment or more. As "modernised", the section now permits them to arrest without warrant anyone they reasonably suspect of *any* criminal offence. And what is more, this means any offence whether currently in the course of commission or committed at some point in the past. So in principle the police, without obtaining a warrant, can now lawfully arrest people on suspicion of past offences not only where they are grave, like murder or terrorism, but even where they are trivial, like using an unlicensed TV, or shaking a mat in the street after 8 a.m.

The new power of summary arrest is limited by section 24(3), which sets out a list of alternative conditions, one of which must be present before the power is exercised. But as the list includes the condition that the arrest is reasonably believed to be necessary "to allow the prompt and effective investigation of the offence or of the conduct of the person in question", the limitation does not look very limiting. Many police forces have taken the view that this condition means that they can now arrest anyone for anything, if they think a spell of custodial interrogation will induce him to confess.

Richardson, a 39-year-old teacher of good character, was reported to the police for a common assault on a student: an offence punishable with only six months' imprisonment, and hence one for which no power of summary arrest existed before 2005. When contacted by the police he agreed to go to the police station for a voluntary interview. But when he got there the police, over the protest of his solicitor, promptly arrested him – and having done so, also took his photograph, his finger-prints and a sample of his DNA, procedures which the police, under their "modernised" powers, may now impose on anyone whom they arrest.

Having heard Richardson's explanation of the incident, and made further enquiries, the police decided to take no further action. At this point Richardson sued them for false imprisonment – namely the arrest. The police countered this by claiming that they believed this to be necessary "to allow the prompt and effective investigation" of his alleged assault. It was true, they said, that he was prepared to give a voluntary interview, but in a voluntary interview he could have got up and left at any time. Had he tried to do so, they could indeed have arrested him as he made for the door; but that "would disrupt the free flow of the interview".

After hearing argument on various cases (including *Alexander* [2009] N.I.Q.B. 20 and *R. (C)* v *Chief Constable of A* [2006] EWHC 2352, noted at p. 181 [2007] C.L.J. 282[26]), Slade J. accepted that in principle an arrest could be justified on the ground the police put forward, but only if there was an "evidential basis for a belief that the claimant would interrupt his interview and leave the police station". In the case in hand there was none. Indeed, the police custody record actually noted that on arrival Richardson was "calm and compliasnt [sic]". So the arrest was not justified – and Slade J. marked the fact by awarding him £1,000 damages for false imprisonment.

This decision, surely, is most welcome. To arrest a person is a serious matter, and the police should not be permitted to do it lightly, particularly where, as here, the offence in question is trivial. Not only is it humiliating and degrading. In our present risk-averse culture, getting arrested, like getting chewing-gum on the sole of your shoe, has unwelcome consequences that are singularly difficult to get rid of. It may lead to various countries excluding you if you wish to visit them. For the purpose of its visa requirements the USA – Sweet Land of Liberty – puts "have you ever been arrested?" on the same footing as "have you ever been convicted?". And the fact of an arrest (irrespective of what happened afterwards) is "soft information" which the police are likely to reveal to those,

---

[26] See p. 181 above.

including a range of potential employers, who are entitled to ask for an "enhanced CRB check". As such it seriously reduces a person's prospects of employment. The trade union official whom Richardson called as a witness told the court that "A teacher who has been arrested is left virtually unemployable because disclosure on enhanced CRB disclosures is generally fatal to an application."

In the light of all this one wonders if the decision goes far enough. Should the police really be able to arrest for questioning someone who is willing to talk to them voluntarily, even supposing they really do believe he might seek to leave if the questioning gets tough – given that, if he does, they can then arrest him at that point? The risk of "interrupting the flow of the police interview" is a small thing to weigh against the risk of blighting the career of a person who may well be innocent.

On 29 July the Court of Appeal discussed the issues debated in this note in *Hayes v Chief Constable of Merseyside* [2011] EWCA Civ 911, [2011] 1 W.L.R. 517. In this case, the police were held to be justified in arresting a person who was prepared to give a voluntary interview, inter alia because they needed to be able to seize his mobile phone and because they wanted to impose bail conditions on his release in order to protect the person whom they believed he was intimidating. But in so holding, the Court recognised that in other situations it might be "quite unnecessary to arrest a suspect who will voluntarily attend an interview, as it was with the schoolteacher in *Richardson* ".

Killa Walks Free
R. v Ford (Kamahl)
CLJ 2011, 70(3) 494–496

Once upon a time it used to be said that, to find out what the law of evidence prescribes, you simply ask what common sense suggests and turn it on its head. The rules of criminal evidence seemed to be a maze of technical irrationality, shutting out material that is logically cogent, and admitting material that is logically weak, more or less in equal measure. Central to this perverse structure was the celebrated "hearsay rule", and conscious of this, in Part 11 of the Criminal Justice Act 2003 Parliament sought, with the aid of the Law Commission's Report No. 245, to inject some rationality into it. But the decision in *Ford* [2010] EWCA Crim 2250 suggests (alas!) that the attempt has at least partly failed – the ancient recipe for determining whether evidence is legally admissible is still to be relied on.

Shortly after his release from prison, Ford (who liked to be called "Killa") started threatening to kill a woman called CW, reinforcing the threats by firing shots through her front window. This led to his return to prison. While he was behind bars, a second gunman came and shot CW's front window out again. When the police arrived a woman who claimed to have seen the shooting gave them a note she had made of the registration number of the attackers' car, and then vanished. Having found the car in question the police arrested the four young men inside, whose mobile phones revealed not only that they had been in discussion with the incarcerated Ford, but also that they were in the area of the second shooting at the relevant time. Deducing they were Ford's associates who had carried out the shooting at his instigation, the police charged Ford with conspiring with them to commit it.

At his trial on the conspiracy counts a key piece of evidence was the passer-by's note of the registration number of the car – a vital link connecting Ford's associates, and hence Ford, with the second shooting. This, in law, was hearsay; but the trial judge held that, under the reformed law, it was admissible. Under the new law, hearsay evidence, if relevant – though still generally inadmissible – goes in if any of a list of specific exceptions set out in the Act applies; and failing those, it can also be admitted under a general "inclusionary discretion" set out in section 114(1)(d), which lets in hearsay otherwise inadmissible if the judge decides, having examined a list of factors set out in section 114(2), that the interests of justice so require. It was under this provision that H.H. Judge Karu admitted it.

In a judgment delivered by Laws L.J. the Court of Appeal ruled that the note was wrongly admitted, in the light of the following dictum of Lord Chief Justice Judge, first uttered in *Mayers* [2008] EWCA Crim 2989, [2009] 1 W.L.R. 1915 (at [113]), and then repeated in *Horncastle* [2009] UKSC 14, [2010] 2 A.C. 373 (at [13]).

> ... we are being invited to re-write the [Criminal Evidence (Anonymity) Act 2008] by extending anonymous witness orders to permit anonymous hearsay evidence to be read to the jury. We cannot do so. Neither the common law, nor the 2003 Act, nor the 2008 Act permits it.

Accordingly they quashed the conspiracy convictions, and with them, that part of Ford's sentence that related to them.

I believe the Court of Appeal's decision to be wrong, for at least four reasons.

First, the Court in *Ford* took Lord Judge's dictum out of context. His resounding condemnation of "anonymous hearsay" was spoken in the general context of the Criminal Procedure (Anonymity of Witnesses) Act, a statute that permits, subject to stringent limitations, a judge to allow a witness to give *oral testimony* in court anonymously, i.e. without identifying himself to the defendant; and in the specific context of a case where the prosecution had tried to go one further, and serve up what their anonymous witness had to say in the form of a written statement, so saving him from being cross-examined as well as having to explain who he was. That is a very different issue from the one in the present case, which was whether the prosecution could put in evidence a piece of information received from a member of the public whose identity they did not know, with no question of their trying to avoid calling her as a witness.

Secondly, imposing on the hearsay provisions of the Criminal Justice Act a general gloss that they can never be used to admit hearsay from an unidentified source does violence to the wording of the statute. In the suite of sections setting out the terms of the exceptions to the hearsay rule there is one – section 116 – that explicitly provides that the original maker of the statement must be identified. However, no such limiting words are present in the other sections. Normal principles of statutory construction therefore suggest that, in those other sections, hearsay from unidentified sources can be admitted. And indeed, this is what those who drafted the provisions undoubtedly intended. When explaining the scope of what is now section 114(1)(d), applied by Judge Karu in this case, the Law Commission (in §8.143 of their Report) said "The declarant need not even be identified".

Thirdly, imposing this gloss on the hearsay provisions of the Criminal Justice Act 2003 gravely disrupts the reform. It means, for example, that section 117, which renders admissible hearsay contained in "records", can only now be used if the person who originally fed the information into the record can be identified. The practical effect of this would be to make the new law of hearsay even more restrictive than the old law it was meant to modernise. (It would, for example, resurrect the deplorable decision in *Myers v DPP* [1965] A.C. 1001, which older readers familiar with the law of evidence will remember with a shudder; which held that, to establish which engine was originally fitted in which now-ageing car, you cannot use the records routinely made by the unidentified factory workers who were on the assembly line that day.)

Finally, the practical result is disastrous. It means that, for purely technical reasons, a piece of highly cogent evidence is excluded, so preventing the court from reaching an outcome in accordance with the truth. The result here was the acquittal of a guilty person. But next time it could equally well be the conviction of someone who was innocent.

Ford, surely, is an aberration: a rogue decision, in an unreserved judgment, given by an overworked court which, on this occasion, made an uncharacteristic blunder. Let us hope that later courts recognise it as such and disavow it.

Controlling the Discretion to Prosecute
R. (E, S and R) v DPP
CLJ 2012, 71(1) 27–29

An article of faith for English lawyers is that the Crown has a discretion to prosecute, rather than a duty to bring proceedings wherever there is evidence of a crime – as is the case with public prosecutors in some other legal systems. But the discretion to prosecute, like the duty to prosecute, has its own particular problems: namely, ensuring that the discretion is exercised intelligently and fairly. With that in mind, the law now imposes on the Director of Public Prosecutions the duty to publish his prosecution policy, and influenced by this, the courts now treat the decision to prosecute as susceptible of judicial review. Up to now, most of the case-law has involved prosecutorial inaction: coppers "copping out" and prosecutors unwilling to proceed. But, as *R. (E, S and R) v DPP* [2011] EWHC 1465 (Admin), [2012] 1 Cr. App. R. 6 now clearly shows, it can sometimes be invoked against the opposite problem of excessive zeal.

When she was 12, E videoed herself performing indecent acts with her two little sisters, then aged four and two. Two years later, officers from the national Child Exploitation and Online Protection Centre discovered this on the internet. E's story was that she had been groomed and pressured to do this by an adult paedophile – an explanation that seemed plausible, given the presence on the internet of other indecent videos, this time of E alone, being "remotely abused".

Informed of this, the local authority called a case-conference with a "strategy group" composed of social workers, representatives of the NSPCC, the probation service, the child and adolescent mental health service, the children's school and the police. All participants believed that E was herself a victim and in need of help rather than of punishment, except for one. This was the police, who thought she should be prosecuted. They sent the papers to the Crown Prosecution Service, which endorsed their view. In consequence, E found herself facing a Crown Court trial.

At this point the children's mother, acting on their behalf, sought to have the decision of the CPS judicially reviewed. Her challenge succeeded, and the decision to prosecute was quashed on the ground that it conflicted with the prosecution policy of the CPS as officially proclaimed.

When read together, three documents – the Code for Crown Prosecutors (published under section 10 of the Prosecution of Offences Act 1985), the CPS's published policy for handling child abuse cases and the CPS's official policy on the safeguarding of children involved in criminal proceedings – stress the need for prosecutors to consider the welfare of children, and also to consider the views of the victim's family. In its report the strategy group had explained why it would be not only bad for E herself if she were prosecuted, but also devastating for her family (including the little sisters who were the victims of her offence). Yet when announcing its decision to prosecute, the CPS, though stating that the strategy group's report had been "considered", had failed to address any of the arguments contained in it.

In her legal challenge to the CPS decision the mother also deployed arguments based on the UK's international obligations: in particular, under the European Convention on Human Rights and under the United Nations Convention on the Rights of the Child. These arguments, by contrast, were rejected. This aspect of the case is interesting; but for reasons of space I shall leave it to others (e.g. Malkhani, [2011] Crim. L.R. 943) and deal here with just two different points.

The first relates to forum. The proceedings by which the decision to prosecute was challenged in this case were civil ones: an application for judicial review, made in the Administrative Court. Whilst readily admitting judicial review as a proper method for challenging prosecutorial inaction, the civil courts have hitherto discouraged its use to challenge allegedly improper decisions to proceed. The right place to challenge a decision to prosecute, they have said, is the criminal court that is dealing with the prosecution. A criminal court can stay a prosecution if it considers it to be an abuse of process; and so a defendant who claims to be the victim of an improper exercise of the discretion to prosecute should raise the matter by inviting the criminal court to exercise this power. This point was made, inter alia, by Lord Steyn in *ex parte Kebiline* [2000] 2 A.C. 326, and his remarks were endorsed and applied by the Administrative Court in *R. (Pepushi) v Crown Prosecution Service* [2004] EWHC 798 (Admin). But, said the Administrative Court, all these earlier cases involved applications for judicial review made by disgruntled criminal defendants. Different considerations apply in cases where, as here, the applicants include the victims of the offence – who, unlike the defendant, have no official standing before the criminal courts. In taking this position, the Administrative Court has added to the list of recent cases which, when viewed together, show a growing tendency to enhance the legal status of the victim – for long the "forgotten person" in the criminal justice system.

The second general point concerns the potential application of the law forbidding sexual acts with juveniles to defendants who are juveniles themselves. This part of the criminal law exists to protect children from sexual exploitation by predatory adults. In its present form, however, it applies equally to sexual acts – even the most trivial ones – when done by juveniles with other juveniles; and this is so even where, unlike in the present gruesome case, the persons are of the same age and willingly consent. Nine years ago, when what is now the Sexual Offences Act 2003 was before Parliament, the Government was invited to support the decriminalisation of sexual acts between consenting juveniles, and resisted. No such exemption was required, it said, because the CPS would publish guidelines to regulate its prosecution policy in such cases, and these would prevent needless or oppressive prosecutions being brought. Sceptics were dissatisfied with this response. What recourse would there be, they asked, if the guidelines are not applied? This new and welcome decision suggests at least a partial answer.

Police Officers on Juries
Hanif and Khan v United Kingdom
CLJ 2012, 71(2) 254–257

ANDY CAPP, the cartoon character in the *Daily Mirror,* was once shown as the referee in a football match. Not only was his lower lip adorned, as always, by the ever-present half-smoked cigarette: his referee's shirt was ornamented by a big rosette, as worn by team supporters. To a player, who had noticed it, he was saying "Sumthin' botherin' yer?" Translated into legal terms, this was *Hanif and Khan v UK* (2012) 55 E.H.R.R. 16.

On the second day of the defendants' trial in 2007 for conspiracy to supply heroin, a juror warned the judge that he was a police officer and knew one of the police witnesses, whose evidence was crucial against Hanif. The judge, astonishingly, ruled this did not matter and in due course his fellow jurors made him foreman. The jury, readers will be unsurprised to learn, convicted – and long prison sentences were imposed.

The defendants appealed, arguing that the presence of the police officer meant that the tribunal which had tried them was not independent. In 2008 a strong Court of Appeal, containing both the Lord Chief Justice and the President of the Queen's Bench Division, upheld their convictions.

Three years later the Fourth Division of the Strasbourg Court took a very different view. In its judgment, given on 20 December 2011, it said:

> [148] … leaving aside the question whether the presence of a police officer on a jury could ever be compatible with Article 6, where there is an important conflict regarding police evidence in the case and a police officer who is personally acquainted with the police officer witness giving the relevant evidence is a member of the jury, jury directions and judicial warnings are insufficient to guard against the risk that the jury may, albeit subconsciously, favour the evidence of the police …

It followed, said the Court, that Hanif's right to a fair trial under Article 6(1) of the Convention had been violated because the tribunal that tried him was not "independent"; and as the two defendants' cases were so closely intertwined, Khan's right to a fair trial had been violated too. The UK was ordered to pay compensation to the defendants; and at some point the Court of Appeal will presumably be hearing the appeal again, this time on a reference from the Criminal Cases Review Commission.

To readers unfamiliar with the twists and turns of criminal justice legislation in the last ten years the puzzle will not be the outcome of the case at Strasbourg, but how it ever got there in the first place. How come the Court of Appeal upheld a conviction in a case where one of the jurors was a policeman – let alone a policeman who knew another policeman who was a key prosecution witness in the case?

Traditionally, police officers were ineligible to serve on juries. In their inability to do so they were not alone: their ineligibility was part of a complicated maze of disqualifications, exemptions and potential excusals, the overall effect of which was to relieve a wide range of professionals of the need to serve on juries and to ensure that, in the main, juries were composed of persons who had nothing else to do. This was criticised, for two reasons. First, it spread the burden of jury service unfairly among the social classes, and secondly, it meant the intellectual level of juries tended to be low. (The last point was summed up in a graffito that once allegedly appeared in the urinal at the Crown Court at Snaresbrook: "Here your fate is in the hands of 12 good men too stupid to get out of jury service".)

This issue was drawn to public attention by Sir Robin Auld in his *Review of the Criminal Courts* in 2001. In the course of his researches he had visited New York, where jury service was truly universal, and was favourably impressed. On the basis of what he had seen there, he recommended that most of the existing disqualifications, exemptions and excusals should be scrapped: most spectacularly, those that kept out lawyers, judges and policemen. Like most of his other recommendations that could be sold as "tough on crime", the previous government endorsed it. By Schedule 33 of the Criminal Justice Act 2003, jury service became (in essence) obligatory for all adults between 18 and 70 other than mental patients and convicted criminals.

But how far, if at all, were juries with policemen and CPS employees sitting on them compatible with the basic requirement of a tribunal that is independent? In *Abdroikov* [2007] UKHL 37, [2007] 1 W.L.R. 2679 the House of Lords held that employees of the CPS – a single body operating nationwide – must not normally serve on juries in cases prosecuted by the CPS. With police officers, who are not members of one single force and who do not prosecute, the answer, they said, must depend on the facts of the individual case. As the court was split 3-2 and the majority judges delivered separate speeches saying subtly different things, the decision left it unclear as to exactly what the facts are that the answer should depend upon. However, one thing the majority all said was that a policeman should not be a juror if he shared the "same service background" as a police witness on whose contested evidence the issue of guilt or innocence would turn.

In *Hanif and Khan* the Court of Appeal interpreted these words as legitimating the presence of a policeman on a jury who knows another policeman who is a key witness for the Crown, provided (as in Hanif's case) the defence are saying that he is "mistaken" in his evidence rather than that he is telling lies: and on that basis they upheld the conviction. They did so in a composite judgment in which appeals in five separate cases, all turning on related points, were all dismissed. The aim, presumably, was to signal that appeals in this type of case would normally be ill received; and in the following years this policy was carried through. In seven later cases, all cited and discussed in the Strasbourg judgment, convictions were upheld in all but one. This was *R. v L* [2011] EWCA 65, where the jury contained not only a serving police officer but, for good measure, a retired one and an employee of the CPS.

If the Court of Appeal had qualms in taking this hard line, it suppressed them in deference to what it perceived to be the democratic will. "Parliament, in its wisdom, has decided that police officers can be jurors, and so …". The Strasbourg Court, by contrast, did not feel obliged to start its analysis of the issue from the premise that Parliament, like God, must be considered to be wise. In its judgment it surveyed 14 jurisdictions, including Scotland and both parts of Ireland, in Europe and elsewhere, where jury trial is used, and found that police officers are banned from serving in all but two of them. And in Belgium and New York, the two exceptions to the rule, defendants have a right of "peremptory challenge": that is, the right to object to any juror without giving reason – a right they formerly enjoyed in England too, but lost in 1988 in an earlier "rebalancing of justice". In consequence, England seems to be the only jurisdiction where a police officer is eligible to serve, and if he does so, the defendant is forced to put up with it. The Strasbourg Court limited itself to condemning the UK on the narrow ground that the independence of the tribunal was compromised by a police officer on the jury who knew a prosecution witness. But the tenor of the judgment suggests that, if it had been obliged to decide the point, it would have ruled that the mere presence of any police officer on a jury is enough to violate the defendant's right to a fair trial.

If it was a good idea in general terms to make a bonfire of the tangled mass of disqualifications and exemptions from jury service, in retrospect it surely was a bad idea to make police officers eligible to serve. In practical terms, the need for judges to question police jurors about their relationships (if any) with witnesses adds a new and needless complication to the trial, and where one does serve and the defendant is convicted, a new and needless ground for possible appeal. And in theoretical terms, however honest the individual officer, in public perception a policeman is a member of the opposing team; and so like Andy Capp with his rosette, he should not be acting as a referee.

The government should now make a virtue out of necessity and, taking the initiative, reverse the change its predecessor made before another Strasbourg condemnation forces it to do so.

Incest and Article 8 of the European Convention on Human Rights
Stubing v Germany
CLJ 2013, 72(1) 5–7

Patrick Stubing was removed from his natural family at the age of three and his foster parents later adopted him. As an adult he renewed contact with his natural family and found he had a grown-up sister. The two of them began to live together (in the fullest sense of the expression) and over the next four years, until he underwent a vasectomy, she regularly bore him children. For his ongoing sexual relationship with his sister he was prosecuted and convicted no less than three times for the offence of incest contrary to §173 of the German Criminal Code. On the third occasion he was sentenced to 16 months' imprisonment; his sister, who this time was also prosecuted, was convicted too, but because of her mental state excused from punishment. Stubing then complained to the

German Constitutional Court, arguing that his conviction was unconstitutional. When, by a majority, this Court turned him down he applied to the European Court of Human Rights in Strasbourg, arguing that his conviction violated his right to "respect for his private and family life" as protected by Article 8 of the European Convention.

In *Stubing v Germany* (2012) 55 E.H.R.R. 24 a Division of the Strasbourg Court declared his application admissible, but rejected it. In so doing, the judges accepted that a legal ban on sexual intercourse with his willing sister was an interference with his right to respect for his private life, and hence that Article 8 was properly engaged. But Article 8(2), they pointed out, permits the state to interfere with private lives where this is "necessary in a democratic society... for the protection of health or morals, or for the protection of the rights and freedoms of others". In the context of restrictions on people's sexual freedom, they said, such interferences are only "necessary" where there is a "pressing social need" for them. But, said the court, in deciding whether such a pressing social need exists, contracting States enjoy a wide "margin of appreciation". As to whether incest between consenting adults should constitute a criminal offence the legal systems of the Contracting States, the judges pointed out, are currently divided. Furthermore, though some countries that once punished it have decriminalised it in recent years, others have retained the offence, or even widened it. In the light of this division of national opinion the Court concluded that the punishment of Stubing for consensual sexual intercourse with his adult sister fell within the German "margin of appreciation", and his application therefore failed.

In principle, the issue in this case is the same as the one that arose some decades back in relation to the criminalisation of homosexual acts between consenting adult males. When, if ever, should the criminal law punish sexual acts between consenting adults carried out in privacy? Once upon a time, a sufficient answer would have been "When those acts are contrary to the moral values generally accepted by society". Whether such an answer was sufficient was, of course, the central point of the celebrated debate between Hart and Devlin in the 1960s, Devlin claiming that it was, and

Hart arguing that it was not. And as far as homosexual acts are concerned, it was of course the Hart view that eventually prevailed. For England and Wales, Parliament changed the law to legalise homosexual acts between consenting adult males in 1967, and 13 years later it did the same for Scotland too.

A move to change the law in Northern Ireland too, however, was temporarily abandoned in the face of furious opposition. The Reverend Ian Paisley's "save Ulster from sodomy" campaign – in which, unusually, he stood shoulder to shoulder with the Catholic bishops – quickly attracted 70,000 signatures to its petition demanding that, in this part of the United Kingdom, the existing law should be maintained. And so it was until in *Dudgeon v UK* (1982) 4 EHRR 149 a majority of the Strasbourg Court, also accepting the Hart view of the matter, condemned the UK over this for violation of Article 8 of the Convention. A few years later, in *Norris v Ireland* (1991) 13 EHRR 186, the Strasbourg Court similarly dispatched the identical ban which still lingered on in the Republic.

In reaching the opposite conclusion in the *Stubing* case the Strasbourg Court sought to apply its reasoning in these two earlier cases, rather than to reject it. So it was not prepared to say that the punishment of adult incest fell within the German national margin of appreciation simply because German morality was outraged by it. Instead, taking the lead from the majority of the German Constitutional Court and the arguments of the German government, it looked for utilitarian reasons by which to distinguish the criminalisation of incest from the criminalisation of homosexual acts.

The arguments it found were two. One was the risk of genetic abnormalities in any children that might result from the union, and other was the risk that sexual relations between siblings could "seriously damage family structures". Whether taken on their own or in conjunction, these risks do not make much of a case for imposing criminal liability. The enhanced risk of genetic abnormality, though it exists, is relatively small – and very much smaller than the risk when lawful sexual intercourse takes place with someone who is the carrier of a genetically transmissible disease, like Huntington's chorea or haemophilia.

(And even this small genetic risk, of course, only arises where both of the incestuous parties are fertile, unlike the Stubings after Mr. Stubing's vasectomy.) And the risk of the behaviour breaking up the happy home – or making an unhappy one yet more dysfunctional – is even less convincing as a reason. If it were generally accepted as sufficient ground for criminalising sexual acts, the prisons of the Western world would be even more overcrowded than they are.

With utilitarian arguments as weak as these, it is unsurprising that the German government and the Strasbourg Court also sought to justify the criminalisation of adult incest by invoking other arguments as well: in particular, "the background of a common conviction that incest should be subject to criminal liability" (at [63]) and the need "to maintain the taboo against incest" (at [50]). But these, surely, are the same sort of arguments which were deployed, in previous decades, in support of maintaining the criminalisation of homosexual acts between consenting males; as indeed they were at one time also used to support the criminalisation of sexual relations between those of different races. As against this, it could be said that the taboo against incest appears to be more general in time and space than the taboos against other forms of sexual practice which different societies have frowned upon at different times and different places. But if the criminalisation of a type of sexual behaviour cannot properly be justified by the fact that many people are disgusted by the thought of it, can it be justified by the fact that nearly everybody is? And if the incest taboo is so strong that nearly everybody deeply disapproves of it, is it really necessary to imprison those who break it in order to ensure it is maintained?

In truth it is hard to resist the conclusion that it was really the "yuck factor", rather than the utilitarian reasons, which ultimately led the Strasbourg Court to decide this case as it did. And the same can be said of the legislative decision to retain and extend the criminalisation of adult incest in sections 63 and 64 of the Sexual Offences Act 2003. Fuelled by a mixture of political correctitude and moral panic, Parliament replaced the previous offence of incest, defined as vaginal intercourse between a limited range of blood relatives, with a new offence of "sex with an adult relative", covering any act of penetrative sex between any of an extended range of adult relatives, and extending to "homosexual incest" between related adult males. Even a weak utilitarian argument for this new offence would be difficult to find.

Signature, Consent, and the Rule in
L'Estrange v Graucob
CLJ 1973, 32(1) p.104–122

It seems to be generally accepted that a person who signs a contractual document may not dispute his agreement to any of the terms which it contains, unless he can establish one of three defences: (a) fraud, (b) misrepresentation, or (c) *non est factum*.[27]

The case which is usually taken to be authority for this proposition is the decision of the Divisional Court[28] in *L'Estrange v F. Graucob Ltd.*[29] in which Scrutton L.J. said[30]: "Where a document containing contractual terms is signed, then, in the absence of fraud, or, I will add, misrepresentation, the party signing it is bound, and it is wholly immaterial whether he has read the document or not," and where Maugham L.J. said much the same, but added the further possibility of a plea of *non est factum*.[31] In fact, the rule was laid down four years earlier and with greater authority by the Court of Appeal in *Blay v Pollard and Morris*, [32] and there is a first instance decision to similar effect eight years earlier still- *The Luna*.[33] Neither of these cases was cited or relied on in *L'Estrange v Graucob*, where

---

[27] *Sutton and Shannon on Contracts*, 7th ed., p. 106; Cheshire and Fifoot, *The Law of Contract*, 8th ed., p. 129; *Salmond and Williams on Contracts*, p. 79.

[28] It was a decision of the Divisional Court, with Scrutton and Maugham L.JJ. sitting as additional judges in the King's Bench Division. It is often mistaken for a decision of the Court of Appeal, *e.g.*, *McCutcheon v MacBrayne* [1964] 1 W.L.R. 125 at p. 134, *per* Lord Devlin, quoted *post*, p. 249. This has probably given the case a weight of authority it does not really possess.

[29] [1934] 2 K.B. 394.

[30] *Ibid.* at p. 403.

[31] *Ibid.* at p. 406.

[32] [1930] 1 K.B. 628.

[33] [1920] P. 22.

the court based the rule solely on a dictum of Mellish L.J. in *Parker v South Eastern Railway Co.*,[34] which is probably its original source. However, even if *L'Estrange v Graucob* is not its real origin, it was that case which made the rule famous – or infamous. The facts of the case were hard enough to attract public attention,[35] and the application of the rule in that case to standard form contracts showed how wide its potential effect would be.[36] So it is good sense, even if it is bad legal history, to refer to the rule as *"the rule in L'Estrange v Graucob,"* and that is what it will be called in this article.

Is the rule in *L'Estrange v Graucob* right? Is a person who disputes the terms of a signed contract really limited to the three defences of fraud, misrepresentation and *non est factum?* An attempt will be made here to show that the rule is wrong, and that there is a fourth defence which ought to be open to him – the defence that he simply did not agree to the term in question. The rule will be attacked on the ground that it contradicts the settled theory of agreement which underlies the law of contract generally.

THE COMMON LAW THEORY OF AGREEMENT

Everyone says that the common law theory of agreement is "objective," which means that the parties have to be judged by what they outwardly appeared to decide rather than by what they inwardly meant to decide. This is vague, however, and to see what this "objective" theory really is we must look at the cases upon which it is based.

One of these cases is *Smith v Hughes.*[37] The case usually features in books in the chapter headed "mistake" rather than in the one headed "agreement." However, when the common law deals with the sort of mistake where P thought the terms of the contract to be ABC and D thought them to be XYZ – what Cheshire and Fifoot

---

[34] (1877) 2 C.P.D. 416 at p. 421. The court also referred to *Roe v Naylor (No. 2)* (1918) 87 L.J.K.B. 958, which contains similar dicta. See 87 L.J.K.B. 958 at p. 964, *per* Scrutton L.J.

[35] It was described as "a menace to the community" by P. A. Landon in his note on the case, 51 L.Q.R. 272. The author is indebted to this case-note.

[36] The Supply of Goods (Implied Terms) Bill will greatly reduce the effect of *L'Estrange v Graucob* as regards contracts for the sale and supply of goods, although the general problem of onerous terms in signed contracts, especially those in standard form, will still remain.

[37] (1871) L.R. 6 Q.B. 597.

call "mutual " and " unilateral " mistake[38] – it solves the problem by asking which set of terms (if any) are those to which, as a matter of law, the parties agreed. In other words, mistake is often no more than the other side of agreement.[39] So *Smith v Hughes* is an authority quite as relevant to agreement as it is to mistake.

The facts of *Smith v Hughes* are well known. P delivered some oats he claimed to have sold to D, who refused to pay for them because he said that he had not agreed to buy the kind of oats which P had sent him. The case was heard in the county court before a jury, which found for D. P then appealed to the Court of Queen's Bench on the ground that the county court judge's direction to the jury on the question of agreement had been defective. The Court of Queen's Bench thought that the judge had misdirected the jury, and ordered a new trial, having first laid down what his direction should have been. Blackburn J.'s statement is particularly famous.

> I apprehend that if one of the parties intends to make a contract on one set of terms, and the other intends to make a contract on another set of terms, or, as it is sometimes expressed, if the parties are not *ad idem*, there is no contract, unless the circumstances are such as to preclude one of the parties from denying that he has agreed to the terms of the other. The rule of law is that stated in *Freeman v Cooke*.[40] *If,* whatever a man's real intention may be, he so conducts himself that a reasonable man would believe that he was assenting to the terms proposed by the other party, and that other party upon that belief enters into the contract with him, the man thus conducting himself would be equally bound as if he had intended to agree to the other party's terms.[41]

According to *Smith v Hughes*, then, the "objective" test of agreement means this. Words are to be interpreted as they were reasonably understood by the *man to whom they were spoken*, not as they were understood by the *man who spoke them*. Thus if A went to an auction, and being unused to the ways of the country and unable

---

[38] *The Law of Contract*, 8th ed., pp. 202–203.

[39] Slade, "The Myth of Mistake in the English Law of Contract," 70 L.Q.R. 385; Atiyah, *Introduction to the Law of Contract*, 2nd ed., p. 49.

[40] (1848) 2 Ex. 654; 154 E.R. 652. *Freeman v Cooke* has nothing to do with contract. The court, however, expounded estoppel in general terms, and this exposition was picked up and applied to a contract case, first in *Cornish v Abington* (1859) 4 H. & N. 549; 157 E.R. 956, and again in *Smith v Hughes*.

[41] (1871) L.R. 6 Q.B. 597 at p. 607.

to appreciate the finer points of distinction between a cow and a bull, bid for B's bull under the impression that it was a cow that B was contracting to sell him, there would be a contract between A and B for the purchase and sale of a bull. Although the minds of the parties did not meet, A has misled B into thinking that he was offering to buy his bull. A is therefore not allowed to go back on the impression he has created, because it would be unfair to B to enable him to do so.[42]

However, there are at least two cases where it *is* fair to B to allow A to deny his apparent consent.

(i) It is fair to allow him to do so if B knew, or ought to have known,[43] that A was mistaken. In this case, B has not been misled by any appearance of consent in A, so there is no reason why A should not be allowed to say that the minds of the parties did not really meet.[44] Thus if B knew that A did not really mean to bid for B's bull, A is not bound by a contract to buy it.[45] For example, in *Hartog v Colin and Shields*[46] D offered P 30,000 skins at prices per *pound* when he meant to offer to sell at prices per *piece*. P accepted the offer, well knowing that D had made a mistake and that the prices he appeared to offer were much lower than the prices he intended to offer. The court refused to give P damages for breach of contract.

---

[42] *Cf. Gill v McDowell* [1903] 2 I.R.K.B. 463, where a hermaphrodite was mistaken for either a bullock or a heifer, it is not clear which, and *Thwaites v Morrison* (1918) 14 Alta. Rep. 8, where a stallion was mistaken for a gelding. If nothing else, these two cases show that no imaginary example can ever be more improbable than one from real life.

[43] Singleton J.'s judgment in *Hartog v Colin and Shields, infra*, appears to cover both the cases where B had actual knowledge of A's mistake and the case where he had constructive knowledge only. He said: "The plaintiff could not *reasonably* have supposed that the offer contained the offeror's real intention."

[44] *Smith v Hughes* (1871) L.R. 6 Q.B. 597 at p. 610, *per* Hannen J.; *Gill v McDowell, supra; London Holeproof Hosiery v Padmore* (1928) 44 T.L.R. 499; *Hitchman v Avery* (1892) 8 T.L.R. 698 (discussed *post, p.* 254); *cf. Ewing & Lawson v Hanbury & Co.* (1900) 16 T.L.R. 140.

[45] As in *Gill v McDowell, supra*, where the court found that A intended to buy either B's heifer or his bullock (it is not clear which), that B intended to sell his hermaphrodite, and that B well knew A to be mistaken as to what he was buying. The court therefore held the contract to be void. On the facts as found, the decision is undoubtedly correct. One wonders, however, whether the facts were not really as found, but rather that A was buying a *specific animal,* wholly indifferent as to its sex, if any. Had these facts been found, there ought to have been a valid contract, because the parties would then have been perfectly *ad idem.*

[46] [1939] 3 All E.R. 566.

(ii) It is also fair to allow A to deny his apparent consent if it was really B's fault that A appeared to agree to something he did not. Thus if before the sale, B in some way confused A, and as a result of this A bid for the bull in the belief that it was a cow, then A will also be allowed to plead his mistake, and will not be bound to accept and pay for B's bull.[47] Thus in *Scriven v Hindley*,[48] D bid at an auction for a lot which he believed to be bales of hemp, whereas P meant to sell him bales of tow, which were worth much less. D's mistake was, however, partly due to P's confusing arrangement of the lots. P's action for the price failed, the court holding that a contract "cannot arise when the person seeking to enforce it has by his own negligence or by that of those for whom he is responsible, caused, or contributed to cause, the mistake." The case is a strong one, since there was also an express finding that D himself was also careless.

A RIVAL THEORY OF AGREEMENT

The notion behind what has been said so far is that A's words must be judged as they appeared to B, the person to whom they were directed. There is nothing new or original in this: in fact, it has been repeated so often in the past[49] that some readers may wonder why it has been necessary to labour the point. The reason is that in recent years an even more objective theory of agreement has emerged, according to which A's words must be judged, not as they appeared to B, but as they would have appeared to C, a reasonable man

---

[47] In *Gill v McDowell, supra,* the seller put the animal, itself "a sort of living lie" [1903] 2 I.R.K.B. 463 at p. 469, *per* Gibson J., among other animals which were either bullocks or heifers, so that its peculiarity was concealed. *Cf. Roe v Naylor (No. 1)* [1917] 1 K.B. 712. For a case in equity, see *Torrance v Bolton* (1872) 8 Ch.App. 118.

[48] [1913] 3 K.B. 564. The case has suffered bad mangling at the hands of those who wish to make it fit their theory. In *Principles of the Law of Contracts,* by Salmond and Winfield, p. 179, it was wrongly explained as turning on the fact that the auctioneer knew the purchaser was mistaken (which he did not). This was corrected when the book re-emerged as *Salmond and Williams on Contracts* (p. 209). Cheshire and Fifoot explain the decision as one where "the evidence is so conflicting that there is nothing sufficiently solid from which to infer a contract in any final form without indulging in mere speculation," so that the court must "of necessity declare that no contract whatsoever has been created " (8th ed., p. 222). This, with respect, is also misleading.

[49] Treitel, *The Law of Contract,* 3rd ed., p. 1; *Salmond and Williams on Contract,* Chap. V; Smith and Thomas, *A Casebook on Contract,* 4th ed., pp. 3–4; Slade, *op. cit.,* 70 L.Q.R. 385.

eavesdropping on the negotiations. The test is not what the other party would have thought, but how things would have appeared to the reasonable fly on the wall. This rival theory has begun to gain ground at the expense of the more orthodox theory which we have just examined, and it is time we examined it closely to see what its implications are.

In some cases, the two theories produce the same results. Thus according to either theory, the unobservant A will usually be bound to buy the bull he bid for thinking it was a cow; if the *Smith v Hughes* theory is used, this is because A led B to believe A was contracting to buy a bull; if the later theory is used, it is because a reasonable bystander would have thought A was contracting to buy a bull. On these facts, it makes no difference which theory is used – "you pays your money and you takes your choice". However, the theories produce conflicting results in cases like *Hartog v Colin and Shields* and *Scriven v Hindley*, where A's mistake was either known to B, or partly the fault of B. According to the *Smith v Hughes* theory, there is no contract at all in these cases.[50] According to the more objective "fly on the wall" theory, however, there *is* a contract in both these cases. No matter how things appeared to B, the parties appeared to be in agreement to the reasonable eavesdropper, C. So the protagonists of this theory would say that there ought to have been a valid contract in both *Hartog v Colin and Shields* and in *Scriven v Hindley*, despite what the courts in each case said.[51] They would explain the result reached in these two cases by saying that in this sort of situation the court may set the contract aside "on equitable grounds" – in the opinion of most lawyers, a very dubious proposition.[52]

---

[50] *Ante*, p. 106.

[51] In *Solle v Butcher, infra*, Denning L.J. said that nowadays the contract in *Smith v Hughes* would be held voidable only, and likewise the contract in *Cundy v Lindsay* (1876) 1 Q.B.D. 348; (1877) 2 Q.B.D. 96; (1878) 3 App.Cas.459. *Sed quaere.*

[52] Slade, "The Myth of Mistake in the English Law of Contract" 70 L.Q.R. 385, 390, 396. *Torrance v Bolton* (1872) 2 Ch.App. 118 lends some support to this view. The court rescinded a contract which a man had made at an auction because he mistook what he was buying, the mistake being partly the fault of the vendor who had prepared misleading particulars of sale – the facts being very similar to *Scriven v Hindley*. But the fact that a court of equity granted rescission does not exclude the possibility that the contract would, like *Scriven v Hindley*, have been void at common law: *Cooper v Phibbs* (1867) L.R. 2 H.L. 149 appears to be a case in which the courts of equity "rescinded" a contract void at common law.

The dissemination of the "fly on the wall" theory of agreement appears to be largely the work of Lord Denning M.R.[53] In *Solle v Butcher*[54] he said:

> once a contract has been made, that is to say, once the parties, whatever their inmost states of mind, have to all outward appearances agreed with sufficient certainty in the same terms on the same subject-matter, then the contract is good unless and until it is set aside for failure of some condition on which the existence of the contract depends, or for fraud, or on some equitable ground. Neither party can rely on his own mistake to say it was a nullity from the beginning, no matter that it was a mistake which to his mind was fundamental, *and no matter that the other party knew that he was under a mistake.*[55]

To support this theory, Denning L.J. invoked the authority of the House of Lords in *Bell v Lever Bros.*[56] It is hard to criticise him for taking this view of *Bell v Lever Bros.;* it would, however, be equally hard to criticise him for taking any other view of *Bell v Lever Bros.* The case is, of course, a final authority for whatever it decides, but there has been considerable discussion as to what this is.[57] The real origin of the "fly on the wall" theory appears to be not the House of Lords, but Williston.[58] He loudly proclaimed an extreme "objective" theory of consent, which has had wide influence on legal thinking in the United States, and which is reflected to some extent in the American Law Institute's *Restatement of the Law of Contract.*[59]

---

[53] *Solle v Butcher, infra.* Denning L.J. approved his own views there expressed in *Leaf v International Galleries* [1950] 2 K.B. 86, 89, and applied them in *Rose (Frederick E.) (London) Ltd. v Pim (Wm. H.) Junior & Co. Ltd.* [1953] 2 Q.B. 450, 460. See also *Gallie v Lee* [1969] 2 Ch. 17, 33 (affirmed *sub nom. Saunders v Anglia Building Society* [1971] A.C. 1004), and *Lewis v Averay* [1972] 1 Q.B. 198.

[54] [1950] 1 K.B. 671 at p. 691.

[55] Author's italics.

[56] [1932] A.C. 161.

[57] *Anson's Law of Contract*, 23rd ed., p. 261.

[58] *Williston on Contracts*, ss. 1536, 1537. Williston, " Mutual Assent in the Formation of Contracts" (1919) 14 *Illinois Law Review*, p. 85, reprinted in *Selected Readings on the Law of Contracts* (New York), p. 119. Williston's views are not universally accepted in the U.S.A. See *Corbin on Contracts*, s.106, where they are strongly refuted; and *Rickett v Pennsylvania Railroad Co.*,153 F. 2d 757. Williston himself admitted that his theory did not square with English cases so well as with those from his own country – see his article, *supra*, at p.120.

[59] ss. 70 and 71, especially 71 (c), Illustration (2). But the theory set out in the *Restatement* is not so extreme as that of Lord Denning, since it accepts that no contract is concluded in a case like *Hartog v Colin and Shields, see* s. 71 (c).

Indeed, so far from being based on English case law, the "fly on the wall" theory goes against the English cases almost without exception. For a start, it does not fit with *Smith v Hughes* – as Denning L.J. himself admitted in *Solle v Butcher*.[60] Yet *Smith v Hughes* has been approved and applied time out of number, both in general terms,"[61] and on the test of consent which it laid down.[62] It has been accepted as authoritative in Canada[63] and Australia.[64] It is also interesting to note that *Smith v Hughes* was approved by Lord Atkin in *Bell v Lever Bros.*, the case on which the "fly on the wall" theory is supposedly based. Furthermore, if the "fly on the wall" theory is correct, then *Hartog v Colin and Shields* is wrong, or must be explained on other grounds, and the same must go for all the other cases where, although the parties were outwardly agreed, the court held there to be no contract because A knew B to have misunderstood the terms of the bargain.[65] Lastly, *Cundy v Lindsay*[66] and the other mistaken identity cases do not fit well with the "fly on the wall" theory. Denning L.J. accepted this in *Solle v Butcher*, and got around the difficulty by saying that a modern court would therefore not hold the contract in *Cundy v Lindsay* to be void, but only voidable. With due respect, this is to look through the wrong end of the telescope. If the theory does not square with one of the best known decisions of the House of Lords in the last hundred years, surely it is the theory rather than the decision of the House of Lords which is wrong!

---

[60] [1950] 1 K.B. 671 at p. 693*Post*, n. 56

[61] *Pope & Pearson v Buenos Aires New Gas Co.* (1892) 8 T.L.R. 758.

[62] *London Holeproof Hosiery v Padmore* (1928) 44 T.L.R. 499; *Sullivan v Constable* (1932) 48 T.L.R. 369; *Ewing & Lawson v Hanbury & Co.* (1900) 16 T.L.R. 140; *Hitchman v Avery* (1892) 8 T.L.R. 698. See also the following cases, which were decided on the *Smith v Hughes* theory of agreement, but without reference to the case itself: *Cornish v Abington* (1859) 4 H. & N. 549; 157 E.R. 956; *Harris v Great Western Railway* (1876) 1 Q.B.D. 515 and *Tamplin v James* (1880) 15 Ch.D. 215.

[63] *Riley v Spottswood* (1873) 23 U.C.C.P. 318; *Lindsay v Heron* (1921) 50 O.L.R. 1; *Colonial Investment Co. of Winnipeg v Borland* (1911) 1 W.W.R. 171; (1912) 2 W.W.R. 960. Cf. *Hobbs v Esquimalt and Nanaimo Ry*. (1899) 29 S.C.R. 450.

[64] *Goldsborough Mort & Co. v Quinn* (1910) 10 C.L.R. 674, 695; Cheshire and Fifoot, *The Law of Contract*, 2nd Australian edition, p. 333.

[65] *London Holeproof Hosiery v Padmore* (1928) 44 T.L.R. 499; *Gill v McDowell* [1903] 2 I.R.K.B. 463; *Hitchman v Avery* (1892) 8 T.L.R. 698; *cf. Ewing & Lawson v Hanbury & Co.* (1900) 16 T.L.R. 140.

[66] (1876) 1 Q.B.D. 348; (1877) 2 Q.B.D. 96; (1878) 3 App.Cas. 459.

Are there any English cases which do support the "fly on the wall" theory of agreement?

There is the line of cases starting with *Solle v Butcher*[67] in which Lord Denning has repeated the theory several times over. In all of these cases except one, the "fly on the wall" theory of agreement was not essential to the decision, which turned on points which had little or nothing to do with agreement at all;[68] thus what was said about agreement there was only *obiter dicta*. The exceptional case is *Rose (Frederick E.) (London) Ltd. v Pim (Wm. H.) Junior & Co. Ltd.*,[69] which could have gone the other way had a different theory of agreement been applied to the facts. And this case can also be explained on other grounds.[70]

Apart from these cases in which Lord Denning was involved, there seems to be only one case which can be used to support the "fly on the wall" theory of agreement, and that is *Upton-on-Severn R.D.C. v Powell*.[71] D was entitled to the free services of the fire brigade in whose area he lived, whereas he could have the services of the fire brigade in adjoining areas only if he paid for them. Believing that he lived in the Upton fire brigade area he called the Upton fire brigade, which came to the fire, also believing that D lived in their area. D meant to call a free service, the P fire brigade meant at the time to give him one. Neither party intended to make a contract at all, and neither side discovered that D really lived in another fire brigade area, and so was not entitled to the free services of the P fire brigade, until afterwards. Nevertheless the Court of Appeal held D was contractually bound to pay for the services P had rendered him.

---

[67] *Leaf v International Galleries* [1950] 2 K.B. 86; *Rose v Pim* [1953] 2 Q.B. 450; *Gallie v Lee* [1969] 2 Ch. 17 (affirmed *sub nom. Saunders v Anglia Building Society* [1971] A.C. 1004); *Lewis v Averay* [1972] 1 Q.B. 198.

[68] In *Solle v Butcher* there was no dispute as to what the parties had agreed – the question was whether the court could relieve P on account of a mistake of fact which was shared by both parties. *Leaf v International Galleries* turned on rescission for misrepresentation, and everything that is said about agreement is clearly *obiter*. *Gallie v Lee* is a *non est factum* case pure and simple, and was so treated by the House of Lords when it affirmed the decision *sub nom. Saunders v Anglia Building Society* [1971] A.C. 1004. In *Lewis v Averay* the other members of the Court of Appeal held that there had been a mistake of attributes, not of identity, and assumed that the contract would have been void had there been a mistake of identity, however the transaction would have appeared to the "reasonable fly on the wall".

[69] [1953]1 2 Q.B. 450.

[70] *Post*, n. 56.

[71] [1942] 1 All E.R. 220.

The case could be explained by saying that although neither P nor D intended to make a contract, the reasonable eavesdropper, C, would have assumed that they did: therefore there was in law a contract between them. However, this explanation does not feature in Lord Greene M.R.'s single-page judgment. In fact, no explanation at all is given in the judgment, which appears to be most singularly innocent of any *ratio decidendi*. All that clearly emerges is that the court was most annoyed with Powell, who, it thought, was trying to get something for nothing. This suggests that the case is best relegated from the law of contract altogether, and seen as one where the court gave a restitutionary remedy to prevent unjust enrichment through services rendered under a mistake.[72]

Not only is the "fly on the wall" theory of agreement apparently contrary to authority, it is often difficult and uncertain to apply. It will work well enough where the parties are negotiating face to face. Then the reasonable eavesdropper is notionally at the keyhole, enthusiastically drawing inferences from what he hears within. But what if one of the parties is at Land's End and the other at Llandudno? At whose keyhole is the reasonable eavesdropper notionally listening then? – at the offeror's, or at the offeree's – or has he ears on infinitely extensible leads, enabling him to apply one to each keyhole simultaneously? The difficulty is that the inference he will draw will depend on how much he knows, and what he will know will often depend on where he is. Furthermore, unless *Solle v Butcher* has reversed a long line of cases, the reasonable eavesdropper will need a good deal of specialised and esoteric knowledge. He must have overheard all the previous negotiations,[73] he will need to know all the ships sailing from Bombay to Liverpool,[74] he will need to be an expert in cracking codes,[75] and if we bring other Canadian cases into consideration, he will have to understand fluent German,[76] Ukrainian[77] and Finnish.[78] In the law

---

[72] See Stoljar, *Quasi-Contract*, p. 186; Wade, *Restitution, Cases and Materials* (U.S.A.), 2nd ed., p. 108. Although *Anson's Law of Contract*, 23rd ed., pp. 30, 280, goes into the case, neither Treitel nor Cheshire and Fifoot think it is worth attention.

[73] *Lindsay v Heron* (1921) 50 O.L.R. 1.

[74] *Raffles v Wichelhaus* (1864) 2 H. & C. 906; 159 E.R. 375.

[75] *Falck v Williams* [1900] A.C. 176.

[76] *Streimer v Nagel* (1909) 11 W.L.R. 325 (Man.).

[77] *Free Ukranian etc. Credit Union v Hnatkiw* (1961) 44 D.L.R. (2d) 633 (Ont.).

[78] *Freeman v Kaltio* (1963) 39 D.L.R. (2d) 496 (B.C.).

of tort the reasonable man has to be imbued with qualities which are said to include the agility of an acrobat and the foresight of a Hebrew prophet.[79] To fit him for his new role as the eavesdropper in the law of contract, this excellent but odious creature[80] will also need the omnipresence of Puck and the learning of the *Encyclopaedia Britannica*. These difficulties arise from importing the fiction that a third party is listening to the negotiations when he is not, and they disappear if we abandon that fiction. We run into all sorts of difficulties if we ask ourselves "how would C, overhearing A and B's negotiations, have interpreted them?" which never arise if we ask the more sensible question, "How should B, the other party, have interpreted what A said?"

The "fly on the wall" theory is also open to the objection that it leads to absurd results. What happens if the parties are *inwardly* agreed, but *outwardly* at variance, or agreed on something else? Suppose, for example, that Ali and Benedetto, two immigrants with little knowledge of English, agree on the purchase and sale of a "bull," both of them intending to deal with a cow, and in the belief that the word "bull" means the female of the species. According to the "fly on the wall" theory of agreement, they have made a contract to buy and sell a bull, although A does not want one and B has not got one to sell.[81] This is ridiculous. Yet this is the result reached in the Court of Appeal by Denning L.J. in *Rose v Pim*.[82] The facts as interpreted by Denning L.J. were that A and B made a written agreement for the purchase and sale of "horsebeans", by which both A and B meant "feveroles", which, again according to Denning L.J., are something "essentially different". Denning L.J. held that although both parties meant to deal with feveroles, they

---

[79] Lord Bramwell, quoted in *Winfield and Jolowicz on Tort*, 9th ed., p. 26, n. 24.

[80] A. P. Herbert, *Uncommon Law*.

[81] *Cf. Restatement-Contracts*, s. 71 (c), illustration (2). "A says to B, 'I offer to sell you my horse for $100.' B, knowing that A intends to offer to sell his cow, not his horse for that price, and that the use of the word 'horse' is a slip of the tongue, replies ' I accept.' There is no contract for the sale of either the horse *or the cow.*" *Sed quaere.* If neither party has misunderstood the other, surely the answer ought to be that there is a contract for the sale of the cow.

[82] [1953] 2 Q.B. 450. The decisions of the other members of the Court of Appeal seem to be based rather on the assumption that feveroles are simply a special kind of horsebean, that there was no dispute as to *what* the parties agreed to buy and sell, but simply a mistake of both parties as to the qualities of what they agreed to buy and sell. So the case was one where the parties had reached agreement, but under a common mistake which did not go to the root of the transaction.

were contractually bound to buy and sell horsebeans, because their agreement as outwardly expressed, both orally and in writing, was for "horsebeans". It is a platitude to say that the law of contract exists to enforce agreements, and that agreements are what people have agreed to do, not what officious people with no interest in the matter would think they had agreed to do.[83] It may be acceptable for the law occasionally to force upon *one* of the parties an agreement he did not want; but surely there is something wrong with a theory which forces upon *both* of the parties an agreement which *neither* of them wants. If the "fly on the wall" theory does this, that is an excellent reason for rejecting it.

If we reject the "fly on the wall" theory of agreement, we are back to the less extreme theory of apparent consent established in *Smith v Hughes*, according to which A's words are judged as B, the addressee, understood them, and not as C, an eavesdropper, would have understood them. Here it might be convenient to summarise the *Smith v Hughes* theory as follows:

(a) Where A leads B to believe that he agrees to B's terms, A is bound by his apparent consent, although he did not in fact agree to the terms as B understood them.

BUT

(b) A is *not* bound by his apparent consent where B knew that A's mind did not go with his apparent consent,

(c) nor is A bound by his apparent consent where B originally misled A, so that it is partly B's fault that A's mind did not go with A's apparent consent.

Smith v Hughes and the Signed Document Cases

Let us now look afresh at the facts of *L'Estrange v Graucob*,[84] taking that case as the archetype of those in which a person has been held bound by a term in a contractual document of which he was unaware.

---

[83] See Glanville Williams, 23 Can. Bar Rev. 380 at p. 387, and also 17 M.L.R. 154. See also Slade, 70 L.Q.R. 385, 396, n. 50.

[84] [1934] 2 K.B. 394.

Miss L'Estrange, the proprietor of a café in Llandudno, was visited by two of Graucob Ltd.'s salesmen, who persuaded her to order a cigarette machine, to be sold to her by their company. They produced an order form, which she signed without reading properly. It contained a mass of clauses, including the following: "Any express or implied condition, statement or warranty, statutory or otherwise, not stated herein, is hereby excluded." She did not realise this term existed until she later tried to sue the company for breach of section 14 (1) of the Sale of Goods Act 1893 in selling her an article which was unfit for the purpose for which it was sold, when the company set this exemption clause up as a defence. Nevertheless, it was held that the exemption clause formed part of the contract which she had made, that it exempted the company from liability under the Sale of Goods Act, and that Miss L'Estrange accordingly lost her action.

Was this right? When Miss L'Estrange signed the order form on which were written various terms, she gave the appearance of agreeing to everything that was written on the document. To borrow the words from *Smith v Hughes* itself,[85] she so conducted herself "that a reasonable man would believe that she was assenting to the terms proposed by the other party." It would usually follow from this that she was bound by her apparent consent to all those terms. However, a person is not bound by apparent consent where the other party knew that his mind did not go with his apparent consent, or where the other party is responsible for the mistake which has been made. Didn't the facts of the case bring Miss L'Estrange within the scope of these exceptions to apparent consent?

The order form which Graucob Ltd. provided seems to have been drawn up in a most confusing way. Maugham L.J. said "... I could wish that the contract had been in a simpler and more usual form. It is unfortunate that the important clause excluding conditions and warranties is in such small print."[86] Not only was this clause printed in small print, but it was also printed on brown paper, which must have made the small print even harder to read. The general layout of the form also appears to have been confusing, too, the exemption

---

[85] (1871) L.R. 6 Q.B. 597 at p. 607, *per* Blackburn J.
[86] [1934] 2 K.B. 394 at p. 407.

clause being in a part of the document where it easily escaped notice. Then was this not one of those cases where although A apparently consented to B's terms, he did so because B had earlier confused him as to what those terms should be? In principle, the case is surely the same as *Scriven v Hindley*,[87] where A was allowed to deny his apparent consent to a contract to buy tow, because the auction catalogue had been confusing, and had contributed to form A's belief that he was offering to buy, not tow, but hemp.

Perhaps Miss L'Estrange could have gone even further than this, and also denied her apparent consent to the exemption clause on the ground that the company either knew or ought to have known that her mind did not go with her apparent consent. Why did Graucob Ltd. use order forms printed on brown paper containing obscure exemption clauses in minute print in unexpected places? Was it because it knew that if it said what it meant more plainly, its customers would understand the document they were being asked to sign, and would refuse to do so? Who in their right mind would sign a document headed "I agree to pay for your goods even if they are useless, and not to sue you even if they injure me?" Even if Graucob Ltd. had used the words it did use – "any express or implied condition, statement or warranty, statutory or otherwise, not stated herein is hereby excluded" – Miss L'Estrange might still have refused to sign if those words had been printed clearly where they could be seen. She would not have understood them, of course, but like the plaintiff in *Curtis v Chemical Cleaning and Dyeing Co. Ltd.*,[88] she might have asked the salesmen what the words meant. If the salesmen had explained correctly, presumably she would not have signed. If he had explained incorrectly, then the company would have misrepresented the legal effect of the form, and, like the Chemical Cleaning and Dyeing Co., would have been unable to rely on the exemption clause.

The truth is that whatever may have been Graucob Ltd.'s intentions disreputable companies put harsh exemption clauses in minute print in order to "put one over" people like Miss L'Estrange. Then why should people in her position not be allowed to deny their apparent consent to the clause because the company either

---

[87] 1913] 3 K.B. 564.
[88] [1951] 1 K.B. 805; *Jaques v Lloyd* [1968] 1 W.L.R. 625.

knew or *ought to have known* that their mind did not go with their apparent consent?[89]

Yet the Divisional Court, which felt sorry for Miss L'Estrange, did not allow her to deny her assent to the exemption clause by alleging either that Graucob Ltd. were to blame for her mistake, as in *Scriven v Hindley,* or that they had actual or constructive knowledge of the mistake she had made, as in *Hartog v Colin and Shields.* Why not?[90]

A similar puzzle is set by *Blay v Pollard and Morris.*[91] Pollard and Morris were partners in a garage. They decided to dissolve the partnership, and Pollard's father, a solicitor, drew up a contractual document to put their decision into legal effect. Morris signed this document without understanding it properly, and without noticing that a clause in the contract made him liable to indemnify Pollard against claims for arrears of rent. Blay, the landlord of the garage, sued Pollard for rent due, and Pollard in turn sought indemnity from Morris. Morris denied liability. He said that he never intended to agree to indemnify Pollard, and what is more, *that Pollard knew this when he, Morris, signed.* This allegation, if proved, should have enabled him to deny his apparent consent, as the defendant was allowed to do in *Hartog v Colin and Shields,* for example. The trial judge found Morris's allegation proved, and gave judgment for him, but the Court of Appeal reversed the decision, holding that the argument was not open to him. He could plead fraud, or *non est factum,* as defences, and nothing else.[92] Why was this?

The reason why the courts in both *L'Estrange v Graucob* and *Blay v Pollard and Morris* refused to admit the usual defences based on

---

[89] As the defendant was allowed to do in the analogous Canadian case, *Colonial Investment Co. of Winnipeg v Borland* (1911) 1 W.W.R. 17.1; (1912) 2 W.W.R. 960, and in the American case, *International Transportation Assn. v Atlantic Canning Co.* (1933) 249 N.W. 240, discussed *post,* p. 255 n. 123.

[90] It could be that neither of these arguments were raised, of course. We know that counsel tried unsuccessfully to prove a misrepresentation about the legal nature of the document, but little else about how he put his case. Alternatively, the court may have seen any such argument as amounting to a charge of fraud against Graucob Ltd., which in the circumstances could not be raised. See [19341 2 K.B. 394 at p. 403, *per* Scrutton L.J. See also n. 93, *post.*

[91] [1930] 1 K.B. 628.

[92] In this case, the court did not even mention the possibility of a defence of innocent misrepresentation, which was later allowed in *L'Estrange v Graucob.* In *Blay v Pollard and Morris* a claim for rectification of the document, based on the allegation that it failed to give effect to the prior agreement of both parties, was also made. This failed, because Morris could not prove the document to have been signed under a common mistake.

Smith v Hughes, and restricted the range of available defences to fraud, misrepresentation and *non est factum,* appears to be that both courts thought that there was something special about a signed document.[93] Where there is a signed document, the courts thought that some kind of magic operated to take the contract out of the usual rules that govern the formation of contracts, and to bind the signatory almost absolutely.

At any rate, this is certainly how later commentators have explained the cases. *Kerr on Fraud and Mistake* says "But where there is no fraud then unless *non est factum* is available the deed[94] will stand even between the parties",[95] and in *McCutcheon v MacBrayne* Lord Devlin said "Unless your Lordships are to disapprove the decision of the Court of Appeal *[sic]* in *L'Estrange v Graucob* – and there has been no suggestion in this case that you should-the law is clear, *without any recourse to the doctrine of estoppel,*[96] that a signature to a contract is conclusive."[97]

Why did the courts think that signed contracts deserved special treatment? Two ideas probably led them to apply special rules to such a case, although neither of these ideas was precisely expressed in either *Blay v Pollard and Morris* or in *L'Estrange v Graucob.* Both ideas will be examined now, and, it is hoped, shown to be misconceptions.

THE PAROL EVIDENCE RULE

In an earlier case[98] which was cited and relied on in *L'Estrange v Graucob,*[99] Scrutton L.J. had this to say. "There is no doubt as to the

---

[93] A further reason why both parties failed is that Scrutton L.J. apparently saw a defence based on *Smith v Hughes* as amounting to an allegation of fraud, which could be made in neither case, because it should have been (and had not been) raised expressly in the pleadings; see [1930] 1 K.B. 628 at pp. 633–634; [1934] 2 K.B. 394 at p. 403. *Sed quaere.* To say that the parties did not agree is not the same as to say that one cheated the other. There is no suggestion that a defence of no *consensus* amounts to fraud in *Smith v Hughes* itself, nor in the Court of Appeal decision in *London Holeproof Hosiery v Padmore* (1928) 44 T.L.R. 499.

[94] It is clear from the context that the author is not talking about deeds alone, but is referring to all kinds of signed instrument.

[95] 7th ed., p. 448.

[96] Author's italics.

[97] [1964] 1 W.L.R. 125 at p. 134

[98] *Roe v Naylor (No. 2)* (1918) 87 L.J.K.B. 958 at p. 964.

[99] [1934] 2 K.B. 394.

general rule that, when a contract has been reduced into writing, it is not open to give oral evidence to show that a term in the written document is not part of the contract. ..." This suggests that in reaching its decision in *L'Estrange v Graucob*[100] the Divisional Court had the parol evidence rule at the back of its mind.

The parol evidence rule says that external evidence may not be adduced to vary the terms of a written contract. As Salmond and Williams put it, "the instrument is exclusive and conclusive evidence of the contract."[101] The form in which the parol evidence rule usually appears is this – "the document is the *whole contract*" – and neither party may seek to set up terms which are not part of the writing. Does the parol evidence rule have a second limb as well – *"the document is nothing but the contract"* – which prevents one of the parties alleging that a written term is *not* part of the contract, whatever the position according to *Smith v Hughes*[102] may be? Some authority certainly suggests that this is so. Chitty wrote the following:

> Where the terms of a promise admit of more senses than one, the promise is to be performed in that sense in which the promisor apprehended at the time that the promisee received it...'[103] This rule appears to be as true in law as in ethics; subject, perhaps, to this general principle of the law of evidence, that parol testimony cannot be received to contradict the evident independently of the written instrument, that the promisor meant to make a different bargain.[104]

It is submitted that what Chitty said in 1834 is not the law today, however. The parol evidence rule has been so whittled down over the years that nowadays it is said to amount to no more than a rebuttable presumption "that a document which *looks* like a contract is to be treated as the *whole* contract."[105] Even this presumption is not

---

[100] The Court of Appeal in *Blay v Pollard and Morris* [1930] 1 K.B. 628 and the Court of Appeal in *Roe v Naylor (No. 2)* had a common factor in the person of Scrutton L.J. So the court in *Blay v Pollard and Morris* probably had the parol evidence rule in mind, too. It is also worth noticing that *L'Estrange v.Graucob* was cited with approval in a leading parol evidence rule case, *Hutton v Watling* [1948] Ch. 398.

[101] p. 147, relying on *Goss v Nugent* (1833) 5 B. & Ad. 58; 110 E.R. 713.

[102] (1871) L.R. 6 Q.B. 597.

[103] Quoting Paley, *Moral Philosophy.*

[104] Chitty's *Law of Contracts* (1834) (later *Chitty on Contracts)*, p. 63.

[105] Wedderburn [1959] C.L.J. 58, 62

applied so strictly as it used to be.[106] There is a host of exceptional cases where terms not appearing in a contractual document may be proved by parol evidence.[107] And there are also various cases in which the courts have allowed a man to produce parol evidence to prove that he did not really agree to terms which did form part of the document, the most remarkable of these cases being *City and Westminster Property v Mudd*.[108] Textbooks on contract law generally say that notwithstanding the parol evidence rule, parol evidence may be given to prove mistake.[109] So it seems unlikely that the parol evidence rule enables B to hold A bound by a term of a contract which A has signed not knowing it was there, if B either caused or connived at A's mistake.

NON EST FACTUM[110]

The second idea behind *L'Estrange v Graucob* and *Blay v Pollard and Morris* appears to be a mental confusion arising from *non est factum*. The courts knew that *non est factum* is a defence of mistake which may only be pleaded in connection with signed documents. From

---

[106] *Ibid.* p. 63.

[107] See authority collected in Treitel, 3rd ed., p. 152 *et seq.*

[108] [1959] Ch. 129. *Cf. Couchman v Hill* [1947] K.B. 554; *Curtis v Chemical Cleaning and Dyeing* [1951] K.B. 805; and *Jaques v Lloyd* [1968] 1 W.L.R. 625.

[109] Salmond and Williams, p. 162; Treitel, 3rd ed., p. 152.

[110] When the two cases under discussion were decided, the rules of *non est factum* were substantially different from those obtaining today. In 1934, a defence of *non est factum* was only available to someone who had signed a document under a mistake about the class of document in question; a mistake about its *contents*, however serious, would not do; *Howatson v Webb* [1907] 1 Ch. 537; [1908] 1 Ch. 1. Neither Miss L'Estrange nor Morris could have raised the defence because each understood the class of document they had signed, and both had made a mistake about its contents only. In 1971, the House of Lords gave *non est factum* a face-lift. In *Saunders v Anglia Building Society* [1971] A.C. 1004, the House of Lords virtually overruled *Howatson v Webb*, holding that in future, any really serious mistake about the document signed could give rise to *non est factum*, whether it was a mistake as to class or as to contents. However, neither Miss L'Estrange nor Morris would be in any better position under the new version of *non est factum* than they were under the old. The House of Lords stressed that the mistake must still be such as to make the transaction radically different from what the signatory imagined, and to judge from the examples their Lordships gave, the mistakes which Miss L'Estrange and Morris made would be wholly insufficient to raise a defence of *non est factum* even today. In fact, both persons would probably be worse off under the new rule than they were under the old. Formerly, it was irrelevant that the signatory had been careless in not reading the document – *Carlisle & Cumberland Banking Co. v Bragg* [1911] 1 K.B. 489. But the House of Lords overruled *Bragg's* case and held that carelessness of this kind precludes the defence altogether.

this they deduced that *non est factum* is the only defence of mistake which may be pleaded in connection with a signed document – a different proposition from the first, and one which does not follow from it.

There is a preliminary objection to this argument. Why, if it is right, may fraud and misrepresentation be raised as defences to a claim brought on a signed contract? Fraud and misrepresentation are both, after all, only special kinds of mistake. A mistake is a state of mind not in accordance with the facts.[111] Fraud, then, is mistake which is deliberately induced by the other party, and innocent misrepresentation is mistake which is innocently induced by him. If in the case of a signed document, mistake may only be set up by a plea of *non est factum*, logically fraud and misrepresentation should not be allowed as defences any more than a plea of mistake based on *Smith v Hughes*. Yet *L'Estrange v Graucob* and *Blay v Pollard and Morris* expressly allow such defences to be raised.

There is a second and historical objection to the idea that *non est factum* excludes any defence based on failure to agree within the rules set out in *Smith v Hughes*.[112] It is that such a rule ignores the distinction between *non est factum* as applied to deeds and *non est factum* as applied to simple contracts, and that it also ignores the differences between situations involving two parties and those in which there are three.

Non est factum evolved as a defence to an action on a deed before the law of simple contracts had been developed. If A, a party to a deed, was sued by B, the other party, A certainly could not allege a mistake about the terms of the instrument unless it fulfilled the requirements of *non est factum*, and this is a rule which probably holds good for deeds today. But that does not mean the same is true where A and B are parties to a simple contract that has been reduced to writing.

Non est factum was first applied to a simple contract in *Foster v Mackinnon* in 1869.[113] Except for *L'Estrange v Graucob* and *Blay v Pollard and Morris*, all the cases [114] in which *non est factum* has been applied to

---

[111] *Restatement – Contracts*, s. 500; *Williston on Contracts*, s. 1535.

[112] See Landon, 51 L.Q.R. 272 at p. 274.

[113] (1869) L.R. 4 C.P. 704

[114] *Hunter v Walters* (1871) L.R. 7 Ch.App. 75: *Lewis v Clay* (1897) 67 L.J.K.B. 224: *National Provincial Bank v Jackson* (1886) 33 Ch.D. 1; *Howatson v. Webb* [1907] 1 Ch. 537; [1908] 1 Ch.

simple contracts since 1869 have had this feature in common: they were all *three party situations.*[115] In each one, B duped A into signing an instrument which, unknown to A, conferred some presumed benefit on C, an innocent third party – the *Cundy v Lindsay*[116] situation, in other words, but involving instruments instead of chattels. These cases say that A may not raise any defence except *non est factum against C,* but there is nothing in any of them to suggest that where we are dealing with a simple contract, as against a deed, the only defence which A may raise *against B* is one of *non est factum.*

Nowadays it is generally admitted to have been an error of policy as well as of legal history to apply *non est factum* to simple contracts at all.[117] Surely, then, the courts in *L'Estrange v Graucob*[118] and *Blay v Pollard and Morris*[119] were wrong to extend *non est factum* as applied to simple contracts to the two party situation at all – let alone to say that in such a situation, it operates to exclude any other kind of defence of mistake altogether.

CONCLUSION

It seems to have been a misunderstanding of two other rules, then, which led the courts to lay down the rule in *L'Estrange v Graucob.* It is therefore submitted that they were wrong so to restrict the defences open to someone who signs a contractual document under a mistake as to the terms which it contains. Instead, they ought to have allowed him the possibility of pleading that he did not mean to consent to the disputed term, and that although he appeared

---

1; *Bagot v Chapman* [1907] 2 Ch. 222; *Carlisle & Cumberland Banking Co. v Bragg* [1911] 1 K.B. 489; *Mercantile Credit v Hamblin* [1965] 2 Q.B. 242; *Muskham Finance v Howard* [1963] 1Q.B. 904; *Saunders v Anglia Building Society* [1971] A.C. 1004.

[115] A further exception is the decision of the Privy Council in *Hasham v Zenab* [1960] A.C. 316, where despite counsel's submission that mistake and *non est factum* overlap [1960] A.C. 316 at p. 329, the court appeared to think they did not. However, the decision is not binding in England, being a decision on the interpretation of the Indian Contracts Act in force in East Africa.

[116] (1876) 1 Q.B.D. 348; (1877) 2 Q.B.D. 96; (1878) 3 App. Cas. 459.

[117] Cheshire and Fifoot, 8th ed., p. 236; *Saunders v Anglia Building Society* [1971] A.C. 1004 at p. 1024, *per* Lord Wilberforce.

[118] [1934] 2 K.B. 394.

[119] [1930] 1 K.B. 628.

to consent to it, the other party either caused or connived at his mistake. When *L'Estrange v Graucob* and *Blay v Pollard and Morris* were decided, there was authority on which the courts could have reached the result which is advocated here. *Hitchman v Avery*[120] is an example. Hitchman, a dairyman, persuaded Avery, his roundsman, to sign a contractual document containing a covenant forbidding him to set up a rival business if he left Hitchman's service. Hitchman knew that Avery could not read, although he had learnt to write his name in the army. Wright J. held that although Avery would ordinarily have been estopped from denying his consent to the term, no such estoppel arose, because Hitchman knew Avery could not read. Thus Avery was not bound by the covenant, of which he was unaware when he signed the paper.

It is instructive to compare a Canadian approach to the problem of confusing documents which are signed but not fully understood. In *Colonial Investment Company of Winnipeg v Borland*,[121] D went to the P company to obtain a loan. He was induced by P's employees to sign a document which, unknown to him, imposed on him a number of stringent obligations in addition to the duty to repay the money with interest. When the P company tried to enforce the contract, Beck J., in the Supreme Court of Alberta, refused to entertain the claim based on the parts of the document of which D had been unaware. The document, Beck J. held, was drawn up in a confusing way, and this led D to sign it without understanding it properly. In the circumstances, the company must be taken to have known that someone in D's situation would make such a mistake. Accordingly Beck J. applied the rules set out in *Smith v*

---

[120] (1892) 8 T.L.R. 698. This case must go some way to counterbalance *The Luna* [1920] P. 22, another decision at first instance, which goes the other way. See also *Roe v Naylor (No. 1)* [1917] 1 K.B. 712, where at p. 716 Atkin J. said " If a party signs the document he is taken to have assented to the terms contained in it. If although he has not signed the document, he has received it without dissent, he would also prima facie be taken to have assented to the terms. But in both cases the issue might arise whether a particular clause was one of the terms so assented to. In that case the question would be, was the document in such a form that a reasonable man reading the document with reasonable care might and did fail to see that the particular clause in question formed part of the contractual terms?" See also *Alan v Mawson* (1814) 4 Camp. 115; 171 E.R. 37, and the case referred to by Lord Hardwicke in 2 Atk. 32; 26 E.R. 416. None of this authority was cited in *L'Estrange v Graucob* or in *Blay v Pollard and Morris*.

[121] (1911) 1 W.W.R. 171. Affirmed (1912) 2 W.W.R. 960.

Hughes,[122] and allowed D to deny his apparent consent to all the terms when he signed the document.[123]

Policy considerations, but of different kinds, no doubt lay behind both the Canadian and the English approaches to this problem. The Canadian court was impressed by the abuses which would result – and, in England, *have* resulted – from enabling companies to hold ignorant signatories to the letter of sweeping exemption clauses contained in contracts in standard form. The English courts, however, were much more impressed with the danger of furnishing an easy line of defence by which liars could evade contractual liabilities freely assumed.[124] "It would be very dangerous to allow a man over the age of legal infancy to escape from the legal effect of a document he has, after reading it, signed, in the absence of any express misrepresentation by the other party of that legal effect."[125] Forty years later, most lawyers would admit that the English courts made a bad choice between two evils. They tried to leap over the mud, only to land in the mixen. Now it will take the best efforts of the House of Lords, or, more probably, the Law Commission, to pull them out.

---

[122] (1871) L.R. 6 Q.B. 597.

[123] *Cf.* an American decision, *International Transportation Association v Atlantic Canning Co.* (1933) 249 N.W. 240, and two further Canadian decisions, *International Transportation Association v Winnipeg Storage Ltd.* [1931] 2 W.W.R. 664 (Manitoba), and *International Transportation Association v Capital Storage* [1928] 4 D.L.R. 480 (Saskatchewan). P sent D a document requesting information about his business for a trade directory. Among a mass of clauses was hidden one whereby D promised to pay P $100 for the privilege. On these facts, D was allowed to deny his consent to a contract.

[124] When the courts rule out a particular line of defence altogether lest liars abuse it, the results are usually too harsh, because by so doing they prevent an honest man from telling an unlikely tale on the rare occasion when it happens to be true. *Cf.* the "objective " test of *mens rea* established in *D.P.P. v Smith* [1961] A.C. 290, reversed after public outcry by the Criminal Justice Act 1967, s. 8.

[125] *Blay v Pollard and Morris* [1930] 1 K.B. 628 at p. 633, *per* Scrutton L.J.

Annex: List of Selected Publications

Books

Jackson's Machinery of Justice (8th edn. of R.M. Jackson's Machinery of Justice in England), (Cambridge University Press, 1989).

(With Ray Bull, Rhona Flin and Gordon Nicholson, eds.) *Children's Evidence in Legal Proceedings – an International Perspective* (Collected papers from an international conference on children's evidence; published and distributed by the Law Faculty, 1990.) also online at http://www.law.cam.ac.uk/docs/view.php?doc=3503

(With Rhona Flin) *The Evidence of Children – the Law and the Psychology* (Blackstone Press 1990); 2nd edn. 1993

La procédure pénale anglaise (Presses universitaires de France, Que sais-je? Series, 1998).

(With Mireille Delmas-Marty) *European Criminal Procedures*. Cambridge University Press 2002, paperback 2005. (English version of (ed. Delmas-Marty) *Procédures pénal es d'Europe* (1995); wrote chapters 1 (1–75), 3 (142–217) and 11 (594–640) and supervised the translation of the rest.)

(With Antje du-Bois-Pedain, eds.) *Freedom and Responsibility in Reproductive Choice* (Hart Publishing 2006)

Evidence of Bad Character (Hart Publishing 2006); 2nd edn. 2009.

Hearsay Evidence in Criminal Proceedings (Hart Publishing 2008); 2nd edn. 2014.

(With Michael E. Lamb, eds.) *Children and Cross-Examination: Time to Change the Rules?* (Hart Publishing, 2012); wrote chapters 1 (1–20) and 9 (171–201).

(With Alicia Hinarejos and Steve Peers) *Opting out of EU Criminal Law: What is actually involved?* (Cambridge Centre for Legal Studies, 2012).

Chapters in New Editions of Books by Others, Edited

Clerk and Lindsell, *The Law of Torts*, 14th edn. 1975. Chapters on occupiers' liability and on breach of statutory duty.

Clerk and Lindsell, *The Law of Torts*, 15th edn. 1982. Chapters on self-help and self-protection, discharge of torts, occupiers' liability and breach of statutory duty

Simester and Sullivan's *Criminal Law*, 4th edn. 2010 and 5th edn. 2013. Chapters on sexual offences, theft, related offences, and fraud.

Articles in Journals and Chapters in Collective Books:

(1) English Criminal Law, Criminal Procedure And Criminal Evidence

"Criminal Libel – a Skeleton in the Cupboard" [1977] Criminal Law Review 383–394; 465–474

"The Metamorphosis of s.6 of the Theft Act" [1977] Criminal Law Review 653–660

"The Press and the Reform of Criminal Libel" in (ed. Glazebrook) *Reshaping the Criminal Law* (Stevens, 1978) 266–286

"The Theft Act 1978" [1979] Criminal Law Review 24–39

"Criminal Libel in Action – the Snuffing of Mr Wicks" [1979] Cambridge Law Journal 60–78

"The Mishandling of Handling" [1981] Criminal Law Review 682–687

"Blasphemy – the Law Commission's Working Paper" [1981] Criminal Law Review 810–820

"Criminal Law and Criminal Appeals – the Tail that Wags the Dog" [1982] Criminal Law Review 260–282

"Criminal Libel – the Law Commission's Working Paper" [1983] Criminal Law Review 524–534

"Handling, Theft and the Mala Fide Purchaser" [1985] Criminal Law Review 92–96

"No Prosecution Appeal Against Sentence?" (1985) 149 Justice of the Peace 262–264

"Motor Vehicles as Weapons of Offence" [1985] Criminal Law Review 29–41

"Do We Need a Prosecution Appeal Against Sentence?" [1987] Criminal Law Review 724–736

"Road Traffic Law: a Review of the North Report" [1988] Criminal Law Review 707–721

"Public Nuisance: a Critical Examination" [1989] Cambridge Law Journal 55–84

"The Neutral Expert: an Implausible Bogey" [1991] Criminal Law Review 106–110

"Hearsay and the Evidence of Absent Witnesses" [1994] Criminal Law Review 628–644

"The Criminal Appeal Act 1995" [1995] 9 Archbold News 3–6

"Law Commission Consultation Paper No. 138 on Hearsay: Hearsay Reform – a Bridge not Far Enough" [1996] Criminal Law Review 29

"English Criminal Procedure and the Human Rights Act 1998" (1999) 33 Israel Law Review 1–14

"When is a Conviction Unsafe?" [1998] 5 Archbold News 5–8

"The Case for a Code of Criminal Procedure" [2000] Criminal Law Review 519–531

"The Youth Justice and Criminal Evidence Act 1999: the Evidence Provisions" [2000] 1 Archbold News 5–8

"Inscrutable Verdicts, the Duty to Give Reasons and Article 6 of the European Convention on Human Rights" [2001] 1 Archbold News 5–8

"Furnishing Someone With the Means by Which They Kill Themselves" [2002] 5 Archbold News 6–8

"The Sexual Offences Act 2003: Child and Family Offences" [2004] Criminal Law Review 328–360

"Criminal Liability for the Desecration of a Corpse" [2004] 6 Archbold News 7–9

Noted, but not invariably approved

"Attorney-General's Reference (No.4 of 2002) and Sheldrake v DPP" [2004] 9 Archbold News 5–6

"Prosecution Powers to Gather Evidence: the Case for Reform" [2005] 8 Archbold News 6–9

"Codifying Criminal Procedure" Guest editorial, [2006] Criminal Law Review 279–280

"Does Our Present Criminal Appeal System Make Sense?" [2006] Criminal Law Review 677–694

"Can Juvenile Offenders be 'Named and Shamed' When They are Adults?"(2006) 170 Justice of the Peace 644–647

"Hearsay Under the Criminal Justice Act 2003: the Case Law One Year On" [2006] 8 Archbold News 8–11

"Quashing Convictions, and Squashing the Court of Appeal" (2006) 170 Justice of the Peace 790–793

"Are Foreign Convictions Admissible as Evidence of Bad Character?" [2007] 2 Archbold News 6–9 and 7 Archbold News 4

"Quashing Convictions for Procedural Irregularities" [2007] Criminal Law Review 835–848

"Special Measures and Unusual Muddles" [2008] 6 Archbold News 7–9

"Messing up Murder" [2008] 8 Archbold News 5–6

"Intercept Evidence – the Case for Change."(2008) 172 Justice of the Peace 651–655 and 671–672

(With Graham Virgo) "Encouraging and Assisting Crime: Legislate in Haste, Repent at Leisure" [2008] 9 Archbold News 7–9

"The Drafting of Criminal Justice Legislation – Need it be so Impenetrable?" [2008] Cambridge Law Journal 585–605

Chapter 32 (on the criminal law) in (ed Blom-Cooper, Dickson and Drewry), *The Judicial House of Lords 1876–2009*, Oxford University Press 2009) 594–61

"Juries and the Life Sentence" [2009] Criminal Law and Justice Weekly 165–167

"The Victim and the Prosecutor" in (ed Bottoms and Roberts) *Hearing the Victim, Adversarial Justice, Crime Victims and the State* (Willan, 2010) 143–162

"The codification of criminal procedure," in (ed. Chalmers and others) *Essays in Criminal Law in Honour of Sir Gerald Gordon* (Edinburgh University Press, 2010) 341–364

"Squaring up to Strasbourg: Horncastle in the Supreme Court" [2010] 1 Archbold Review 6–9

"Compensation for Wrongful Imprisonment" [2011] Criminal Law Review 803–822

"Hearsay Evidence at Strasbourg: a Further Skirmish, or the Final Round?" [2012] 1 Archbold Review 5–8

"Sex by Deception" [2013] 9 Archbold Review 6–9

(2) Children's Evidence

"Child Witnesses, Video-technology and the Law of Evidence" [1987] Criminal Law Review 76–83

"Child Witnesses, Corroboration and Expert Evidence" [1987] Criminal law Review 239–251

"Thoughts for the Home Office on Child Witnesses and Video Technology" [1987] Journal of Criminal Law 444–463

"Pigot and Children's Evidence: the Criminal Justice Bill 1990" [1991] Journal of Child Law 34–36

(With Danya Glaser) "Sentencing, Children's Evidence, and Children's Trauma" [1990] Criminal Law Review 371–382

Persuading the Courts to Listen to Children, in (eds. Anne Bannister, Kevin Barrett and Eileen Shearer), *Listening to Children* (Longman and NSPCC, 1990) 110–121

Two chapters in (eds. Kathleen Murray and David A Gough) *Intervening in Child Sexual Abuse* (Scottish University Press, 1991); 'The English Legal System' (76–94), and 'Diversion in the English Legal System' (143–145)

"Reforming the Law on Children's Evidence in England: the Pigot Committee and After," in (eds. Helen Dent and Rhona Flin) *Children as Witnesses* (Wiley, 1992) 113–129

"Children's Evidence: the New Law" (1992) 17 Archbold News 6–8

"Children's Evidence: Two Troublesome Points" [1993] 6 Archbold News 7–8

"Children as witnesses: a blunder averted" [1994] 6 Archbold News 7–8

"Evidence in Child Abuse Cases: Too High a Price for Too High a Standard?" [1994] Tolley's Journal of Child Law 160

"The Memorandum: an International Perspective," in (eds. Helen Westcott and Jocelyn Jones) *Perspectives on the Memorandum* (Arena, 1997) 95–107

(With Helen Westcott and Graham M. Davies) "Children, Hearsay and the Courts: a Perspective From the United Kingdom" (1999) 5 Psychology, Public Policy and Law, No. 2, 1–22

"Children's Evidence: the Barker case, and the Case for Pigot" [2010] 3 Archbold News 5–8

"Evidence and Cross-examination", in (ed. Michael E Lamb and others) *Children's Testimony – A Handbook of Psychological Research and Forensic Practice* (Wiley-Blackwell, 2nd edn., 2011) 285–305

(3) On Comparative Criminal Law and Procedure

"Nulla Poena Sine Lege in English Criminal Law" (1980) (3) Cambridge-Tilburg Lectures 35–57

Chapter on criminal law in (ed J A Jolowicz) *Précis de droit anglais* (Dalloz 1986); 2nd edn. 1992.

"Experts: can England Learn a Lesson from France?" (1992) 45 Current Legal Problems 213–236

"Les limites en matière de preuve – aspects actuels" Revue de Science Criminelle, 1992, 42–51

"La preuve pénale en droit comparé: rapport sur le droit anglais" (1992) Revue Internationale de Droit Penal 83–103

(With Barbara Deleuze and David Vorms) "La preuve: une question inclassable" (1993) 15 Archives de politique criminelle 33–53

"French and English Criminal Procedure – a Brief Comparison" in (ed. Basil Markesinis) *The Gradual Convergence* (Oxford University Press, 1994) 33–45

"Le ministère public en Angleterre" in *Vers un nouveau Ministère Public?* (Ecole Nationale de la Magistrature, 1995) 45–55

"La célérité de la procédure pénale" (1995) Revue internationale de droit pénal 413–432

"Improving the Position of the Victim in English Criminal Procedure" (1997) 31 Israel Law Review 286–299

"Le rôle des médias dans les procédures judiciaires" in *La présomption d'innocence en droit comparé* (Societé de législation comparée, 1998) 83–90

"Quelques observations préliminaires sur la rédaction de la décision de justice" in *Juges et jugements: l'Europe plurielle* (Société de législation comparée 1998) 73–76

"Le procès pénal en Angleterre" in (ed. M Delmas-Marty) *Procès pénal et droits de l'homme* (Presses Universitaires de France, 1998) 117–130

"The Role of Experts in the Common Law and the Civil Law" in (eds. Stephen Ceci and Helene Hembrooke) *Expert witnesses in child sexual abuse cases: what can and should be said in court?* (American Psychological Association, 1998) 29–58

"Proactive Policing and the Principles of Immediacy and Orality" in (eds. Stewart Field and Caroline Pelser) *Invading the Private? State accountability and new investigative methods in Europe* (Dartmouth 1998) 359–375

"La procédure pénale anglaise française: les ressemblances" in (ed .Louis Vogel) *Unifier le droit: le rêve impossible ?* (Editions Panthéon-Assas 2001-1) 59–72

"How Safe is Forensic Evidence?" in (eds. J F Nijboer and W J J M Sprangers) *Harmonisation in forensic science* (Thela Thesis, Amsterdam 2000) 543–555

Section on England in (ed. Jaap van der Hulst) *ECHR and Criminal Proceedings – the impact of the European Convention on Human Rights on Criminal Proceedings in the European Union* (Erasmus University, Rotterdam, 2001) 11–23

"An English lawyer's Reactions to Strafvordering 2001" in (eds. C H Brants, P A M Mevis, E Prakken and J M Reijntjes) *Op zoek naar grondslagen* (Boom, Den Haag, 2003) 29–42

"Brief Comments From an English Perspective" in (ed. Klaus Tiedemann) *Wirtschaftsstrafrecht in der Europäischen Union* (2002) 435–445

"Lay participation in justice in England and Wales" in (ed. A Mangas) *Human Rights; Crime-Criminal Policy; essays in honour of Alice Yotopoulos-Marangopoulos* (Athens 2003) 1235–1241

"Dix ans après la réforme de 1994 : quel regard d'Outre-Manche?" Actes des Xèmes journées d'étude de l'Institut de sciences criminelles de Poitiers (2005) 185–197

(With Antje Pedain) "Approaches to Strict and Constructive Liability in Continental Criminal Law" in (ed. Andrew Simester) *Appraising Strict Liability* (Oxford University Press 2005) 237–283

Chapter on English law in (ed. Geneviève Giudicelli-Delage) *Le droit pénal des affaires* (Presses Universitaires de France, 2006) 62–116

(With Sabine Gless), "Effienz und Individualrechtsschutz im Dreiecksverhaeltnis der sonstigen Rechtshilfe" Strafverteidiger 5, 2006, 269

"Chronique de droit anglais (années 2003–2005)" (2006) Revue pénitentiaire et de droit pénal, No.1, 183–189

"La procédure pénale française vue par un Anglo-saxon" in (sous l'égide de la Cour de cassation) *La procédure pénale en quête de cohérence* (Dalloz, Paris, 2007) 227–239

"Intentional killings in French law" in (ed. Jeremy Horder) *Homicide Law in Comparative Perspective* (Hart Publishing, 2007) 39–53

"Chronique de droit anglais (années 2006–2007)" (2008) Revue pénitentiaire et de droit pénal, No.3, 691–698

(With M-A Brajeux) "Criminal Liability for Negligence – a Lesson From Across the Channel?" (2010) 59 International and Comparative Law Quarterly 1–12.

"The Rise and Fall of the 'Bad Character Evidence' Rule in English law" in (eds. Anat Horovitz and Mordechai Kremnitzer) *Current Trends in Criminal Procedure and Evidence, a Collection of Essays in*

Annex: List of Selected Publications

Honor or Professor Eliahu Harnon (Hebrew University of Jerusalem, 2010) 157–175

"Telephone-tap Evidence and Administrative Detention in the UK," in (eds. Mariane Wade and Almir Maljevic) *A War on Terror?* (Springer 2010) 373–400

"L'indemnisation des victimes des erreurs judiciaires vue des deux côtés de la Manche" in Les voyages du Droit : Mélanges Breillat (LGDJ, Paris, 2011) 535–547

"Chronique de droit anglais (années 2008–2012)" (2012) Revue pénitentiaire et de droit pénal, No.3, 475–483

"La criminalité organisée en droit anglais" in (eds. Jean Pradel and Jacques Dallest) *La criminalité organisée* (LexisNexis, Paris, 2012) 345–354.

(4) Corpus Juris Project and EU Criminal Law

(With Delmas-Marty and others) *Corpus Juris – introducing penal provisions for the purpose of the financial interests of the European Union,* Economica, 1997

(With Delmas-Marty, John Vervaele and others), contributions to *The implementation of the Corpus Juris in the Member States* (3 volumes) Intersentia, 2000), and http://www.law.uu.nl/wiarda/corpus/index1.htm

"The Corpus Juris Project and the Fight Against Budgetary Fraud" (1998) 1 Cambridge Yearbook of European Legal Studies 77–105

"The Corpus Juris project – Has it a Future?" (1999) 2 Cambridge Yearbook of European Legal Studies 355–367

"The European Convention and the Rules of Criminal Procedure and Evidence in England" in *The Human Rights Act and the Criminal Justice and Regulatory Process* (University of Cambridge Centre for Public Law, Hart Publishing 1999) 57–63

"Why is the Harmonisation of Criminal Law Necessary?" in (eds. André Klip and Harmen van der Wilt), *Harmonisation and harmonising measures in criminal law* (Koninklije Nederlandse Akademie van Wetenschappen, 2002) 43–53

"The Impact of Accession on the Criminal Law and Procedure of the New Member States" in (ed. Christophe Hillion) *EU Enlargement, a Legal Approach*, (Hart Publishing, 2004) 170–179

"European Criminal Procedure – Fantasy or Fact?" [2003] 4 Archbold News 5–9.

"The concept of European evidence" ERA Forum 2/2003 29–38.

"The European Arrest Warrant" (2003–4) 7 Cambridge Yearbook of European Legal Studies 201–217

"La réception du mandat d'arrêt européen au Royaume Uni", in (ed. Marie-Elisabeth Cartier) Le mandat d'arrêt européen (Bruyant 2005) 186–199

"An Academic Critique of the EU acquis in Relation to Transborder Evidence-gathering", ERA Forum, Special Issue 2005, 28–40.

(With Nicola Padfield) "L'intégration des droits européens en droit britannique", [2006] Revue des sciences criminelles 537–550

"The Problem of Trans-border Evidence, and European Initiatives to Resolve Them", (2007) 9 Cambridge Yearbook of European Legal Studies 465–480.

(With Giulietta Gamberini), chapter on the law of the UK in relation to people-trafficking, in (eds. Anne Weyembergh and Veronica Santamaria) *The Evaluation of European Criminal Law* (Editions de l'Université de Bruxelles, Brussels, 2009) 342–377.

"People-trafficking: Some Reflections on the EU legislation, and its Implementation in the UK" (2009) 11 Cambridge Yearbook of European Legal Studies 189–210

Chapter on mutual recognition in the United Kingdom in (eds. Gisèle Vernimmen-van Tiggelen, Laura Surano and Anne Weyembergh) *The future of mutual recognition in criminal matters in the European Union* (Editions de l'Université de Bruxelles, 2009) 523–548.

"Implementing the European Arrest Warrant: a Tale of How Not To Do It," (2009) 30(3) Statute Law Review 184–202

(With Dirk van Zyl Smit) "The European Dimension to the Release of Sentenced Prisoners" in (eds. Nicola Padfield and Dirk van Zyl Smit) *Release from Prison* (Willan, 2010) 9–46.

"Fonctionnement du procureur européen – selon quel système?" in *Quelles perspectives pour un ministère public européen ?* (Dalloz, Sur l'égide de la Cour de cassation, 2010) 213–219

"The Green Paper on Obtaining Evidence From One Member State to Another and Securing its Admissibility", Zeitschrift für internationale Strafrechtsdogmatik 9/2010, 602–606.

"EU Fair Trial Rights – Progress at Last" (2010) 1 New Journal of European Criminal Law 445–457

"EU Criminal law – the Present and the Future?" in (ed. Anthony Arnull and others) *A Constitutional Order of States – essays in honour of Alan Dashwood* (Hart Publishing, 2011) 341–364

"'No thank you, we've already got one!' Why EU Anti-terrorist Legislation has Made Little Impact on the Law of the UK," in (eds. Francesca Galli and Anne Weyembergh) *EU Counter-terrorism Offences – What Impact on National Legislation and Case-law?* (Editions de l'Université de Bruxelles, 2012) 117–132

"Opting out of EU Criminal Justice?" [2012] 7 Archbold Review 6–9

"Mutual Recognition and Choice of Forum" in (ed. Michiel Luchtman) *Choice of forum in Co-operation against EU Financial Crime, Eleven International Publishing*, The Hague (2013), 61–72

Chapter on Il principio del mutuo ricononoscimento in (ed. Roberto Kostoris) *Manuale di procedura penal e europea* (Giuffrè, 2014) (in press).

"EU Criminal Law" in Catherine Barnard and Steve Peers, *European Union Law*, OUP, Oxford, 2014 (in press)

(5) Contract and Tort

"The Defective Premises Act 1971 – Defective Law and Defective Law Reform" [1974] Cambridge Law Journal 307–323; [1975] Cambridge Law Journal 48–78

"Products Liability in England" in (ed. Alpa) *Danno da Prodotti e Responsibilita Dell' Impresa* (1980) 113–164

"Motor-cars and the Rule in *Rylands v. Fletcher*: a Chapter of Accidents in the History of Law and Motoring" [1983] Cambridge Law Journal 65–84

"La quantification du dommage dans les pays du Common Law" in (ed. André Dessertine) *l'Evaluation du préjudice corporel dans les pays de la CEE* (1990) 179–183

"Civil Liability for Crimes" in (ed. Matthew Dyson) *Unravelling and Organising Tort and Crime* (Cambridge University Press, 2014) (in press)